Design and Deploy Microsoft Defender for IoT

Leveraging Cloud-based Analytics and Machine Learning Capabilities

Puthiyavan Udayakumar
Dr. R. Anandan

Apress®

Design and Deploy Microsoft Defender for IoT: Leveraging Cloud-based Analytics and Machine Learning Capabilities

Puthiyavan Udayakumar,
Ph.D Research Scholar
Department of CSE – Technology,
VISTAS.
Chennai, Tamil Nadu, India

Dr. R. Anandan M.S., Ph.D., D.Sc., C.Eng.
Professor & Head,
Department of CSE – Technology,
VISTAS.
Chennai, Tamil Nadu, India

ISBN-13 (pbk): 979-8-8688-0238-6
https://doi.org/10.1007/979-8-8688-0239-3

ISBN-13 (electronic): 979-8-8688-0239-3

Managing Director, Apress Media LLC: Welmoed Spahr
Acquisitions Editor: Smriti Srivastava
Development Editor: Laura Berendson
Editorial Assistant: Kripa Joseph

Cover image designed by Freepik (www.freepik.com)

Distributed to the book trade worldwide by Springer Science+Business Media New York, 1 New York Plaza, Suite 4600, New York, NY 10004-1562, USA. Phone 1-800-SPRINGER, fax (201) 348-4505, e-mail orders-ny@ springer-sbm.com, or visit www.springeronline.com. Apress Media, LLC is a California LLC and the sole member (owner) is Springer Science + Business Media Finance Inc (SSBM Finance Inc). SSBM Finance Inc is a **Delaware** corporation.

For information on translations, please e-mail booktranslations@springernature.com; for reprint, paperback, or audio rights, please e-mail bookpermissions@springernature.com.

Apress titles may be purchased in bulk for academic, corporate, or promotional use. eBook versions and licenses are also available for most titles. For more information, reference our Print and eBook Bulk Sales web page at http://www.apress.com/bulk-sales.

Any source code or other supplementary material referenced by the author in this book is available to readers on GitHub. For more detailed information, please visit https://www.apress.com/gp/services/source-code.

Paper in this product is recyclable

Table of Contents

About the Authors

Puthiyavan Udayakumar is an infrastructure architect with over 14 years of experience modernizing and securing IT infrastructure, including the cloud. He has authored over nine information technology books in various domains of virtualization, cloud computing, networking, and security. He has designed, deployed, and secured IT infrastructure from on-premises and cloud, including virtual servers, networks, storage, and desktops for various industries, including pharmaceutical, banking, healthcare, aviation, federal entities, etc. He is an Open Group Master Certified Architect.

Dr. R. Anandan completed his undergraduate degree and doctorate in Computer Science and Engineering and postdoctoral degree (D.Sc.) in Computer Science and Engineering in Mexico. He is an IBM S/390 Mainframe professional and a Chartered Engineer from the Institution of Engineers in India and received a fellowship from Bose Science Society, India. He completed seven certification courses (mainly from CISCO). He has published more than 140 research papers in various international journals such as Scopus and SCI. He has presented 90 papers at various international conferences. He received 18 awards from national and international agencies. He authored and edited 27 books. He is also an editor for publishing companies such as Springer, Wiley, World Scientific Press, and Nova.

About the Technical Reviewer

 **Mittal Mehta** is an experienced technologist who specializes in DevOps automation, configuration, and release management process for on-premises and cloud applications. He is always eager to learn new technologies related to automation application lifecycle management. He worked on Microsoft technologies like C#, .Net, Azure DevOps, PowerShell, etc. Mittal currently works as a Senior Manager, DevOps, for enterprise applications in Bangalore, India. He specializes in setting up cloud automation and Azure DevOps processes. He has completed the technical review of many books on Azure DevOps, Git, and release management.

Acknowledgments

I would like to express my sincere appreciation to the Acquisitions Editor, Smriti Srivastava, whose invaluable insights, guidance, and unwavering support played a pivotal role in shaping and refining this manuscript. She takes Apress to the next level. Special thanks to Shobana Srinivasan for her tireless efforts in materializing the book. Thanks to all Apress production team members.

—Puthiyavan Udayakumar

Acknowledgments

Introduction

The Internet of Things (IoT) is a network of interconnected devices embedded with sensors, software, and connectivity to facilitate data exchange. This expansive ecosystem spans smart home devices, industrial machinery, wearables, and vehicles, offering enhanced efficiency and data-driven decision-making across diverse industries. As IoT devices proliferate, the significance of cybersecurity intensifies. These devices handle sensitive data, and any compromise could lead to severe consequences, such as unauthorized access, data breaches, and potential disruptions to critical systems. The diverse nature of IoT devices and varying security levels present a challenge, emphasizing the vital need for robust cybersecurity measures.

The book *Design and Deploy Microsoft Defender for IoT* is a valuable resource for IoT engineers seeking to enhance the security of their IoT deployments. Its five chapters offer a structured approach to understanding, implementing, and managing Microsoft Defender for IoT.

Chapter 1, "Get Started with IoT," offers insights into IoT fundamentals, emphasizing the necessity for security. The chapter introduces Microsoft Defender for IoT and its role in safeguarding IoT ecosystems.

Chapter 2, "Develop Security Strategy for IoT/OT with Defender for IoT," delves into the intricacies of designing a robust security strategy for IoT environments. Integrating Microsoft Defender for IoT into the broader security framework is thoroughly explored.

Chapter 3, "Plan Microsoft Defender for IoT," provides practical guidance for planning and preparing to deploy secure IoT solutions. The chapter also addresses considerations for incorporating Microsoft Defender for IoT into the planning phase.

Chapter 4, "Deploy Microsoft Defender for IoT," offers step-by-step instructions for securely deploying IoT solutions. Integrating Microsoft Defender for IoT during deployment is a focal point, ensuring a comprehensive security approach.

The final chapter, Chapter 5, "Manage Microsoft Defender for IoT," underscores the importance of continuous monitoring for IoT security. It provides insights into utilizing Microsoft Defender for IoT to monitor and effectively manage the entire IoT ecosystem.

This book equips IoT engineers, developers, and cybersecurity architects with knowledge and practical insights, guiding them in implementing a robust security framework using Microsoft Defender for IoT. By doing so, it ensures a more secure and resilient IoT infrastructure.

CHAPTER 1

Get Started with IoT

The Internet of Things (IoT) refers to the network of physical objects or "things" that are embedded with sensors, software, and other technologies to connect and exchange data with other devices and systems over the Internet or other communication networks. These objects range from simple, everyday items like light bulbs and thermostats to more complex procedures like autonomous vehicles or industrial machines. IoT involves extending Internet connectivity beyond standard devices, such as desktops, laptops, smartphones, and tablets, to a diverse range of things and environments.

The Internet of Things (IoT) is considered necessary for several reasons, as it has the potential to impact various aspects of our daily lives, industries, and the global economy. Here are some key reasons why IoT is considered important: efficiency and productivity, data-driven decisions, cost savings, improved quality of life, safety and security, environmental and societal benefits, economic growth and innovation, global scale and reach disaster prevention and response, and enhanced customization and personalization.

In summary, the importance of IoT lies in its immense potential to improve economic and operational efficiencies, enhance safety and security, drive innovation and new business models, improve the quality of life, and help address various societal and environmental challenges. However, it also presents significant challenges, such as security, privacy, and ethical considerations, which must be addressed as its adoption grows.

By the end of this chapter, you should be able to understand the following:

- Introduction to Internet of Things (IoT)

- IoT vs. OT vs. IIOT comparative overview

- IoT architecture

- Building blocks of IoT

© Puthiyavan Udayakumar and Dr. R. Anandan 2024
P. Udayakumar and Dr. R. Anandan, *Design and Deploy Microsoft Defender for IoT*,
https://doi.org/10.1007/979-8-8688-0239-3_1

- Microsoft Azure IoT solution offerings

  - Overview of Azure IoT Central

  - Overview of Azure IoT Hub and Azure Digital Twins

  - Overview of Azure IoT Edge

  - Overview of Azure Sphere

  - Overview of Windows for IoT

  - Overview of Azure RTOS

Introduction to Internet of Things (IoT)

In this section, let us get started by understanding what Internet of Things (IoT) is.

The Internet of Things relates to a network of interconnected physical devices that communicate and exchange data with each other through the Internet. These devices, or "things," can be anything from simple sensors to sophisticated appliances and machinery. They are embedded with sensors, software, and other technologies that allow them to collect data, process it, and communicate with other devices or systems. IoT extends Internet connectivity from traditional devices like computers and smartphones to a wide array of objects and environments.

Imagine a world where your refrigerator can detect when you're low on milk and then automatically order it for you or where your plant pot sends a notification to your phone when it needs water. Picture city infrastructure that adapts to real-time traffic patterns reducing congestion and optimizing energy usage. These scenarios may sound futuristic, but they are rapidly becoming our reality. The phenomenon known as the Internet of Things (IoT) is the driving force behind these innovations.

What Is IoT?

The Internet of Things is a tremendous network of linked physical devices that can collect and share data without human intervention. These devices, often embedded with sensors, software, and other technologies, can range from everyday household items like washing machines and thermostats to industrial tools in factories and wearable health devices.

Why Is IoT Important?

The following key points highlight the importance of Internet of Things:

- Interconnectivity: With IoT, devices can communicate and collaborate, fostering a seamless integration of the physical and digital worlds.

- Automation and Control: Systems can be more efficient and adaptive by making decisions based on real-time data without human involvement.

- Data Collection and Analysis: Devices can generate a wealth of data, which can then be analyzed to extract meaningful insights, enhance user experiences, and improve decision-making.

- Efficiency and Productivity: By understanding and optimizing processes, businesses and homes can reduce waste and improve their bottom line.

Potential and Growth

From smart homes to intelligent transportation systems, the possibilities with IoT are almost limitless. Predictions suggest that by the end of this decade, tens of billions of IoT devices will be online, indicating the magnitude of its impact. Industries across the board, from agriculture and healthcare to retail and energy, are reaping the benefits of IoT, creating more innovative solutions and transforming how we live and work.

However, with great potential come challenges. Concerns about security, privacy, and interoperability are at the forefront of discussions around IoT. Understanding and addressing these issues will be paramount as we journey into the age of connected devices.

In essence, the Internet of Things is not just a technological revolution but a cultural one. It's shaping our future, and its influence on personal and global scales is just beginning to be realized.

The Internet of Things (IoT) is considered a significant advancement because it allows for unprecedented levels of communication between devices, leading to automation and control that were not possible before. It enables devices to act independently without human intervention, making systems more efficient, reducing waste, and improving service delivery.

Key Benefits

The following are the key benefits of Internet of Things (IoT).

- Efficiency and Productivity: IoT enables the automation of tasks and processes, reducing human intervention and increasing efficiency and productivity.

- Data-Driven Decisions: The data collected from IoT devices can be analyzed to inform better and more timely decision-making for individuals and organizations.

- Cost Savings: IoT can lead to significant cost reductions, from minimizing equipment failure through predictive maintenance to reducing energy consumption through smart home devices.

- Improved Quality of Life: IoT can make life more convenient and comfortable, such as through intelligent home systems that automate lighting, heating, and security.

- Safety and Security: IoT can enhance personal safety and security through applications such as smart alarms and surveillance systems.

- Health Monitoring: Wearable IoT devices can monitor various health metrics and provide patients and healthcare providers with real-time feedback.

- Environmental Monitoring and Sustainability: IoT can be used to monitor environmental conditions and foster sustainability through applications like precision agriculture and intelligent energy grids.

- Innovation and New Business Models: IoT opens the door to new business opportunities, creating new services and revenue streams for companies.

Use Cases of IoT

The Internet of Things (IoT) is one of the key technologies driving digital transformation and is expected to have a widespread impact on various industries and everyday life.

The adoption of the Internet of Things (IoT) signifies a transformative shift across various industries, reshaping how businesses operate, how consumers interact, and how data is used to drive decision-making.

Early Stages of Adoption: In the initial stages, the potential of IoT was primarily recognized by industries involved in manufacturing and logistics. Companies identified the advantage of using sensors and smart devices to monitor equipment health, track goods in real time, and optimize supply chain operations. Early adopters were primarily large enterprises with substantial resources and the ability to invest in new technologies.

Consumer Adoption: Parallel to industrial uptake, the consumer sector began embracing IoT, especially with the proliferation of wearable tech like fitness trackers and smartwatches. The concept of smart homes started gaining traction, with devices like smart thermostats, security cameras, and voice assistants becoming more commonplace. This consumer-facing side of IoT has grown exponentially, driven by a combination of falling hardware costs, improved connectivity options, and increased consumer awareness.

Challenges and Concerns: The adoption curve was steep but needed challenges. Concerns about data privacy, security vulnerabilities, and the lack of standardization across devices and platforms emerged. These challenges necessitated a more cautious approach, especially in industries handling sensitive data, like healthcare and finance.

Recent Trends: As technology matured, sectors like agriculture, healthcare, and urban planning began leveraging IoT for precision farming, patient monitoring, and smart city initiatives, respectively. The introduction of 5G is also set to supercharge IoT adoption, with its promise of faster speeds, near-zero latency, and the ability to handle many connected devices simultaneously.

Future Outlook: The future trajectory of IoT adoption is poised to be even steeper. As the benefits become more evident and challenges are systematically addressed, smaller businesses and previously hesitant sectors are also jumping on the IoT bandwagon. The fusion of IoT with other disruptive technologies like artificial intelligence, machine learning, and blockchain promises to open up even more innovative use cases, ensuring that the IoT adoption wave continues its upward trend.

The Internet of Things (IoT) is used in various sectors and applications, transforming how we live, work, and interact with the world. Here's a general overview of some prominent areas where IoT is being utilized:

- Smart Homes

  - An example of a smart thermostat is the Nest Learning Thermostat, which learns your schedule and adjusts your home's temperature accordingly. Remote control of smart lighting systems is possible with smartphone apps.

- Wearable Health Devices

  - Example: Fitness trackers like Fitbit or Apple Watch track physical activity, heart rate, sleep patterns, and more. They can sync this data to a smartphone, allowing users to monitor their health metrics over time.

- Smart Cities

  - Example: In a smart city, IoT sensors can be used to optimize traffic flow through intelligent traffic lights that respond to real-time traffic situations, reducing congestion and improving energy efficiency.

- Industrial IoT (IIoT)

  - Example: In a manufacturing plant, IoT sensors on machinery can monitor equipment in real time. Suppose a machine shows signs that it may fail soon (e.g., vibrations indicating misalignment or rising temperature). In that case, maintenance can be scheduled proactively to fix the issue before a failure occurs, avoiding costly downtime.

- Precision Agriculture

  - Example: IoT devices can monitor soil moisture levels in different parts of a farm and use that data to optimize irrigation, apply water only where and when needed, conserve water, and improve crop yield.

- Retail and Supply Chain Management

  - Example: IoT sensors can track products moving through a supply chain. This provides real-time inventory data, making managing stock levels and reducing costs easier. In retail environments, intelligent shelves can alert staff when they need to be restocked.

- Environmental Monitoring

  - Example: Sensors in rivers or oceans can monitor water quality in real time, providing early warnings about pollution or other issues.

In summary, IoT represents a significant evolution in how devices and systems interact, with wide-ranging applications that offer substantial benefits in terms of efficiency, convenience, safety, and more. However, with these advantages come challenges, particularly regarding security and privacy. Since IoT devices are connected to the Internet, they are susceptible to hacking and other forms of cyberattacks, and the vast amounts of data they collect can also raise significant privacy concerns.

What Is the Best Way for Businesses to Approach IoT?

IoT empowers your enterprise to tackle challenges and identify opportunities by leveraging your own data resources. The Internet of Things transcends the mere concept of interconnected gadgets; it's a transformative technology that focuses on the invaluable data generated by these devices. This data can be analyzed to produce immediate and impactful insights that drive business transformation. You can substantially cut costs by optimizing resource usage, eliminating waste, and enhancing operational workflows by employing IoT solutions. Furthermore, the real-time data analytics enabled by IoT can pave the way for diversifying into novel business segments that were previously unfeasible. In a competitive landscape, IoT offers the strategic advantage of converting data into actionable insights, enabling informed and timely decision-making for your business.

The Internet of Things (IoT) presents a transformative opportunity for businesses, enabling them to gain insights, improve operational efficiencies, and create new revenue streams. However, implementing IoT is challenging, including technical complexities, security risks, and integration issues.

Here's a comprehensive outline on how businesses should approach IoT.

Initial Assessment and Planning

- Identify Objectives: Clearly articulate what you hope to achieve with IoT. Is it about increasing efficiency, improving customer experience, or creating new revenue streams?

- Scope and Scale: Determine the scope and scale of the IoT project. Will it be a pilot project or a full-scale implementation?

- Stakeholder Involvement: Engage key stakeholders from IT, operations, finance, and other relevant departments.

- Budget and ROI: Prepare a budget and calculate potential return on investment (ROI).

- Regulatory Compliance: Understand the legal requirements that could affect your IoT implementation, such as GDPR for data protection.

Technology Selection

- Hardware: Choose appropriate sensors, actuators, and other hardware components.

- Connectivity: Decide the best way to connect your devices – Wi-Fi, Bluetooth, LoRaWAN, etc.

- Platform: Select an IoT platform that fits your needs, whether it's cloud based, on-premises, or hybrid.

- Data Storage: Choose where the collected data will be stored and ensure it's secure and scalable.

- Software Stack: Decide on the software stack for data analytics, machine learning models, etc.

Implementation and Deployment

- Pilot Testing: Start with a small-scale pilot to test assumptions and understand real-world challenges.

- Integration: Ensure that the IoT system integrates well with existing infrastructure.

- Security: Implement security measures at every layer – device, connectivity, data storage, and application.

- Data Analytics: Deploy analytics tools to make sense of the collected data.

- Monitoring and Management: Ensure systems are in place to monitor device health, security, and performance.

Post-deployment

- Scaling: If the pilot is successful, plan for scaling the project.

- Ongoing Maintenance: Regularly update software and security features.

- Data Analysis: Continuously analyze data for insights and make necessary adjustments to your operations.

- User Training: Keep the staff trained and updated on how to use the new IoT systems.

- Feedback Loop: Establish a feedback mechanism to improve the system continuously.

Best Practices

- Security First: Always consider security a priority.

- Data Governance: Have a clear policy for using, sharing, and storing data.

- Collaboration: Encourage collaboration between IT and other departments for successful implementation.

- Vendor Relations: Maintain good relationships with vendors for hardware and software solutions.

- User Experience: Always consider the end-user experience, whether an employee, customer, or machine.

By systematically approaching IoT implementation in these stages, businesses can mitigate risks and increase the chances of successful deployment.

IOT vs. OT vs. IIOT Comparative Overview

IoT (Internet of Things), OT (operational technology), and IIoT (industrial Internet of Things) are distinct but increasingly interconnected technologies used in the modern industrial and business landscape.

IoT (Internet of Things)

IoT is a technology paradigm encompassing a vast network of interconnected devices capable of collecting, sharing, and acting upon data. Its fundamental components include sensors, data communication, cloud computing, and data analytics. IoT is widely used in applications ranging from smart homes to precision agriculture, allowing for data-driven insights and automation. However, the openness and interconnected nature of IoT systems make them susceptible to security threats, emphasizing the importance of robust cybersecurity measures.

OT (Operational Technology)

OT represents the technology used in industrial and operational settings to monitor, control, and automate physical processes and equipment. Critical components of OT include SCADA systems, PLCs, HMI (Human-Machine Interface) devices, and industrial communication protocols. OT is vital for sectors like manufacturing, energy, and utilities. Given its role in critical infrastructure and industrial processes, ensuring the security of OT systems is crucial. Cyberattacks on OT systems can result in operational disruptions and physical damage and even endanger human lives.

The growing ubiquity, susceptibility, and integration with cloud technology of Internet of Things (IoT) and operational technology (OT) devices signify an expanding and frequently unmonitored risk landscape that impacts a broader spectrum of industries and organizations. The rapid proliferation of IoT devices enlarges the potential points of entry and surfaces for cyberattacks. As operational technology increasingly connects to the cloud and the gap between IT and OT narrows, it grants attackers access to less secure OT systems, thereby heightening the risk of detrimental infrastructure attacks.

Operational technology (OT) encompasses the utilization of hardware and software to oversee and manage industrial machinery, primarily focusing on interfacing with the tangible, real-world aspects of operations. OT includes a variety of industrial control systems (ICSs), including programmable logic controllers (PLCs), distributed control systems (DCSs), and Supervisory Control and Data Acquisition (SCADA) systems.

In OT settings, the emphasis is on monitoring and governing physical processes in sectors such as manufacturing, energy production, healthcare, building management, and environmental ecosystems.

Operational technology, known as OT, differs fundamentally from information technology, or IT, which primarily revolves around managing data systems. While OT systems are chiefly designed for interfacing with the physical world, IT systems are primarily employed to address business challenges for end users, such as telecommunications service providers. To put it succinctly, OT networks facilitate communication with physical machinery, while IT networks handle information and data.

The Internet of Things (IoT) involves

- The practice of linking everyday physical objects to the Internet

- Ranging from common household items like lightbulbs to healthcare devices

- Wearables

- Smart gadgets

- Even entire smart cities

Some of these devices may feature dedicated apps, but all serve diverse purposes. These IoT-enabled devices connect to wireless IT networks, transmitting and receiving data, often with the assistance of data centers, with minimal human intervention.

Within the IoT realm exists a subset known as the industrial Internet of Things (IIoT), which encompasses connected devices utilized in manufacturing, energy production, and other industrial settings. IIoT is closely associated with OT and is vital in introducing increased automation and self-monitoring to industrial machinery. Coupled with edge computing, IIoT accelerates problem-solving in manufacturing, aids end users in making informed business decisions, and enhances overall plant productivity.

It's also common to hear discussions about IIoT systems in the context of Industry 4.0, often called the Fourth Industrial Revolution. Both terms essentially refer to the same concept, encompassing elements like artificial intelligence and machine learning (AI/ML), machine-to-machine communication, and big data, which are closely intertwined with the principles of Industry 4.0.

IIOT (Industrial Internet of Things)

IIoT, or the industrial Internet of Things, is a transformative technological concept that extends the principles of the IoT (Internet of Things) into industrial and manufacturing processes. It involves the integration of smart devices, sensors, and advanced data analytics within industrial settings to optimize operations, improve efficiency, and enhance decision-making. IIoT leverages the power of connectivity to collect, exchange, and analyze data in real time, allowing industries to make more informed and timely decisions.

At the core of IIoT are the vast arrays of sensors and devices that capture data from various points within industrial processes, such as machinery, production lines, and supply chain logistics. These devices continuously collect data on temperature, pressure, humidity, and other relevant variables. This data is then transmitted to central systems, undergoing real-time analysis. IIoT not only provides real-time insights but also enables predictive analytics, allowing industries to anticipate and prevent potential issues, thereby reducing downtime and operational costs.

The impact of IIoT is felt across a broad range of industries, including manufacturing, energy, healthcare, and agriculture. In manufacturing, it helps optimize production lines, monitor equipment health, and enhance supply chain management. In energy, it aids in efficiently distributing resources and minimizes waste. In healthcare, it allows for remote patient monitoring and predictive maintenance of medical devices. IIoT is transforming the industrial landscape, ushering in a new era of data-driven decision-making and operational excellence.

Table 1-1 offers a comparative table of IoT vs. OT vs. IIoT from various aspects.

Table 1-1. *IoT vs. OT vs. IIoT Comparative Overview*

Aspect	IoT (Internet of Things)	OT (Operational Technology)	IIoT (Industrial Internet of Things)
Definition	IoT refers to the network of interconnected physical devices and objects that collect and exchange data, enabling them to make intelligent decisions and actions.	OT comprises the specialized technologies and systems used to monitor and control physical devices and processes in industrial environments.	IIoT is an extension of IoT, specifically focused on industrial applications, where sensors and devices are integrated into industrial processes to enhance efficiency and productivity.
Primary focus	IoT primarily focuses on data collection, analysis, and communication between various devices for a wide range of applications, including smart homes, healthcare, and logistics.	OT primarily focuses on managing and controlling the operation of industrial processes and equipment, such as manufacturing, energy production, and critical infrastructure.	IIoT extends the capabilities of OT by leveraging IoT technologies to optimize and streamline industrial processes, leading to increased efficiency and cost savings.
Devices	IoT devices include a broad range of consumer and industrial devices, such as sensors, wearables, smart appliances, and connected vehicles.	OT devices are specialized and industry-specific, including SCADA (Supervisory Control and Data Acquisition) systems, PLCs (programmable logic controllers), and industrial robots.	IIoT devices are tailored for industrial use and are designed to integrate seamlessly into manufacturing and industrial processes.

(continued)

13

Table 1-1. (*continued*)

Aspect	IoT (Internet of Things)	OT (Operational Technology)	IIoT (Industrial Internet of Things)
Data types	IoT deals with diverse data types, including structured and unstructured data, often generated from various sources, for purposes like environmental monitoring or user interaction.	OT primarily deals with structured data, focusing on real-time data, telemetry, and control data generated within industrial processes and systems.	IIoT deals with various data types, including process data, telemetry, and sensor data, which are used to enhance real-time control and decision-making in industrial settings.
Latency	IoT applications may tolerate some latency, making them suitable for non-time-critical tasks like remote monitoring or home automation.	OT requires low or near-zero latency to ensure real-time control and safety within industrial processes, making it critical for operations.	IIoT demands low latency for real-time control and optimization of industrial processes, but it may tolerate slightly higher latencies compared to OT.
Network	IoT often uses standard Internet protocols (e.g., HTTP, MQTT) and may rely on public networks like the Internet for data transmission.	OT networks are typically proprietary and isolated from public networks to ensure security and reliability.	IIoT networks often leverage standardized communication protocols (e.g., MQTT, OPC UA) to connect industrial devices and systems while maintaining strict security measures.
Security focus	IoT security focuses on protecting data and privacy and may involve encryption, access control, and authentication.	OT security emphasizes the protection of industrial processes, safety, and critical infrastructure, often involving physical security and strict access control.	IIoT security combines elements of IoT and OT security, emphasizing the integrity and reliability of industrial processes while protecting sensitive data and operational continuity.

(*continued*)

Table 1-1. (*continued*)

Aspect	IoT (Internet of Things)	OT (Operational Technology)	IIoT (Industrial Internet of Things)
Cybersecurity importance	The importance of cybersecurity in the IoT world cannot be overstated. IoT devices are vulnerable to various cyber threats, including data breaches, device manipulation, and network intrusions. Ensuring the security of IoT ecosystems is essential to safeguard sensitive data, privacy, and the functionality of connected devices.	OT cybersecurity is paramount, as breaches can have immediate and severe consequences, including physical harm and economic damage. OT systems must be protected against cyberattacks to maintain the stability and safety of industrial processes, making cybersecurity measures an integral part of OT technology.	IIoT security is critical in optimizing industrial processes while ensuring the protection of critical infrastructure, sensitive data, and operational continuity. Cybersecurity measures in IIoT are essential to balance efficiency and security.

Fundamentals of IoT (Internet of Things)

IoT is a technology paradigm encompassing a vast network of interconnected devices capable of collecting, sharing, and acting upon data. Critical components of IoT include the following:

- Devices: A wide array of devices, from sensors and actuators to smart appliances and wearables, form the foundation of IoT.

- Data Communication: IoT relies on various communication protocols like MQTT, CoAP, and HTTP to facilitate data exchange between devices and cloud platforms.

- Cloud Computing: Cloud-based services collect, store, and process data from IoT devices, allowing for scalable and efficient data analysis.

- Data Analytics: IoT leverages data analytics to extract actionable insights from the vast data connected devices generate.

- Security: IoT security includes encryption, authentication, and access control to protect data and devices from cyber threats.

Fundamentals of OT (Operational Technology)

OT is the technology used in industrial settings to monitor, control, and automate physical processes and equipment. Key components of OT include the following:

- SCADA Systems: SCADA (Supervisory Control and Data Acquisition) systems monitor and control industrial processes.

- PLCs (Programmable Logic Controllers): PLCs are hardware devices that control machinery and industrial processes.

- HMI (Human-Machine Interface): HMIs provide a visual interface for operators to monitor and control industrial equipment and processes.

- Telemetry: OT relies on real-time telemetry data from sensors and devices within the industrial environment.

- Industrial Communication Protocols: Proprietary protocols like Modbus and Profibus are commonly used for secure and reliable data transmission in OT.

Fundamentals of IIoT (Industrial Internet of Things)

IIoT extends OT by leveraging IoT technologies to optimize and streamline industrial processes. Critical components of IIoT include the following:

- Industrial Sensors: IIoT devices include specialized sensors for monitoring and controlling industrial processes.

- Data Integration: IIoT integrates data from various sources, including sensors and industrial equipment, for analysis and decision-making.

- Real-Time Analytics: IIoT employs real-time analytics to enhance industrial processes, increase efficiency, and reduce downtime.

- Standardized Communication Protocols: IIoT often uses standardized protocols like MQTT and OPC UA to ensure interoperability between devices and systems.

- Security Measures: IIoT implements robust security measures to protect industrial processes, data integrity, and operational continuity.

Cybersecurity Importance in IoT and OT/IIoT Across Industries

IoT Cybersecurity Importance Across Industries

- Healthcare: IoT is vital for remote patient monitoring and medical device connectivity. Cybersecurity ensures the confidentiality and integrity of patient data.

- Smart Manufacturing: In smart factories, IoT enhances production processes. Cybersecurity protects sensitive manufacturing data and ensures uptime.

- Agriculture: IoT is used in precision agriculture to optimize resource use. Cybersecurity safeguards crop and environmental data.

- Transportation: IoT in transportation enhances vehicle connectivity and autonomous systems. Cybersecurity protects against potential vehicle hacking and data breaches.

- Smart Cities: IoT in smart city initiatives improves infrastructure management. Cybersecurity prevents disruptions to city services and data breaches.

OT Cybersecurity Importance Across Industries

- Energy: In the energy sector, OT controls power generation and distribution. Cybersecurity is crucial to prevent power outages and critical infrastructure disruptions.

- Manufacturing: OT technology is vital in manufacturing for process automation. Cybersecurity ensures safety and production continuity.

- Water and Utilities: OT systems manage water treatment and distribution. Cybersecurity is essential to prevent contamination risks and service disruptions.

- Oil and Gas: OT controls drilling, extraction, and refining operations. Cybersecurity prevents environmental disasters and financial losses.

- Transportation: In transportation and logistics, OT is vital for supply chain management. Cybersecurity protects against disruptions and data breaches.

IIoT Cybersecurity Importance Across Industries

- Manufacturing: IIoT enhances manufacturing processes by providing real-time data and predictive maintenance capabilities. Cybersecurity protects against equipment failures and production interruptions.

- Utilities: IIoT is used in utility management for more efficient resource utilization. Cybersecurity safeguards critical infrastructure and prevents service disruptions.

- Agriculture: IIoT improves farming practices by optimizing resource use. Cybersecurity ensures data privacy and operational reliability.

- Healthcare: IIoT in healthcare offers real-time monitoring of medical equipment and patient data. Cybersecurity is critical to protect patient privacy and device reliability.

- Oil and Gas: IIoT enhances remote monitoring and predictive maintenance in the oil and gas industry. Cybersecurity protects against equipment failures and environmental risks.

In all three domains – IoT, OT, and IIoT – cybersecurity measures are essential to protect critical data, maintain operational continuity, and ensure the safety and privacy of individuals and organizations. The interconnected nature of these technologies exposes them to various security threats, making robust cybersecurity a top priority. As these technologies evolve, cybersecurity remains paramount to address new and emerging threats.

Building Blocks of Internet of Things (IoT)

The Internet of Things (IoT) is a complex system involving various elements working together to collect, transmit, analyze, and act on data. The Internet of Things (IoT) building blocks can be customized significantly based on the detailed use case and requirements. Figure 1-1 depicts the widely accepted building blocks of Internet of Things (IoT).

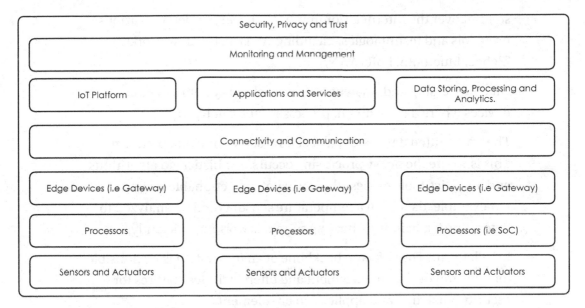

Figure 1-1. *Internet of Things – building blocks*

These blocks interact to enable the seamless functioning of an IoT system, from data collection and transmission to analysis and action.

- Sensors and Actuators: Devices that collect data from the environment or perform commands-based actions. The first step in an IoT system is data collection. Sensors or devices are deployed to collect data from the environment. This could be anything from temperature readings, light levels, motion detection, health metrics, and more. These devices are often small and have some level of computing power.

- Edge Devices/Gateways: Hardware that connects sensors and actuators to the network, often performing initial data processing.

- Connectivity and Communication: Network protocols and communication channels transmit data between devices and central systems (e.g., Wi-Fi, cellular networks, Zigbee, LoRaWAN).

  Once the data is collected, it must be sent to a central system for further processing. This is usually done over a network connection. The sensors/devices are connected to an IoT gateway or edge device that serves as an intermediary, which preprocesses the data and sends it over the Internet. Communication can happen via various protocols and technologies, including Wi-Fi, cellular networks, Zigbee, Bluetooth, LoRaWAN, etc.

- Data Processing and Analytics: Servers, cloud systems, or edge devices where data is stored, processed, and analyzed.

The transmitted data is sent to a central server or cloud platform. This is where the heavy processing occurs. Sophisticated algorithms and analytics tools process the raw data into actionable insights. For example, data from a temperature sensor could be analyzed to determine if a building's heating system is working efficiently.

- IoT Platform: The software backbone of an IoT system is responsible for data and device management and often includes features for security, analytics, and application enablement.

- Applications and Services: Software applications that use the processed data to perform actions or present information to users in a usable way.

The system can make decisions and take appropriate actions based on the processed data and analysis. This can be as simple as sending an alert to a user or as complex as automatically adjusting the settings on a machine. For example, if the system detects that the temperature in a room is too high, it might send a command to lower the thermostat.

The actions are often performed by actuators in the IoT system. An actuator is a motor or mechanism that moves or controls a system or mechanism. It is operated by a source of energy – typically, electric current, hydraulic fluid pressure, or pneumatic pressure – and converts that energy into motion.

Many IoT systems have a feedback loop where the results of the action taken are monitored, and the data is used to refine the system's decision-making process over time. For instance, a smart irrigation system might adjust its watering schedule based on past results to use water more efficiently.

- Security: Technologies and protocols protect data, devices, and networks from unauthorized access and attacks (e.g., encryption, authentication, authorization).

  Security is a critical aspect of IoT. Since IoT devices are connected to the Internet, they are susceptible to hacking and other cyberattacks. Secure data transmission, authentication, encryption, and regular security updates are vital.

  Privacy is also a significant concern, especially for consumer IoT devices like smart home products. Ensuring that users' data is handled and stored securely and in compliance with relevant regulations is a fundamental part of IoT operation.

- Monitoring and Management: Tools and processes for managing devices, data, and the overall health and performance of the IoT system.

  IoT systems usually include tools for managing the devices themselves (like updating their software) and tools for monitoring the system's health (like alerts if a device goes offline). This is critical for large-scale IoT deployments with thousands or millions of devices.

These building blocks are the core components of most IoT architectures, enabling the system to collect data from various devices, send it through a network, process and analyze it, and then make informed decisions based on the analysis. The specific implementation and technologies used can vary widely depending on the use case and requirements of the IoT system.

Internet of Things Architecture

The Internet of Things (IoT) architecture is a layered structure that ensures efficient data flow from physical devices to the end-user application and vice versa. The IoT architecture can be broadly divided into four layers such as Device Layer (Sensing Layer), Communication Layer (Network Layer), Processing Layer (Management Layer), and Application Layer. Figure 1-2 illustrates the layers of IoT architecture.

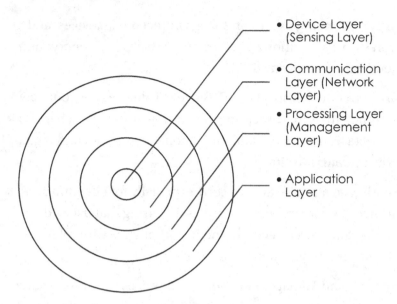

- Device Layer (Sensing Layer)
- Communication Layer (Network Layer)
- Processing Layer (Management Layer)
- Application Layer

Figure 1-2. *IoT layers*

Let's delve deeper into each layer:

- **Device Layer (Sensing Layer)**

  Description: This is the layer where physical devices, such as sensors and actuators, reside. These devices collect environmental data, like temperature, humidity, or light levels. Conversely, actuators perform physical actions based on commands received, like turning on a light or adjusting a thermostat.

  Illustration: Imagine a smart thermostat in a home. The temperature sensor measures the current room temperature and sends this data for processing.

- **Communication Layer (Network Layer)**

  Description: Once the devices collect the data, it needs to be transmitted to the next layer for processing. This layer comprises communication protocols, gateways, and network infrastructure, ensuring data is securely and efficiently transferred.

  Illustration: The smart thermostat sends the room temperature data over Wi-Fi to a local gateway or the cloud. It might use protocols like MQTT or CoAP to ensure the data reaches its destination.

- **Processing Layer (Management Layer)**

  Description: Data received from devices is processed in this layer. It involves data storage, data analytics, and decision-making processes. Depending on the data and the use case, specific actions might be taken automatically, or insights might be generated for end users or other systems.

  Illustration: The cloud server receives the temperature data from the smart thermostat. It processes this data, comparing it with the desired temperature the user sets. If the room is colder than desired, a decision is made to activate the home's heating system.

- **Application Layer**

  Description: This is where the end user interacts with the IoT system. Applications present the data as user-friendly and allow users to make decisions or adjust settings. Depending on the IoT use case, this could be a mobile app, a web dashboard, or even another automated system.

  Illustration: The homeowner opens a mobile app connected to the smart thermostat. They can view the current room temperature and adjust the desired temperature. If they increase the desired temperature, a command is sent through the system to adjust the heating.

The IoT architecture provides a structured way to understand the flow of data from the physical world to digital applications and back. Each layer has a crucial role in ensuring that data is accurately collected, transmitted, processed, and presented or acted upon meaningfully. Understanding this architecture will be essential for developing efficient, secure, and user-friendly IoT solutions as IoT systems evolve.

Let us consider a smart thermostat in a home as an example of the Internet of Things to understand a simplified version of understanding IoT inner engineering. Figure 1-3 illustrates the workflow of thermostat showing real-world IoT architecture.

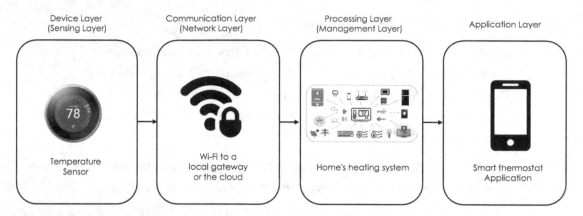

Figure 1-3. *Thermostat IoT architecture*

Let's break down how a smart thermostat with a step-by-step workflow, a popular example of an IoT device, works within the building block of the Internet of Things. Here's a step-by-step walkthrough.

1. The thermostat, equipped with temperature sensors, collects data on the home's current temperature.

2. This data is transmitted via Wi-Fi to a central cloud server.

3. The cloud server processes this data and compares the current temperature to the desired temperature the homeowner sets.

4. If the current temperature is lower than the desired temperature, the server decides that the heating system should be turned on and sends this command back to the thermostat.

5. The thermostat receives and acts on this command, turning on the heating system.

6. As the heating system operates, the thermostat monitors the temperature and sends this data back to the server, creating a feedback loop.

7. The homeowner can manage and monitor this system via a smartphone app, changing the desired temperature as needed.

8. All this data transmission happens over encrypted channels to maintain security and privacy.

The Internet of Things (IoT) has found applications across a wide range of industries, revolutionizing processes, enhancing productivity, and offering new capabilities. Here's a list of industries where IoT is designed and deployed. The Internet of Things (IoT) has revolutionized industries by introducing smart, interconnected devices that can collect, transmit, and process data to optimize operations, reduce costs, and create new business models. IoT enables predictive maintenance in manufacturing, reducing downtime and ensuring efficient production lines. In agriculture, farmers deploy sensors to monitor soil moisture levels and optimize irrigation. The healthcare sector uses wearable devices to track patients' health metrics in real time, while smart cities implement IoT to optimize traffic flow, enhance public safety, and monitor environmental conditions. Retailers benefit from personalized shopping experiences and streamlined inventory management. IoT offers unparalleled opportunities for industries to innovate, improve efficiency, and provide better services.

The Internet of Things (IoT) has paved the way for real-time monitoring of vehicles and goods in transportation and logistics. Fleet managers can track the location and condition of their vehicles, ensuring timely deliveries and reducing operational inefficiencies. Smart sensors on ships, airplanes, and trucks can provide information about cargo conditions, ensuring that perishable goods or sensitive equipment are transported under optimal circumstances. Moreover, the rise of connected cars equipped with IoT devices promises to reshape urban mobility, enhancing safety through features like collision avoidance and enabling innovative solutions such as autonomous driving.

The Internet of Things (IoT) plays a pivotal role in making grids smarter and more responsive in the energy sector. Smart meters allow for real-time electricity consumption monitoring, helping consumers and providers better manage energy use and costs. Renewable energy sources, like wind and solar farms, integrate IoT devices to optimize power generation based on real-time environmental data. This ensures maximum efficiency and aids in the grid's management and distribution of energy. Moreover, in the realm of consumer electronics, smart homes are becoming a reality with the integration of IoT. Devices like thermostats, security cameras, and refrigerators can now be interconnected and remotely managed through smartphones or voice-activated assistants. This provides homeowners with convenience and efficiency and offers opportunities for energy savings and enhanced security. As the boundaries of what can be connected continue to expand, IoT's potential applications and benefits across all facets of industry and daily life seem boundless. Table 1-2 provides a concise overview of the various industries and their corresponding IoT applications. As the IoT field continues to evolve, the applications within each industry will likely expand and diversify.

Table 1-2. *Industry vs. Current and Forecasted IoT Adoption*

Industry	IoT Applications
Healthcare	– Remote patient monitoring – Wearable health devices – Smart hospital equipment management
Agriculture	– Precision farming – smart irrigation – Livestock monitoring
Manufacturing	– Industrial IoT (IIoT) – predictive maintenance – Supply chain optimization
Retail	– Smart inventory management – Customer behavior analytics – Supply chain tracking
Smart cities	– Traffic management – Waste management – Energy optimization
Energy	– Smart grids – Renewable energy monitoring
Transportation and logistics	– Fleet management – Real-time tracking of goods – Predictive vehicle maintenance
Home automation	– Smart thermostats – Connected security systems – Intelligent appliances
Real estate and infrastructure	– Building energy management – Structural health monitoring
Wearables	– Fitness trackers – Smartwatches
Financial services	– Fraud detection – Insurance telematics

(continued)

Table 1-2. (*continued*)

Industry	IoT Applications
Environmental monitoring	– Air quality sensors – Water quality monitoring
Hospitality	– Smart room controls – Personalized guest experiences
Education	– Smart classrooms – Attendance monitoring
Entertainment and media	– Audience engagement tools – Personalized content delivery

Microsoft Azure IoT Solution Offerings

Microsoft Azure provides a comprehensive suite of services and solutions designed to help organizations develop, deploy, and manage Internet of Things (IoT) applications.

Azure IoT enables you to rapidly transform your ideas into tangible results, offering secure, scalable, and open solutions from edge to cloud within the Microsoft Cloud ecosystem.

Azure IoT bridges the gap between edge and cloud by connecting, analyzing, and automating seamlessly. Forge tailored cloud solutions for your industry on an exclusive platform enriched with smart edge-to-cloud tech underpinned by inherent security, privacy, and compliance standards. Spearhead change and realize your business objectives by crafting innovative ecosystems that enable device and application connection, observation, automation, and representation – all powered by the Microsoft Cloud.

Azure IoT services are uniquely poised to address industry-specific challenges, offering tailored, scenario-centric solutions spanning the edge to the cloud. The Microsoft Cloud boasts an extensive partner ecosystem, numbering in the thousands. This network paves the way for users to harness diverse cloud functionalities and roll out numerous tested solutions tailored for distinct business requirements. With the advent of 5G, businesses can further leverage edge-based solutions tailored for specific workloads, propelling their transformation journey. This not only enhances productivity but also cuts costs and optimizes operational efficiency. It enables data-driven decisions in near real time, which is especially vital for applications sensitive to latency and distinct use cases.

Azure IoT services facilitate the connection, monitoring, and management of billions of edge devices. Users can opt for a fully supervised application platform or, if they prefer, construct more adaptive solutions using the platform's robust services. Azure's open strategy emphasizes effortless development and integration, ensuring developers face minimal friction. Furthermore, Azure offers a holistic device management platform, letting users securely connect, provision, update, and oversee any edge device throughout its life cycle. This platform lets users orchestrate their devices and applications under one unified dashboard, enhance features on the fly, automate firmware updates, and diligently monitor and rectify device performance.

Protection remains paramount with Azure. Organizations can have confidence in the robust security measures, encompassing hardware, software, and cloud components. There's an innate trust in the security of your data landscape as you architect open, adaptable, and scalable solutions, all while being shielded with end-to-end security from the foundational chip level up to the vast cloud.

The Azure Internet of Things (IoT) consists of cloud services, edge elements, and SDKs managed by Microsoft. These tools allow you to connect, oversee, and manage your IoT resources on a large scale. Put more, an IoT solution comprises IoT devices that interact with cloud-based services.

At the core of Azure IoT services is Azure IoT Hub, which acts as the central message hub for bidirectional communication between IoT applications and the devices they manage. It provides secure and reliable device-to-cloud and cloud-to-device messaging capabilities.

Figure 1-4 offers an overview of the elements in a standard IoT setup. This piece highlights primary component clusters: devices, IoT cloud services, additional cloud services, and overarching solution concerns.

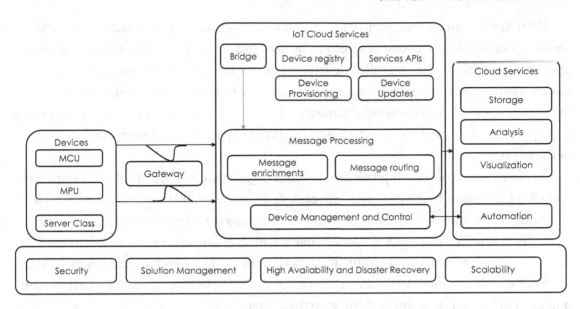

Figure 1-4. *High-level view of Microsoft IoT solution focus areas*

Azure offers a comprehensive suite of tools to drive IoT projects forward. With Azure IoT Central, you can speed up the development of your IoT solutions. Meanwhile, Azure IoT Edge allows you to extend cloud intelligence directly to your edge devices. If you're looking to connect, oversee, and manage billions of IoT assets, Azure IoT Hub has got you covered. Azure Digital Twins is your go-to for those wanting a digital representation of their physical spaces or assets. Dive deep into time-series IoT data as it streams in with Azure Time Series Insights. For robust security in MCU-powered devices, look no further than Azure Sphere. Embedded IoT development and seamless connectivity are made effortlessly simple with Azure RTOS. And for private service consumption on the Azure platform, there's Azure SQL Edge. Together, these tools ensure a holistic and seamless IoT experience.

Azure IoT solutions tackle industry-specific challenges through edge-to-cloud technological answers. Microsoft Cloud boasts a vast partner ecosystem, allowing you to tap into cloud features and implement many established solutions tailored for distinct business requirements. Boost your business transformation by leveraging 5G edge solutions tailored for special workloads, enhancing productivity, cutting costs, and heightening operational efficiency. These solutions facilitate immediate, data-informed decisions, especially crucial for latency-sensitive applications and distinct use cases.

With Azure, you can connect, oversee, and administrate billions of edge devices on a wholly managed application platform or by utilizing potent platform services. Azure's open strategy emphasizes seamless development and integration. Its comprehensive device management platform ensures every edge device is securely connected, managed, updated, and monitored throughout its life cycle. Easily organize your devices and apps, integrate new features on the go, automate upgrades, and keep tabs on device performance.

Azure ensures top-notch protection for your organization across hardware, software, and cloud domains. Rest assured, as you craft flexible, scalable IT and operational tech solutions, Azure's end-to-end security shields your data from chip to cloud.

Thus, Azure IoT services form an extensive and integrated suite that caters to various needs and aspects of an IoT solution, from device connectivity and management to edge computing, data storage, analytics, and security, enabling businesses to fully harness the potential of IoT to transform and enhance their operations.

Overview of Azure IoT Central

Azure IoT Central provides a comprehensive avenue for businesses looking to dive into the world of the Internet of Things (IoT) without the associated complexities. At its core, it's a fully managed IoT solution that aims to simplify the process of building IoT applications.

Azure IoT Central provides an out-of-the-box UX and API interface for seamless device connection and management on a grand scale, ensuring trustworthy data for insightful business decisions. It combines platform-as-a-service (PaaS) solutions, unifying every service under its umbrella and presenting a streamlined, all-inclusive, and secure IoT solution. The following are essential capabilities of Azure IoT Central:

- The rapid linkage between IoT devices and the cloud

- Unified control for hassle-free device modifications and updates

- Graphics and evaluations to decipher IoT data, from overarching views to nuanced specifics

- Adaptability to connect business applications with IoT data, translating insights into tangible actions

Firstly, when we talk about **management**, the primary advantage lies in its scalability and security. Companies, especially those needing more resources for system architecture, can benefit immensely. They can handle the intricacies of scaling up their operations or ensuring the security of their IoT devices. Azure IoT Central's application platform takes care of these aspects, offering a robust system that manages the scale, safety, and overall management of IoT applications and the devices they run on.

Regarding **control**, businesses have abundant flexibility without the associated technical overhead. While Azure IoT Central manages the complex backend processes, companies can still retain their brand identity and customize crucial front-end elements. This includes tailoring the look and feel of their dashboard, defining user roles, specifying devices, and even customizing the telemetry data they collect. This customization ensures that businesses retain their identity and specific requirements, even though they're not involved in the nitty-gritty of the underlying IoT system management.

Lastly, concerning **pricing**, Azure IoT Central understands the importance of financial predictability for businesses. Instead of convoluted pricing models that can often cause budget overruns, Azure IoT Central offers a straightforward and predictable pricing structure. This ensures that companies can budget effectively, knowing there won't be unexpected costs related to their IoT applications.

In essence, Azure IoT Central is for businesses that want the power of IoT without the associated technical challenges. It provides the tools, flexibility, and pricing transparency companies need to thrive in the IoT landscape.

Overview of Azure IoT Hub and Azure Digital Twins

Azure IoT Hub is a pivotal cornerstone for building sophisticated IoT applications, emphasizing two-way communication that bridges the gap between cloud-based solutions and devices on the ground.

At its core, Azure IoT Hub is about fostering a robust connection. It ensures a secure and dependable link between your IoT application and the myriad devices it oversees. By offering a cloud-hosted solution backend, Azure IoT Hub presents an inclusive platform that welcomes almost any device into its fold. But it's not just about connectivity; it's about extending the scope of your solutions. With features such as per-device authentication, the integration allows businesses to stretch their reach from the vast expanse of the cloud right down to the nuanced edges of individual devices. Embedded within this is a strong focus on device management and streamlined provisioning, ensuring that every device remains within your control as you scale.

One cannot emphasize the importance of security in today's digital age, especially with IoT. Azure IoT Hub offers a communication channel fortified with advanced security measures. This ensures that data transmission remains uncompromised, whether sending out commands or receiving feedback from IoT devices.

Complementing this is the "Device Update for IoT Hub" feature. Recognizing the dynamic nature of technology, this tool facilitates over-the-air deployment, ensuring that your IoT devices are always equipped with the latest updates, keeping them current and secure.

But Azure IoT Hub isn't just about devices; it's about simplifying the development process. Its seamless integration with Azure Event Grid and serverless compute gives developers a more straightforward path when building IoT applications. These integrations alleviate everyday complexities, allowing developers to focus on innovating rather than troubleshooting.

Lastly, compatibility with Azure IoT Edge is a game changer for businesses that envision hybrid IoT applications that blend the strengths of cloud and edge computing. It ensures that platform limitations do not constrain you as you craft intricate IoT solutions.

Azure IoT Hub enables two-way communication with countless IoT devices. By leveraging device-to-cloud telemetry data, you can gain insights into the status of your devices and effortlessly direct messages to other Azure services, all without coding. You can dependably dispatch commands and alerts to your integrated devices regarding cloud-to-device messages. Plus, with the added advantage of acknowledgment receipts, you can keep track of message deliveries. Recognizing the challenges of unpredictable connectivity, the system is designed to autonomously resend device messages as required, ensuring continuous and consistent communication.

In summary, Azure IoT Hub is a comprehensive platform, balancing connectivity, security, development simplicity, and compatibility, all tailored to elevate IoT application building to the next level.

At the moment of writing this book, Azure IoT Hub offered two tiers. The following is the comparison of two tiers when evaluating IoT Hubs for their IoT capabilities.

IoT Hub Basic stands as a foundational entry point for businesses venturing into the Internet of Things (IoT) world. Especially for those whose primary needs revolve around unidirectional communication, IoT Hub Basic offers an optimal balance between functionality and simplicity. At its heart, even though it's termed "basic," it doesn't compromise on security – a critical concern in today's interconnected digital landscape. Each device, regardless of the scale of deployment, undergoes rigorous per-device authentication, ensuring that every piece of data and every connection maintains its integrity. The platform is engineered for scalability, so as your business grows and your device count multiplies, IoT Hub Basic is with you, effortlessly accommodating the expansion. Furthermore, it's worth noting that as businesses evolve, their needs might shift from basic to more advanced requirements. Recognizing this dynamic nature, IoT Hub Basic is designed with a smooth upgrade trajectory to **IoT Hub Standard**.

Speaking of IoT Hub Standard, it's a tier that dives deeper into the IoT ecosystem. Beyond just connecting devices, it introduces capabilities such as holistic device management and direct support for Azure IoT Edge. These features are essential for businesses with more nuanced control over their devices and those who wish to leverage the advantages of edge computing.

On another note, Event Hubs emerge as the solution for businesses grappling with vast volumes of data, especially from digital platforms like websites. It's tailored specifically for big-data scenarios. Whether ingesting real-time analytics data from a high-traffic website or collecting large-scale user interactions, Event Hubs streamline the data collection process, making it efficient and organized.

In essence, Azure offers solutions calibrated for each stage and need, whether you're starting out in IoT, looking to manage an expansive device network, or navigating the challenges of large-scale data ingestion.

Azure IoT Hub, paired with its device SDKs, offers a versatile range of protocols to facilitate device connections. These protocols include HTTPS, AMQP, AMQP over WebSockets, MQTT, and MQTT over WebSockets. However, for those situations where an application might not be compatible with any of the listed protocols, there's a solution at hand. Users can expand the functionality of the IoT Hub to cater to custom protocols in two primary ways.

First, one can employ IoT Edge, setting it up as a field gateway to handle protocol translations directly at the edge, close to the devices. Alternatively, there's the option of tailoring the Azure IoT protocol gateway, enabling it to manage protocol translations right within the expansive cloud environment. This flexibility ensures that users can adapt the system to their needs rather than being limited by default configurations.

Azure Digital Twins to craft detailed digital replicas of complete environments. Harness these insights to enhance products, streamline operations, and foster transformative customer experiences. The following are essential capabilities of Azure Digital Twins:

1. Use the Digital Twins Definition Language to craft personalized domain models for any digitally connected setting.

2. Activate your digital twins with a real-time graph display environment.

3. Integrate insights from IoT and enterprise systems, linking assets like IoT devices through Azure IoT Hub, Logic Apps, and REST APIs.

4. Channel twin modification alerts to platforms like Azure Data Explorer, Azure Synapse Analytics, Event Hubs, and additional downstream services.

Monitor historical trends and anticipate the future of any digitally connected setting. Seamlessly design and generate digital depictions of connected scenarios using a flexible modeling language. You can vividly animate these digital twins by tracking their evolution over time, whether it's buildings, factories, farms, energy grids, railways, or even entire metropolises. Harness in-depth insights from these modeled settings through robust query APIs, complemented by integration with Azure's data analytics tools.

Integrate various facets of connected settings:

1. Capture every vital physical space relevant to your enterprise.

2. Integrate data from IoT devices via Azure IoT Hub or any corporate system to formulate a unified live integration layer, offering insights spanning the whole landscape.

3. Construct on a reliable, top-tier platform.

Establish robust IoT connections with the assurance of Microsoft Azure's noted compliance, security, and privacy. Oversee, administer, and refresh IoT devices assuredly and expansively using the Azure IoT Hub. Regulate identity and permissions employing functionalities such as role-based access control (RBAC) and Azure Active Directory (Azure AD).

Azure IoT Hub and **Azure Digital Twins** are more than just technological offerings; they're foundational tools that empower businesses to architect personalized solutions, particularly for intricate IoT scenarios. They're best suited for companies that have hands-on experience with cloud solutions and device management.

From a **management** perspective, these tools are for those who desire a high degree of autonomy over their solutions. Some businesses possess in-house expertise or partnerships that give them a strong foundation in IoT. For them, taking the reins in managing, scaling, and customizing the services becomes not just an option but a preference. Azure IoT Hub and Azure Digital Twins cater to this by allowing these companies to exercise their specialized knowledge. Whether it's onboarding new devices or integrating different services, businesses can use their existing expertise to tailor their IoT environment precisely as they envision.

When it comes to **control**, it's all about the freedom to shape the blueprint of the solution. Companies often have specific requirements dictated by their unique business needs or industry standards. Azure IoT Hub and Azure Digital Twins recognize this and offer a platform that's ripe for complete customization. A one-size-fits-all model doesn't constrain businesses; they can design and control the very architecture of their solution to ensure it aligns perfectly with their objectives.

Lastly, on **pricing**, these Azure offerings present an avenue for cost optimization. Unlike fixed-price models where businesses pay for bundled services – some of which they might never use – with Azure IoT Hub and Azure Digital Twins, businesses can refine and adjust their services. This hands-on approach to service selection means companies can strategically control and often reduce their overall expenditure.

In conclusion, Azure IoT Hub and Azure Digital Twins are essential for businesses keen on leveraging their expertise, maintaining full control, and optimizing costs in their IoT solutions. They offer a blend of flexibility and precision that seasoned businesses in the IoT domain will find invaluable.

Overview of Azure IoT Edge

Leverage Azure IoT Edge on-site to efficiently dismantle data barriers and amass operational data in the Azure Cloud. Administer and deploy cloud-native tasks – like AI, Azure functions, or tailored business algorithms – directly on your IoT gadgets, from a distance and securely.

IoT Edge comprises three primary elements:

- IoT Edge Modules: These are containers designed to operate Azure services, services from third parties, or tailor-made code. Once deployed on IoT Edge–activated gadgets, they function locally on those devices.

- IoT Edge Runtime: Present on every IoT Edge–activated device, this runtime supervises the modules set up on each gadget.

- Cloud-Based Interface: This offers remote surveillance and management of IoT Edge–activated devices.

IoT Edge provides a comprehensive suite of features tailored for seamless device management and operations. It introduces zero-touch provisioning, ensuring effortless onboarding of edge devices. A robust security manager is in place, backed by a hardware-based root of trust for enhanced protection. The platform is adept at handling extended offline operations, ensuring functionality even without constant connectivity. Furthermore, its integration with Azure Monitor grants top-notch observability in device operations. The Automatic Device Configuration Service aids in edge devices' large-scale deployment and settings adjustment. Developers can also benefit from SDKs available in various languages such as C, C#, Node.js, Python, and Java. To streamline module development, tools have been provided for everything from coding and testing to debugging and deployment. Lastly, there's a CI/CD pipeline powered by Azure DevOps for those seeking a smooth transition and update process.

The following are essential capabilities of Azure IoT Edge:

- Certified IoT Edge Equipment: Compatible with your Linux or Windows gadgets that accommodate container engines.

- Runtime: Open source and free under the MIT license for enhanced control and coding adaptability.

- Modules: Azure service or Microsoft partner's Docker-compatible containers, facilitating your edge business operations.

- Cloud Interface: Direct from the cloud, manage and initiate tasks using Azure IoT Hub, including automatic device setup. Transfer AI and analytic functions to the edge.

- Deployment: Launch cloud-constructed and trained models on-site. For instance, deploying a predictive model on a factory cam for quality checks can activate an IoT Edge alert upon anomaly detection. The data is processed on-site or forwarded to the cloud for in-depth examination.

- Streamline Development: Utilize familiar developer tools and code in known languages. IoT Edge's coding is uniform, whether cloud or edge, supporting languages like C, C#, Java, Node.js, and Python.

- Remote Device Monitoring: Oversee IoT Edge devices from afar using Azure Monitor integration. Access comprehensive insights into your edge apps' health and performance via the Azure portal with integrated metrics and selected visuals. Integrate IoT Edge with on-the-fly device logs for top-tier edge insight.

- Cost-Efficient IoT Solutions: Post-analytics, only a minor part of the IoT Edge data holds significance. Incorporate services like Azure Stream Analytics or models trained in the cloud to process data locally, sending only pertinent information to the cloud. This strategy reduces the costs of cloud data transfers while ensuring data integrity.

- Uninterrupted Offline Operation: Guarantee reliable and secure operation of your edge devices, even with offline periods or sporadic cloud connectivity. Azure IoT Edge's device management auto-updates device states upon reconnection, promising uninterrupted functionality.

IoT Edge stands out as one of the most accessible edge platforms in the market today, with Microsoft's unwavering dedication to leveraging open source technologies to bring advancements to the edge. The IoT Edge runtime is freely available under the MIT license (MIT license means a brief and uncomplicated permissive license that mandates only the retention of copyright and license notices. Distributing licensed works, alterations, and larger compositions is permitted under alternative terms, and source code is not mandatory), ensuring users have enhanced control and adaptability over the code. Furthermore, IoT Edge is compatible with the Moby container management system, amplifying the principles of containerization, isolation, and management from cloud-centric environments right down to edge devices.

IoT Edge is versatile, accommodating Azure, third-party, and bespoke logic functioning at the edge. Explore the edge modules available on the Azure Marketplace to tap into edge features. These modules are containerized and validated for compatibility with IoT Edge, ensuring a swifter go-to-market timeline.

IoT Edge is compatible with Windows and Linux operating systems and adept at running on compact devices, including the Raspberry Pi. To discover third-party hardware that's been certified, browse the Azure Certified for IoT device catalog. This certification is grounded on essential functions such as AI integration, device oversight, and security protocols. Minimize cloud expenses while enhancing device responsiveness to local fluctuations, ensuring dependable functioning during prolonged offline intervals.

Microsoft has partnerships with DJI, Qualcomm, SAP, and NVIDIA for IoT Edge services. You can develop IoT Edge Solutions using DJI's high-end GPU-powered commercial drones. Run IoT Edge and AI services on the Snapdragon camera platform using the Vision AI developers kit with Qualcomm. Deploy essential business functions as edge modules with SAP. Get real-time video analytics at the edge by converting video feeds into sensor telemetry with NVIDIA.

Overview of Azure Sphere

Azure Sphere facilitates the crafting, connecting, and maintaining of secure, intelligent IoT devices from the edge to the cloud. It's a comprehensive IoT platform anchored in silicon, spanning the OS and stretching to the cloud. This platform assures seamless connection, management, and safeguarding of new and existing intelligent gadgets.

A vast array of devices in the catalog ensure that you can securely integrate with existing devices or design new, highly secure, intelligent ones. The platform's over-the-air update feature, combined with robust development tools, streamlines the process of rolling out enhancements and fixes to any device. Additionally, security enhancements crafted and initiated by Microsoft stand guard against evolving threats throughout the device's lifespan.

The seamless integration with IoT platform services, including Azure IoT Hub and IoT Central, eases deployment, thus accelerating the realization of business value. Azure Sphere primarily focuses on the following four different areas:

> Safeguard Your Intelligent Devices from Core to Cloud: Guard your devices, data, and networks comprehensively – covering hardware, software, and cloud aspects. Be confident in the integrity of your data landscape with a holistic IoT security solution, facilitating connections with current equipment and the creation of fresh IoT devices. Integrate your present devices with the cloud through Azure Sphere's certified guardian modules, or begin incorporating Azure Sphere in new devices using our developer kit.

Implement Updates and Oversee Device Functions: Adapt swiftly to emerging threats and novel requirements through immediate security patches, system updates, and application enhancements. Every instance of Azure Sphere comes equipped with a decade-long commitment to Microsoft's security services, featuring managed updates. When you're set, introduce over-the-air (OTA) updates in tandem with your application, straight to your IoT device.

Fast-Track Your Market Launch: Place your business vision at the forefront and channel your efforts toward pioneering innovations that amplify your business growth. Allocate your resources to sculpting intelligent edge devices, applications, and immersive experiences that yield tangible business outcomes. Expedite your market entry with adaptable deployment choices and versatile cloud connectivity.

Craft Robust IoT Solutions: Address unique industry demands with solutions designed from the chip all the way to the cloud. Seamlessly integrate and manage both new and legacy devices with IoT security solutions pioneered by our trusted Azure IoT collaborators.

With a broad ecosystem of vendors, Microsoft works with various expert hardware manufacturers to create specialized Azure Sphere–certified chips that satisfy the requirements of different markets. Developing security technology and architecture for each chip requires extensive research and testing.

Azure Sphere comes without recurring charges. The initial payment for your chip encompasses the Azure Sphere OS, cloud-based security services, and lifetime OS updates for your chip.

Azure Sphere guardian devices are designed to safeguard devices and equipment in your enterprise. These guardian modules, which often necessitate minimal to zero equipment modifications, handle data and control machinery without making them vulnerable to network exposures. They shield your operational devices from harmful attacks and streamline device upgrades, enhancing productivity with over-the-air (OTA) updates and IoT connectivity.

Azure Sphere is designed to seamlessly connect with any cloud service, be it public or private. While operating Azure Sphere, you can link with other cloud platforms for application data or enhance productivity by pairing Azure Sphere with Visual Studio and Azure IoT.

Azure Sphere works in harmony with Windows IoT. While Windows IoT offers a top-tier solution for devices that deliver immersive user experiences, Azure Sphere reinforces IoT devices with Microsoft's cutting-edge security developments spanning hardware, software, and cloud realms.

Overview of Windows for IoT

Microsoft's Windows for IoT, commonly known as Windows IoT, is a version of Windows designed to be used in the Internet of Things (IoT) devices. It's tailored for smaller, low-cost devices that are part of a more extensive network of connected devices. Windows IoT comes in different editions to cater to various IoT needs. Here's a brief overview:

- Windows 10 IoT Core: This is designed for small, low-cost devices that are part of a more extensive network of connected devices. It's optimized for minimal resource consumption and can run on devices without a display, like many IoT core devices. Examples include small gateways or wearable devices.

- Windows 10 IoT Enterprise: This is a full version of Windows 10 but is licensed for the Internet of Things (IoT) scenarios. It suits IoT devices with powerful compute requirements and offers a richer user experience. Examples include kiosks, ATMs, or medical imaging devices.

Key Features and Benefits of Windows for IoT

- Integrated Development Environment: Developers can use Visual Studio and the Windows IoT Core Templates to easily create, debug, and deploy applications for IoT devices.

- Security: Microsoft leverages its experience in Windows security to provide trusted boot, BitLocker encryption, and other advanced security features to protect IoT devices.

- Connectivity: Windows for IoT supports various connectivity protocols and standards, making connecting to multiple devices and cloud services easier.

- Device Management: Integrated with Azure IoT Suite, it offers advanced device management capabilities, allowing for the easy management, configuration, and updating of IoT devices.

- Universal Windows Platform (UWP): With UWP, developers can write an application once and have it run across a wide range of Windows 10 devices, including those powered by Windows IoT.

The objective of Windows for IoT is to bring the power of Windows and the ease of use of the Windows development environment to the growing world of IoT devices, ensuring they are secure, robust, and easily manageable.

Enable your organization to construct and operate state-of-the-art technology atop a robust and enduring Windows platform. Leverage the steadfast nature of Windows to realize the potential of IoT fully. Effortlessly design, launch, and expand IoT solutions using a recognized operating system equipped with well-known development and oversight tools. Integrate devices effortlessly with the cloud via Azure IoT, extracting valuable insights that facilitate tailored user experiences, amplify customer interactions, and enhance business performance.

Windows for IoT utilizes the same graphic and media foundation that propels Xbox and Windows gaming, ensuring immersive user interactions. Employ potent and familiar tools for developing and managing Windows for IoT devices. Benefit from decade-long life cycle support, which aids in minimizing device recertification, bolstering device longevity, and mitigating security threats. Experience the open cloud protocol support and the turnkey solution that infuses Azure intelligence into Windows for IoT.

Embark on your Windows for IoT venture with a clear direction to hasten your market entry. Select development tools that resonate with your organization's goals, resources, and ambitions. Capitalize on the expertise of your developers by crafting and overseeing Windows for IoT devices using formidable tools like Visual Studio. From the outset, lay the groundwork for comprehensive IoT solutions tailored for your enterprise.

Establish robust IoT solutions rooted in a foundation supported by over a billion active Windows devices. Safeguard your gadgets with the intrinsic, enterprise-level security of Windows for IoT and ensure consistent user experiences via device lockdown. Adopt a vigilant, zero-trust security approach that's tailored to the intricate nature of today's IoT landscape.

With Azure IoT Edge for Linux on Windows (EFLOW), execute Linux-driven, cloud-centric workloads on Windows for IoT, all while preserving your existing edge management tools on Windows. Develop applications that demand an interactive user interface and potent hardware without exclusively settling on Windows or Linux. Streamline the device-cloud linkage with Azure IoT's open cloud protocol and intuitive initial setup – craft dynamic, forward-thinking, or intelligent applications leveraging Azure AI and its services. Infuse your solutions with AI at the frontier using Windows and Azure's machine learning capabilities, unlocking deeper business insights and paving the way for novel business avenues.

Overview of Azure RTOS

Azure RTOS (real-time operating system) is a comprehensive suite of real-time operating systems and libraries developed by Microsoft to address the specific needs of embedded systems, especially in the IoT (Internet of Things) domain. It's designed to be highly reliable, real time, and compact enough for constrained resources often found in IoT devices.

Experience lightning-fast, consistent operational performance with optimized resource usage. Azure RTOS's ThreadX ensures context switching in under a microsecond, and its NetX Duo delivers almost direct-wire network speeds. All elements are crafted for deterministic action, ensuring consistent speed irrespective of the workload. All Azure RTOS component source codes are accessible on GitHub for inspection and experimentation. As you gear up to shift your code to production, remember: there's no licensing fee for deploying on pre-licensed hardware. Neat, transparent coding not only enhances usability and maintenance but can also minimize ownership expenses. Many certification processes necessitate submitting your software's entire source code, RTOS included. With Azure RTOS, you benefit from top-tier code, and you can also access comprehensive reports confirming the code's adherence to rigorous testing standards.

As devices grow increasingly sophisticated and potent, their potential to gather data, process it, evolve, and predict outcomes is unprecedented – however, this is contingent on a solid cloud connection. Leaping IoT might seem daunting, but we've streamlined the process. Azure RTOS boasts an effortless integration with Azure IoT, enabling smooth device connection, oversight, and management. Establish a connection using IoT protocols, reference designs, or IoT Plug and Play via the Azure IoT device SDK.

Azure RTOS's versatility has found its way into products spanning sectors from avionics to household gadgets, industrial machinery, building systems, and beyond. Developers contending with demanding application development specifications across diverse sectors can tap into Azure RTOS's proven reliability via pre-certification, curtailing development uncertainties and hastening market entry. Notably, Azure RTOS has earned a certification from TUV, meeting the IEC 61508 SIL4 standards.

The following is the list of core features and components:

- Ultra-Low Overhead: Azure RTOS has an impressively small memory footprint, making it ideal for resource-constrained devices. Its performance is optimized to ensure swift, real-time responses.

- ThreadX RTOS: This is the foundational real-time operating system of Azure RTOS. ThreadX is known for its small size, incredible speed, and advanced features like priority inheritance, preemption threshold, and real-time event tracking.

- NetX Duo: This is a dual IPv4/IPv6 stack for Azure RTOS, designed for secure connectivity needs, with features supporting multiple IP interfaces, NAT, DHCP, and more.

- FileX: Azure RTOS's high-performance, fail-safe file system. It supports multiple storage media, including NAND, NOR, RAM, SD, and eMMC.

- USBX: A high-performance USB host, device, and On-The-Go (OTG) stack for Azure RTOS. It's designed for quick integration and supports various USB classes.

- GUIX: A high-performance, compact graphical user interface (GUI) library for Azure RTOS, perfect for devices requiring intuitive interfaces with graphics.

The following is the list of key benefits:

- Ease of Development: Azure RTOS integrates seamlessly with popular development environments and provides developers with extensive tools and resources.

- Seamless Azure Integration: It offers built-in connectivity to Azure IoT, allowing devices to send telemetry data, receive commands, and interact with other Azure services.

- Security: Azure RTOS is designed with security in mind. The system components are regularly audited and updated to protect against known vulnerabilities.

  Azure RTOS ensures security at both the IP and socket layers through globally recognized protocols and adherence to industry standards. It leverages hardware-based encryption and memory protection mechanisms. It backs IP layer security through IPsec and provides socket layer protection using TLS and DTLS protocols. Undergoing meticulous testing, it's certified to align with global security assurance standards. Moreover, it's harmonized with Azure Defender to identify potential threats and address vulnerabilities proactively before they pose a risk.

- Scalability: From tiny microcontrollers to powerful multicore microprocessors, Azure RTOS is versatile and can be scaled according to the device's needs.

- Pre-certified: Azure RTOS solutions come pre-certified for various safety standards, reducing time and costs related to compliance for developers.

- Broad Ecosystem: Azure RTOS supports different chip architectures and is backed by an extensive ecosystem of board support packages (BSPs), middleware, and tools.

Making IoT Development Effortless: Azure RTOS is not just about real-time performance; it's about bridging the gap between constrained devices and powerful cloud platforms like Azure. Azure RTOS significantly simplifies and accelerates the embedded IoT development process by providing a suite of tools that facilitate development, debugging, connectivity, and deployment. Developers can rapidly transition from prototype to at-scale deployment, ensuring that IoT solutions are timely, relevant, and competitive.

In conclusion, Azure RTOS represents Microsoft's commitment to the embedded IoT sector by providing a robust, secure, and efficient platform for developers to bring their IoT visions to life while ensuring seamless integration with the power of the Azure cloud.

Summary

This chapter unfolded a comprehensive exploration of the Internet of Things (IoT), covering key aspects that form the foundation of IoT understanding and implementation.

It offered a comprehensive introduction to the Internet of Things (IoT), providing readers with a foundational understanding of key concepts and technologies. It began with a thorough exploration of IoT, elucidating its significance in connecting and enabling communication between various devices and systems.

The chapter provided a comparative overview, distinguishing between IoT, operational technology (OT), and industrial Internet of Things (IIoT). This comparative analysis serves to highlight the unique features and applications of each, aiding readers in discerning their respective roles in the broader landscape of connected technologies.

A detailed examination of IoT architecture followed, breaking down the intricate structure that underlies the seamless functioning of interconnected devices. The building blocks of IoT were then explored, offering insights into the essential components that constitute the foundation of IoT ecosystems.

The final section of the chapter was dedicated to Microsoft Azure IoT solution offerings. Readers were introduced to a suite of solutions designed to facilitate the implementation of IoT applications. This included an overview of Azure IoT Central, a user-friendly platform for application management, and insights into Azure IoT Hub, which enables communication and data transfer in IoT environments.

In summary, this chapter is a comprehensive guide for individuals embarking on their IoT journey. From laying the groundwork with an introduction to IoT and providing a comparative perspective on related technologies to delving into IoT's architecture and building blocks, the chapter equips readers with a solid foundation. The exploration of Microsoft Azure IoT solutions further enhances the practical understanding of implementing IoT applications in real-world scenarios.

In the book's next chapter, you will read about the method of developing an architecture and cybersecurity strategy for IoT.

CHAPTER 2

Develop Security Strategy for IoT/OT with Defender for IoT

Designing a secure IoT solution requires a multilayered approach that addresses vulnerabilities at each point in the IoT architecture. The first layer of defense starts at the hardware level. Utilize secure microcontrollers and implement trusted computing modules to ensure that devices are tamper-resistant. During the startup process of a device, secure boot mechanisms can also verify the authenticity of the firmware and software loaded.

Network security is another critical domain. All communications between devices and the backend servers should be encrypted using robust encryption algorithms and secure protocols like TLS. Network firewalls and intrusion detection/prevention systems can help monitor and filter malicious traffic. Segmenting the network to isolate IoT devices is also advisable, limiting their exposure to potential threats.

On the software and platform side, opt for secure and scalable IoT platforms like Microsoft Azure IoT, with built-in security features such as identity and access management (IAM), secure data storage, and regular security updates. Security should be built into application programming interfaces (APIs) by requiring authentication and testing them for vulnerabilities like SQL injection.

Cloud security measures must also be in place to protect data at rest, in transit, and during processing. Regular audits, compliance checks, and risk assessments should be part of the routine to ensure ongoing security.

Building a secure IoT solution is not a one-time activity but an ongoing process that involves continuous monitoring, regular updates, and periodic security audits. By

© Puthiyavan Udayakumar and Dr. R. Anandan 2024
P. Udayakumar and Dr. R. Anandan, *Design and Deploy Microsoft Defender for IoT*,
https://doi.org/10.1007/979-8-8688-0239-3_2

implementing security measures across multiple layers – device, network, platform, and cloud – you can build an IoT solution that is functional but also secure and resilient against threats.

By the end of this chapter, you should be able to understand the following:

- IoT's cybersecurity

- How Microsoft Defender for IoT works

- Design framework for IoT cybersecurity solution

- Design principle for IoT cybersecurity solution

- Design elements of Microsoft Defender for IoT

- Microsoft-recommended approach to design security for IoT cybersecurity solution

IoT's Cybersecurity

The Internet of Things (IoT) refers to the vast network of interconnected devices that collect, exchange, and process data. These devices range from everyday household items like smart thermostats and refrigerators to industrial sensors and wearable health monitors. As these devices become increasingly integrated into our daily lives and business operations, ensuring their security is paramount.

IoT cybersecurity focuses on protecting these devices and their networks from various cyber threats. Unlike traditional computing devices, such as PCs or servers, many IoT devices have specific challenges:

- Diverse Ecosystem: IoT encompasses various devices manufactured by multiple companies, often with different operating systems and architectures. This diversity makes a standardized security approach challenging.

- Limited Resources: Many IoT devices have processing power, memory, and storage constraints. This makes it challenging to implement robust encryption or other resource-intensive security measures.

- Prolonged Lifespan: Some IoT devices, especially those in industrial settings, are expected to function for years if not decades. Over such extended periods, vulnerabilities can be discovered, making devices susceptible if they aren't regularly updated.

- Data Sensitivity: IoT devices often collect sensitive data, whether it's personal information from a wearable fitness tracker or operational data from a factory sensor. Unauthorized access to this data can have profound implications.

Given these challenges, IoT cybersecurity requires a multifaceted approach. This includes secure device manufacturing practices, regular software updates and patches, network security measures, and user awareness and training. As IoT continues to grow and evolve, so will the cybersecurity strategies and technologies designed to protect it.

Cybersecurity is critically essential for IoT (Internet of Things) for several reasons:

- Vast Attack Surface: IoT encompasses a wide range of devices, from smart thermostats in homes to medical devices in hospitals to sensors in industrial plants. The sheer number of these connected devices presents a vast attack surface for potential cyber threats.

- Inherent Vulnerabilities: Many IoT devices were designed for functionality and convenience rather than security. As a result, they might lack fundamental security features, making them more susceptible to attacks.

- Data Privacy Concerns: IoT devices often collect personal data. Without proper security, unauthorized individuals can access and misuse this data, leading to privacy breaches.

- Potential for Large-Scale Disruptions: An attack on an IoT system can have broad implications. For instance, if a city's intelligent traffic control system gets compromised, it can lead to massive traffic jams or even accidents.

- Integration with Critical Systems: IoT devices may be linked to critical infrastructure, such as power grids or water supply systems. A security breach in such a device could have catastrophic consequences for communities or entire regions.

- Economic Implications: A security breach can result in significant financial losses. This could be due to direct theft (e.g., intelligent payment systems) or the costs of rectifying a security breach and compensating affected parties.

- Loss of Trust: Consumers need to trust the security of IoT devices to be confident to adopt them. This can hinder the growth and potential benefits of IoT.

- Physical Harm: Unlike traditional cyberattacks that target data, compromised IoT devices can cause physical harm. For example, a hacked medical device could harm a patient, or a compromised car system could lead to an accident.

- Propagation of Attacks: IoT devices, if compromised, can be used as a launchpad for attacks on other systems. For instance, the infamous Mirai botnet used vulnerable IoT devices to launch massive Distributed Denial of Service (DDoS) attacks.

- Regulatory and Legal Implications: As the potential risks of insecure IoT devices become more apparent, there is a growing push for security regulations. Noncompliance with these regulations can lead to legal repercussions for manufacturers and users.

In conclusion, as IoT devices become more intertwined with our daily lives and critical systems, the importance of cybersecurity cannot be overstated. Ensuring the security of these devices is paramount not only for the protection of data but also for the safety and well-being of individuals and communities.

Form of IoT/OT Cybersecurity in the Enterprise: Growing Adoption of IoT and OT

Enterprises across various sectors continue to adopt IoT and OT solutions to enhance productivity, efficiency, and data-driven decision-making. This trend is particularly pronounced in the manufacturing, healthcare, transportation, and energy sectors.

- Increased Risk Exposure: With the proliferation of IoT and OT devices, there is a larger attack surface for cyber threats. Many of these devices were initially designed with a low level of security in mind, leaving them vulnerable to attacks.

- High-Profile Incidents: Several high-profile security incidents involving IoT and OT systems have occurred. These incidents have brought to light the potential risks and have prompted many organizations to reevaluate their security postures.

- Lack of Visibility and Standardization: Many enterprises lack full visibility into their IoT and OT environments, making managing and securing these devices challenging. The IoT world is also diverse, with many vendors, protocols, and standards, which can create security inconsistencies.

- Regulatory Pressures: Governments and regulatory bodies have started acknowledging the potential risks associated with insecure IoT and OT devices. As a result, there's a push toward more stringent regulations and standards for manufacturers and users.

- Shift to Zero Trust: Many enterprises adopt a zero-trust approach for their IoT and OT environments. This means not inherently trusting any device inside or outside the organization's network perimeter.

- Vendor Collaboration: Recognizing the shared risks, there's a growing trend of collaboration between IoT/OT device vendors, cybersecurity firms, and end users. This collaboration aims to develop more secure devices and solutions.

- Need for Skilled Workforce: There's a recognized need for cybersecurity professionals skilled in IoT and OT security. The nuances of these environments require specialized knowledge, and there's a push for more training and certification in this area.

- Integration of AI and Machine Learning: To manage the vast amount of data and potential threats in IoT and OT environments, there's a growing use of AI and machine learning tools. These tools can help identify threats in real time and can be instrumental in proactive threat detection.

- Security by Design: There's a growing emphasis on incorporating security in the design phase of IoT and OT systems. This "security by design" approach ensures that security considerations are integrated from the outset rather than added as an afterthought.

51

In conclusion, IoT and OT offer immense benefits to enterprises but also introduce new cybersecurity challenges. Recognizing these challenges, there's a concerted effort across the industry to enhance the security of these systems, from the design phase to end-of-life considerations. However, it's an ongoing journey, and the landscape is continually evolving as technology advances and threat actors refine their tactics.

IoT Cybersecurity Domains

IoT security is a multifaceted discipline that spans several domains to ensure IoT systems' integrity, confidentiality, and availability. Here is a list of crucial IoT security domains:

Device-Level Security

- Hardware Security: Includes secure boot, trusted computing modules, and other hardware-based security features

- Firmware Security: Ensuring the firmware is tamper-proof and can be securely updated

- Data Encryption: Encrypting data stored on the device

- Access Control: Implementing strong authentication and authorization mechanisms for device access

Network Security

- Secure Communication: Ensuring secure data transmission using encryption and secure protocols like TLS

- Firewalls and IDS: Implementing firewalls and intrusion detection systems to monitor network traffic

- Network Segmentation: Isolating IoT devices in separate network zones to limit exposure

- VPN: Using Virtual Private Networks for secure remote access to devices

Platform and Backend Security

- Data Storage Security: Encrypting data at rest in databases and data lakes

- API Security: Securing APIs used for device-to-server and server-to-server communication

- User Authentication and Authorization: Implementing robust authentication and role-based access control

- Monitoring and Logging: Continuous monitoring for suspicious activities and maintaining secure logs

Cloud Security

- Data Encryption: Encrypting data in transit to and from the cloud

- Identity and Access Management (IAM): Managing identities and permissions for cloud resources

- Compliance: Ensuring cloud services comply with relevant regulations like GDPR, HIPAA, etc.

- Secure Data Backup: Implementing secure and redundant data backup strategies

Application Security

- Code Review: Regularly reviewing and updating the software code for vulnerabilities

- Secure APIs: Ensuring that the application interfaces securely with the backend and other services

- Patch Management: Regularly updating the application with security patches

- Data Validation: Implementing input validation to protect against injection attacks

Physical Security

- Device Tamper Detection: Physical mechanisms to detect and prevent tampering

- Physical Access Control: Restricting physical access to devices and backend systems

- Secure Installation: Ensuring devices are securely installed and can't be easily removed or tampered with

- Environmental Controls: Protecting devices from environmental hazards that could compromise their security

Policy and Compliance

- Security Audits: Regularly conducting security audits to identify vulnerabilities

- Regulatory Compliance: Ensuring the IoT system complies with local, national, and international regulations

- Security Policy: Developing and enforcing a robust IoT security policy

- Risk Assessment: Conduct periodic risk assessments to identify and mitigate security risks

Each domain plays a critical role in establishing a comprehensive IoT security posture. Businesses implementing IoT solutions should consider all these domains to build a resilient and secure IoT ecosystem.

Internet of Things (IoT) Cybersecurity: Challenges, Implications, and Solutions

The Internet of Things (IoT) represents a vision where every object can connect to the Internet and communicate with other devices. IoT is transforming the way we live, work, and play, from smart thermostats and wearable health monitors to connected cars and smart city infrastructures. However, with the widespread adoption of these technologies, significant concerns about security and privacy arise. This essay delves into IoT cybersecurity's challenges, implications, and potential solutions.

Challenges in IoT Cybersecurity

- Diversity of Devices and Standards: The vast array of manufacturers, standards, and protocols means there is more than one-size-fits-all solution for IoT security. The heterogeneity of devices makes it challenging to establish universal security protocols.

- Limited Computational Resources: Many IoT devices are constrained by their processing power, memory, and battery life. These limitations can prevent them from standardizing sophisticated security mechanisms in other domains like PCs or smartphones.

- Lifespan and Updates: Unlike smartphones or computers, which are typically replaced every few years, IoT devices can be used for decades. This long lifespan can lead to outdated security mechanisms and software vulnerabilities if devices aren't regularly updated.

- Physical Security Concerns: IoT devices are often deployed in public or easily accessible locations, making them vulnerable to physical tampering.

Implications of Poor IoT Security

- Data Breaches: Unsecured devices can be accessed to gather sensitive information. For instance, a hacker accessing a smart thermostat might infer when the homeowners are away, making the house a target for burglary.

- Large-Scale DDoS Attacks: In 2016, the Mirai botnet, primarily made up of IoT devices like cameras and routers, was used to launch one of the largest Distributed Denial of Service (DDoS) attacks ever seen, targeting DNS provider Dyn and causing major Internet disruptions.

- Physical Harm: Some IoT devices, like smart cars or health devices, directly influence the physical world. Compromised devices can lead to real-world harm or even fatalities.

- Erosion of Trust: With each security incident, the public's trust in IoT devices diminishes, potentially slowing adoption and stunting innovation.

Solutions and Best Practices

- Standardization: The industry and regulatory bodies should push for standardized device security protocols. Standardization can simplify security measures and ensure a basic level of protection across the board.

- Security by Design: Manufacturers must prioritize security from the inception of product development. This includes ensuring devices have secure boot mechanisms, encrypted communications, and the ability to receive regular security updates.

- Regular Updates: Devices should be designed to receive and install security updates seamlessly. This can help patch vulnerabilities and ensure devices remain secure throughout their lifespan.

- Network Segmentation: Keeping IoT devices on a separate network from critical business or personal networks can prevent potential intruders from accessing sensitive information.

- User Education: Many breaches can be prevented by basic security hygiene. Users should be educated about the importance of changing default passwords, regularly updating firmware, and being aware of the information their devices are transmitting.

While the Internet of Things presents unparalleled opportunities for innovation and convenience, it also brings significant cybersecurity challenges. Balancing the rapid development of these devices with robust security measures is crucial. By addressing the challenges head-on and implementing rigorous security practices, we can harness the full potential of IoT while safeguarding our digital and physical realms.

IoT Architecture in Cybersecurity Terms

The Internet of Things (IoT) architecture can be understood through various layers, each with its own cybersecurity implications. While the specific layers as explained in Table 2-1 can vary depending on the architectural model, a common framework includes the Perception Layer, Network Layer, Middleware Layer, and Application Layer, along with an overarching User Layer interacting with the system.

Table 2-1. *IoT Architecture Layers*

IoT Architecture Layer	Description
Perception Layer	This is the layer where physical sensors, actuators, and embedded systems collect data from the environment. It serves as the gateway for data input into the IoT system.
Network Layer	Responsible for the transmission of data between the Perception Layer and the Middleware or Application Layer. This layer encompasses various networking technologies and protocols.
Middleware Layer	This layer processes, stores, and manages the data collected. It serves as a bridge between the hardware and the application layers and often includes databases, cloud services, and data analytics tools.
Application Layer	This is where the end user interacts with the IoT system, typically through software applications like dashboards, control panels, or mobile apps.
User Layer	While not always explicitly defined, the User Layer includes the human interaction points with the IoT system. This could be through mobile apps, web interfaces, or even voice commands.

Let us get started with Perception Layer in IoT architecture.

Perception Layer

The Perception Layer is the first point of contact in an IoT system, consisting of physical devices like sensors, actuators, and embedded systems. From a cybersecurity standpoint, this layer is susceptible to physical attacks, tampering, and unauthorized data collection. Ensuring the integrity and trustworthiness of the hardware and implementing secure boot processes and hardware-based encryption are key to securing this layer.

The Perception Layer in an Internet of Things (IoT) architecture is the initial interface between the physical and digital realms. This layer comprises sensors, actuators, and embedded systems designed to collect a wide array of data from the environment. These devices could be anything from temperature sensors in a smart home setup to complex industrial sensors monitoring machinery in a factory. The primary role of the Perception Layer is to "perceive" or capture real-world conditions and translate them into digital data that can be further processed and analyzed.

This layer is critical in cybersecurity as it is the first point of data collection and, thus, the first point of vulnerability. Ensuring hardware integrity through secure boot processes, implementing hardware-based encryption, and setting up tamper detection mechanisms are standard security measures employed at this layer. The objective is to establish a trusted foundation right at the point where data enters the IoT system, thereby maintaining the trustworthiness and integrity of the information that flows through subsequent layers.

Current devices in the Perception Layer offer rich illustrations of its capabilities and vulnerabilities. For example, consider a smart thermostat like the Nest Learning Thermostat. It uses sensors to detect room temperature, occupancy, and even humidity. While these features make homes more comfortable and energy-efficient, if not adequately secured, they could serve as entry points for attackers to infiltrate a home network. Another example could be wearable fitness trackers, such as Fitbit or Apple Watch, which collect various health metrics. These devices need to be accurate and secure, as they deal with sensitive personal health data.

In industrial settings, the Perception Layer could include more complex sensors like vibration sensors on heavy machinery or RFID tags for asset tracking. These industrial sensors are often part of a more extensive system known as industrial IoT (IIoT), and the stakes for security in such environments are incredibly high. A compromise at this layer in an industrial context could lead to data breaches, physical harm, and operational downtime.

In summary, the Perception Layer is the cornerstone of any IoT system, translating real-world phenomena into digital data. It's also the layer most susceptible to physical and cyber vulnerabilities, making its security critical to the integrity of the entire IoT architecture.

Network Layer

The Network Layer is responsible for transmitting the data collected by the Perception Layer to the subsequent layers for processing and analysis. The cybersecurity challenges here involve securing the data in transit, preventing unauthorized access, and ensuring data integrity. Secure communication protocols, firewall settings, intrusion detection systems, and data encryption are commonly used to bolster security at this layer.

The Network Layer in an Internet of Things (IoT) architecture is the backbone that connects the Perception Layer to the Middleware and Application Layers. This layer is responsible for the secure and reliable transmission of data collected from various sensors and devices to other parts of the IoT system for further processing and analysis. The Network Layer uses multiple networking technologies and protocols to achieve this, each with its cybersecurity considerations.

From a cybersecurity standpoint, the Network Layer is critical for maintaining the integrity and confidentiality of data as it moves through the system. This involves using secure communication protocols like TLS/SSL, setting up firewalls to filter out unauthorized traffic, and deploying intrusion detection systems to monitor unusual activity. The objective is to ensure that unauthorized entities do not intercept, alter, or access the data during transit.

In terms of network types, the IoT ecosystem often employs a mix. Local area networks (LANs), often using Ethernet or Wi-Fi, are standard in smart homes and smaller installations. For instance, home bulbs, smart speakers, and smart refrigerators may connect to a central Wi-Fi router. On the other hand, wide-area networks (WANs) using technologies like LoRaWAN or rural networks (4G/5G) are more appropriate for larger-scale or outdoor deployments, such as smart cities or agricultural monitoring systems.

Bluetooth and Zigbee are often used for short-range, low-power applications. For example, a Bluetooth-enabled heart rate monitor could send data to a smartphone app, which then uploads the data to the cloud for further analysis. Zigbee is commonly used in industrial settings where a mesh network of sensors might be deployed to monitor various conditions in a factory.

Software-defined networking (SDN) is also becoming increasingly relevant in IoT. SDN allows for more flexible management of network resources, which can be especially useful in complex IoT deployments. For instance, in a smart city project, SDN could dynamically allocate bandwidth for critical services like emergency response systems, ensuring priority over less essential services.

In summary, the Network Layer is a complex but crucial component of IoT architecture that connects many devices and systems. It employs a range of network types and devices, each with advantages, limitations, and security considerations. Ensuring the security of this layer is paramount for the safe and reliable operation of the entire IoT ecosystem.

Middleware Layer

The Middleware Layer, or the processing or platform layer, is where the raw data is processed, stored, and analyzed. Cybersecurity considerations at this layer involve secure data storage, access control, and data processing. Implementing encryption algorithms for data at rest, stringent access control policies, and secure APIs for data exchange are vital for ensuring the cybersecurity of this layer.

The Middleware Layer is the central hub in an Internet of Things (IoT) architecture. It is responsible for aggregating, storing, and processing the data collected from the Perception Layer before it gets utilized by the Application Layer. The Middleware Layer is particularly crucial for data management, analytics, and decision-making, often using cloud computing, machine learning (ML), artificial intelligence (AI), and analytics capabilities to achieve these tasks.

From a cybersecurity perspective, this layer demands stringent measures for secure data storage, access control, and secure data processing. Implementing robust encryption algorithms for data at rest, secure APIs for data exchange, and strict access control lists are some of the key security elements at this layer. The Middleware Layer is the focal point where data can be most effectively monitored and controlled, making it a critical layer for implementing cybersecurity policies and measures.

In today's IoT landscape, cloud adoption at the Middleware Layer is almost ubiquitous. Cloud-based platforms offer scalability, flexibility, and powerful computing capabilities, making them ideal for handling the large volumes of data generated by IoT devices. For instance, platforms like AWS IoT Core or Microsoft Azure IoT Suite provide cloud services tailored for IoT data management and analytics. The cloud can also serve as a central repository where data from multiple sources can be aggregated and analyzed in real time.

Machine learning and AI have increasingly become integral parts of the Middleware Layer, mainly for analytics and decision-making. For example, in an intelligent agriculture system, ML algorithms could analyze data from soil moisture sensors, weather forecasts, and historical crop yields to adjust irrigation schedules automatically. Similarly, AI algorithms could be used in industrial IoT to predict machinery failures before they happen, saving time and reducing operational costs.

Analytics capabilities at this layer provide actionable insights from the collected data. For instance, in a smart home scenario, energy consumption analytics could analyze data from various intelligent appliances and recommend optimizing electricity usage, thereby lowering energy costs.

In summary, the Middleware Layer is a critical component in IoT architecture that handles data management, analytics, and decision-making. With the integration of cloud computing, ML, AI, and analytics, this layer is becoming increasingly sophisticated, offering data storage, intelligent insights, and automation capabilities. However, with these advanced features come increased cybersecurity risks, making robust security measures essential for safeguarding data integrity, confidentiality, and availability.

Application Layer

The Application Layer is where end users interact with the IoT system through various applications, such as monitoring dashboards or control panels. The primary cybersecurity challenges here include secure code development, data confidentiality, and user authentication. Security measures like code reviews, penetration testing, and secure development practices are essential to prevent vulnerabilities that attackers could exploit.

The Application Layer is the uppermost level in an Internet of Things (IoT) architecture and is the layer where end users directly interact with the system. This could be through specialized software applications, web interfaces, mobile apps, or voice-activated systems like smart speakers. These applications take the processed and analyzed data from the Middleware Layer and present it in a user-friendly format, enabling monitoring, control, and decision-making based on real-time or historical data.

From a cybersecurity viewpoint, the Application Layer is vulnerable to various issues, including insecure code, weak authentication mechanisms, and data confidentiality risks. As this layer directly interfaces with the end users, secure code development practices like regular code reviews, penetration testing, and employing secure APIs are paramount. Implementing robust user authentication methods, such as multifactor authentication (MFA), further bolsters security at this layer.

Cloud capabilities play a significant role in enhancing the functionality and scalability of the Application Layer. Cloud-based IoT platforms often come with pre-built application templates, analytics dashboards, and data visualization tools that make developing and deploying IoT applications easier. For example, an IoT-based smart home system might use a cloud-based application to allow users to control lighting, heating, and security systems remotely. The cloud can store user preferences, analyze energy usage patterns, and make automated adjustments based on machine learning algorithms to optimize energy consumption.

Another illustration could be in the healthcare sector, where a cloud-enabled Application Layer can aggregate data from various sources like wearable devices, electronic health records, and medical imaging. This aggregated data can be analyzed using cloud-based AI algorithms to provide insights into patient health, predict potential medical issues, or assist in diagnostics and treatment plans.

In industrial IoT scenarios, cloud capabilities at the Application Layer can facilitate complex tasks like supply chain monitoring, predictive maintenance, and quality control. For instance, a cloud-based application could monitor the real-time status of various machines on a factory floor, predict when they might need maintenance, and automatically schedule repair tasks, minimizing downtime.

In summary, the Application Layer in IoT is the user interface and decision-making platform, made increasingly powerful and flexible through cloud capabilities. While this brings immense benefits in terms of functionality and scalability, it also introduces cybersecurity risks that require diligent attention to secure code development, robust authentication, and data protection measures.

User Layer

The User Layer, though only sometimes explicitly mentioned, is an integral part of the IoT architecture. This is where the human interaction with the IoT system takes place, and it presents its own set of cybersecurity challenges. Issues like weak passwords, phishing attacks, and user negligence can severely compromise the security of the entire IoT system. Educating users on cybersecurity best practices and implementing robust authentication mechanisms are critical for securing this layer.

The User Layer, while not always explicitly defined in every IoT architecture model, serves as the human interaction point within the Internet of Things (IoT) ecosystem. This layer encompasses how users – be they individuals, professionals, or system administrators – interact with IoT devices and applications. These interactions can occur through various interfaces, such as mobile apps, web dashboards, or even voice commands. In the context of operational technology (OT) and industrial IoT (IIoT), the User Layer takes on specific characteristics and challenges distinct from consumer-oriented IoT setups.

In OT and IIoT environments, the users are often engineers, operators, and system administrators interacting with complex industrial systems. These might include manufacturing lines, utility grids, or transportation systems. From a cybersecurity perspective, the User Layer in OT/IIoT is particularly sensitive due to the high stakes involved. A security lapse at this layer could compromise sensitive data and pose significant safety risks, including the potential for physical harm or severe operational disruptions.

The User Layer in OT/IIoT is often closely integrated with specialized industrial control and monitoring software platforms. These platforms are the front-end interfaces where human operators can visualize real-time data, receive alerts, and make command decisions. Given the critical nature of many OT/IIoT applications, these platforms often employ advanced security measures like role-based access control, strong authentication mechanisms, and detailed audit logging to track user activities.

Moreover, in an OT/IIoT context, policies around human-machine interactions are enforced in the User Layer. For example, there may be protocols requiring multi-person authorization for certain high-risk operations, such as shutting down a production line or modifying a utility grid's configurations. This layer also serves as the point where education and training on cybersecurity best practices are most directly relevant. User training in these environments often goes beyond simple password hygiene to include awareness of sophisticated threats like social engineering and targeted phishing attacks that are increasingly common in industrial settings.

The User Layer in OT and IIoT contexts is a critical interface where human operators interact with complex industrial systems. The cybersecurity considerations go beyond data integrity and confidentiality to include operational safety and reliability. As a result, the User Layer in OT/IIoT demands a specialized approach to security, including robust authentication mechanisms, strict access controls, and comprehensive user education and training.

In summary, each layer of the IoT architecture presents unique cybersecurity challenges that require a multifaceted approach for mitigation. The aim is to build an integrated, secure environment that ensures data integrity, confidentiality, and availability while maintaining user trust and privacy.

IoT Security Challenges Across All Layers

The Internet of Things (IoT) architecture is often described in layers to understand better and address the complexities involved. These layers typically include the Perception Layer, the Network Layer, the Middleware Layer, and the Application Layer. Each layer presents its own set of security challenges.

Perception Layer

At the Perception Layer, the ground level of the IoT architecture consisting of sensors and actuators, the security challenges are fundamentally constrained by limited resources. These devices often need more computational power and memory to implement advanced security protocols. Additionally, they are frequently deployed in physically accessible or hostile environments, making them vulnerable to tampering and unauthorized access. The characteristics that make these devices versatile and adaptable – small size, low power, and situational deployment – also make them weak links in the IoT security chain. Consequently, lightweight cryptographic methods, secure boot processes, and physical intrusion detection mechanisms are often recommended to bolster security at this layer.

Network Layer

The Network Layer forms the backbone of IoT systems, facilitating communication between devices and servers. Here, the risks are twofold: the potential interception of data during transit and scalability challenges as the network grows. IoT applications may use varied communication protocols, each with its own vulnerabilities. Therefore, security measures at this layer must be dynamic enough to adapt to different communication standards while robust enough to scale with an increasing number of interconnected devices. Solutions often include

- End-to-end encryption

- Secure key management systems

- Specialized firewalls

- Intrusion detection systems tailored for IoT networks

Middleware Layer

At the Middleware Layer, where data processing and storage occur, the security challenges pivot toward data integrity and authorized access. Data from multiple sources is aggregated and processed here, making it a tempting target for attackers aiming to manipulate or falsify information. Additionally, unauthorized users can access and exploit databases or data streams that are not securely configured. The focus at this layer is not just on securing the data but also on ensuring that the data being processed and stored is accurate and reliable. Data validation, role-based access control, and rate-limiting are commonly employed to enhance security.

Application Layer

The Application Layer presents different challenges oriented toward user interaction and data usage. Security risks at this layer often manifest as weak user authentication methods and insecure application programming interfaces (APIs). The direct interaction with end users exposes the system to vulnerabilities, from weak passwords to social engineering attacks. Moreover, poorly designed APIs can serve as entry points for attackers, compromising the system's integrity. Robust authentication methods, API security measures, and stringent data privacy policies are thus crucial for safeguarding this layer.

User Layer

The User Layer in the Internet of Things (IoT) architecture presents a unique set of security challenges that are often underestimated yet can have significant consequences. Users interacting with IoT devices through various interfaces, like mobile apps, web portals, or voice commands, are often the weakest link in the security chain. One of the primary challenges is poor user awareness and education regarding security best practices, such as the use of strong, unique passwords or the importance of regular software updates. Phishing attacks targeted at users can also compromise the security of the entire IoT ecosystem, as once the User Layer is breached, malicious actors can gain access to the connected devices and potentially the entire network. In addition, user-level data is frequently collected and stored by IoT devices, raising concerns about data confidentiality and privacy. This data can include sensitive information such as location, personal health records, or even behavioral patterns, which, if not adequately protected, can be exploited. Another challenge is the management of device permissions and access controls; users may unintentionally grant excessive permissions to third-party apps or services, leading to unauthorized data access or manipulation. Lastly, the increasing trend of Bring Your Own Device (BYOD) in workplaces with IoT environments complicates the security landscape, as personal devices with varying levels of security can connect to the network, potentially introducing vulnerabilities. Therefore, securing the User Layer requires a multifaceted approach, including user education, robust authentication mechanisms, and stringent data protection policies.

In summary, each layer of the IoT architecture presents unique security challenges that require specialized solutions. A comprehensive security strategy for IoT must, therefore, be multifaceted, considering each layer's vulnerabilities and requirements.

IoT Security Threats and Attacks

Understanding the threats and attacks specific to each layer of the IoT architecture provides a more comprehensive view of IoT security. Here's a breakdown, complete with examples.

Perception Layer

At the Perception Layer, comprising sensors and actuators, physical tampering is one of the most prevalent threats. For instance, an attacker could physically manipulate a temperature sensor in a smart home to trigger a false alarm. This layer is also susceptible to "spoofing" where an attacker could send inaccurate data pretending to be a legitimate sensor. For example, in an industrial setting, a spoofed sensor could send incorrect readings to a control system, leading to faulty operation and potential damage.

The Perception Layer in an industrial Internet of Things (IIoT) or operational technology (OT) setting is the foundational data collection layer. This layer has various industrial sensors, actuators, and embedded systems specifically designed to monitor and control physical processes within manufacturing, energy, transportation, and utilities. These devices range from temperature and pressure sensors in a manufacturing plant to flow meters in a water treatment facility to GPS trackers on shipping containers. These systems often control critical infrastructure, so the cybersecurity implications are magnified.

From a cybersecurity standpoint, the Perception Layer in IIoT/OT is a critical point of vulnerability. Unlike consumer IoT devices, a compromised sensor or actuator in an industrial setting can have severe consequences, including safety hazards, environmental incidents, and significant operational disruptions. Security measures must, therefore, go beyond basic encryption or access control to include real-time monitoring for anomalies, secure boot processes to validate the integrity of devices upon startup, and even hardware-based security features that can resist tampering and physical attacks.

For example, consider a vibration sensor attached to a high-speed turbine in a power plant. This sensor is crucial for monitoring the health of the turbine and preventing catastrophic failures. If the sensor is compromised – either physically tampered with or hacked into – false data could be sent to the control system, possibly leading to incorrect operational decisions that could result in equipment damage or even a catastrophic failure. In such a critical application, the sensor might employ advanced cryptographic techniques to ensure data integrity and might be encased in tamper-evident, ruggedized housing to withstand physical interference.

Another illustration could be RFID tags used in automated warehousing and logistics within a manufacturing environment. These tags help in the real-time tracking of materials and finished goods. If these tags were compromised, it could lead to incorrect data about inventory levels, disrupting the entire supply chain. Therefore, secure authentication methods might ensure that only authorized devices can read or write to these tags.

Given the high stakes, the Perception Layer in OT/IIoT environments must often comply with stringent industry regulations and standards, such as ISA/IEC 62443 for industrial automation and control systems or NERC CIP for the energy sector. These standards outline robust security measures, from device authentication to data encryption, specifically tailored to the needs and challenges of industrial applications.

In summary, the Perception Layer in IIoT and OT is the starting point for data collection and a critical line of defense in the overall cybersecurity strategy. The devices used in this layer are specialized for industrial applications and, as such, come with a unique set of cybersecurity challenges and requirements that often go beyond what is typically seen in consumer-oriented IoT systems.

Network Layer

The Network Layer, responsible for transmitting data between devices and servers, is particularly vulnerable to "Man-in-the-Middle" (MitM) attacks. In a MitM attack, the attacker intercepts and possibly alters the communication between two parties. An example could be an attacker intercepting data from a smart meter on its way to the utility company and altering the consumption figures. Another common attack is "eavesdropping," where the attacker passively listens to network traffic to gather sensitive information, like passwords or device IDs.

The Network Layer in industrial Internet of Things (IIoT) and operational technology (OT) settings serves as the critical conduit for transmitting data from the Perception Layer to the Middleware and Application Layers. This layer employs various communication technologies and protocols often specialized for industrial applications. Examples include industrial Ethernet protocols like PROFINET or Modbus TCP/IP for wired connections and wireless technologies like Zigbee or LoRaWAN for specific use cases that require low-power or long-range communications.

Regarding cybersecurity, the Network Layer in IIoT and OT is a vital battleground for ensuring data integrity, confidentiality, and availability. Given that this layer handles the movement of data between devices and control systems, it is a prime target for various cyberattacks, such as Man-in-the-Middle (MitM) attacks, eavesdropping, or even Denial of Service (DoS) attacks aimed at disrupting communication. Secure communication protocols like TLS/SSL are often implemented, but in industrial contexts, additional security measures like Virtual Private Networks (VPNs), firewalls specifically configured for industrial protocols, and intrusion detection systems tailored for OT environments are commonly employed.

For instance, consider a SCADA (Supervisory Control and Data Acquisition) system used to monitor and control a natural gas pipeline. Communication devices like industrial-grade routers and switches would be deployed to ensure that data from various pressure and flow sensors reach the control center reliably. Given the critical nature of such infrastructure, these networking devices might employ hardware-based security features, robust firewall rules, and real-time monitoring to detect any anomalies in the network traffic, thereby preventing unauthorized access or tampering.

Another example could be a manufacturing line equipped with robotic arms, sensors, and PLCs (programmable logic controllers), all interconnected through an industrial Ethernet network. The network may use advanced authentication and authorization mechanisms to prevent unauthorized commands that could disrupt operations or compromise safety. These include role-based access control (RBAC) and digital certificates to ensure that only authenticated and authorized devices can communicate on the network.

Due to the specific and often critical nature of IIoT and OT environments, standard network security measures are often supplemented with specialized industrial firewalls and intrusion detection systems that understand industrial protocols and can identify attacks that conventional IT security tools might miss. Regulations and standards like ISA/IEC 62443 or NERC CIP often provide guidelines for securing the Network Layer in these industrial contexts.

In summary, the Network Layer in IIoT and OT environments is a critical component that enables seamless and secure communication between various devices and systems. The cybersecurity measures at this layer are often specialized to meet the unique requirements and challenges of industrial applications, going beyond conventional IT security protocols to ensure the safety and reliability of critical infrastructure.

Middleware Layer

This layer is often the target for "SQL injection attacks," especially if it involves a database system. In such an attack, the attacker could manipulate a query to gain unauthorized access to the database. For example, an attacker could exploit vulnerabilities in a smart city's traffic management system to alter traffic light patterns, causing chaos. Additionally, "Denial of Service" (DoS) attacks can be targeted at this layer, overwhelming the servers with excessive requests and rendering them incapable of handling legitimate requests.

The Middleware Layer in industrial Internet of Things (IIoT) and operational technology (OT) environments serves as the data processing and management hub. It takes the raw data collected by the Perception Layer, processes it, and then stores or forwards it for further analysis and decision-making in the Application Layer. This layer often employs databases, cloud services, data analytics platforms, and other software designed for industrial applications. Since it acts as a central repository and processing unit, the Middleware Layer is a critical focus for cybersecurity efforts in IIoT and OT settings.

From a cybersecurity standpoint, the Middleware Layer faces multiple challenges, including securing data at rest, ensuring secure data transfer and access control, and safeguarding data integrity during processing. Advanced encryption techniques are commonly used to protect data at rest, whether stored in on-premises databases or cloud-based storage solutions. Secure APIs and encrypted data channels are often employed for data exchange between different components or systems. Moreover, rigorous access control mechanisms, such as role-based access control (RBAC) or attribute-based access control (ABAC), are essential to ensure that only authorized personnel or systems can access sensitive or critical data.

For example, consider an IIoT system deployed in a manufacturing plant where various sensors collect data on machine performance, temperature, humidity, and other operational parameters. This data might be sent to a centralized industrial database system, like a time-series database, capable of handling high-velocity data streams. Given the critical nature of this data, the database would likely employ hardware-level encryption and multifactor authentication for access. Anomaly detection algorithms may also run real time on this data to identify any signs of machine failure or security breaches.

In energy utilities, the Middleware Layer may include complex analytics platforms capable of processing data from multiple sources like electrical grids, substations, and even consumer smart meters. These platforms could use machine learning algorithms to forecast energy demand, identify inefficiencies, or detect unauthorized access to the grid. Given the compassionate nature of this data and its national security implications, stringent cybersecurity protocols, often mandated by regulations like NERC CIP, would be in place to safeguard it.

Specialized industrial data analytics platforms, often cloud based, are increasingly common in this layer. These platforms offer potent data storage and analytics capabilities and have built-in security features tailored for industrial applications, such as secure data ingestion, real-time monitoring, and robust authentication and authorization mechanisms.

In summary, the Middleware Layer in IIoT and OT is a vital component that handles data storage, processing, and analytics. The cybersecurity challenges here are multifaceted, requiring a blend of encryption, access control, and real-time monitoring to secure various data types and databases. These security measures are often specifically tailored to meet industrial environments' unique requirements and high stakes.

Application Layer

At the Application Layer, "phishing" attacks are common, often targeting the user interface where credentials are entered. For example, a user may receive an email that appears to be from their smart home security provider. The email may contain a link redirecting the user to a fraudulent website where they're tricked into entering their login details. Another prevalent attack is "Cross-Site Scripting" (XSS), where an attacker injects malicious scripts into web applications. For instance, a user could input a malicious script into a vulnerable IoT device management portal, which then gets executed when another user accesses the portal.

The Application Layer in industrial Internet of Things (IIoT) and operational technology (OT) settings is the topmost layer where human-machine interaction occurs. At this layer, processed and analyzed data is presented to end users through specialized software applications, dashboards, and control panels. These applications enable users to monitor real-time operational data, receive alerts, and make critical decisions. In IIoT and OT contexts, the Application Layer is often integrated with cloud services to provide scalable, flexible, and robust computing capabilities. Given its importance in decision-making and direct interaction with users, cybersecurity at this layer is paramount.

The Application Layer faces many challenges regarding cybersecurity, including secure code development, robust user authentication, and data confidentiality and integrity. Security measures like code reviews, penetration testing, and safe development practices are essential to prevent software application vulnerabilities. Multifactor authentication (MFA) and role-based access control (RBAC) ensure that only authorized users can access the applications. Given the sensitive nature of the data involved, encryption, both in transit and at rest, is generally a standard practice.

For example, in an intelligent factory setting, the Application Layer could include a cloud-based dashboard that allows plant managers to monitor the performance of various machines in real time. This application could be hosted on a secure cloud platform, like AWS or Azure, which provides built-in security features such as data encryption, DDoS protection, and activity logging. Given the critical nature of the data, the application might also employ MFA and strict access controls to prevent unauthorized access.

In utility management, such as electrical or water distribution, the Application Layer may include advanced SCADA systems integrated with cloud-based analytics services. These systems could use machine learning algorithms to optimize grid performance, predict equipment failures, and even automatically reroute resources in an emergency. In such scenarios, ensuring the cybersecurity of the application is not just about protecting data; it's also about ensuring the safety and reliability of critical infrastructure. Security measures may include real-time monitoring for abnormal activities, stringent access controls, and robust data encryption protocols.

Increasingly, cloud providers are offering specialized IIoT and OT services that include data storage and analytics, machine learning platforms, and other advanced computational capabilities. These cloud services come with the added advantage of scalability and often have built-in cybersecurity features tailored for industrial applications.

In summary, the Application Layer in IIoT and OT is a critical interface for data visualization, monitoring, and decision-making. It often leverages cloud services to enhance its capabilities. However, this also introduces various cybersecurity challenges that require a multilayered approach, from secure code development and robust user authentication to data encryption and real-time monitoring, to protect against potential vulnerabilities and attacks.

User Layer

The User Layer of IoT systems is susceptible to a range of security threats and attacks that can compromise the integrity, availability, and confidentiality of the IoT ecosystem. One common threat is credential stuffing, where attackers use stolen usernames and passwords to gain unauthorized access to IoT devices or applications. Social engineering attacks, including phishing, are also prevalent at the User Layer, tricking individuals into divulging sensitive information or performing actions that compromising security. Moreover, malicious applications can be disguised as legitimate IoT apps to access user data or control devices. Man-in-the-Middle (MitM) attacks are another concern, where an attacker intercepts communication between the user and the IoT device to either eavesdrop or alter the data being sent.

In some cases, attackers exploit poor device security settings, which users may not have configured correctly, to gain unauthorized access. Data leakage is another significant issue; personal or sensitive data collected from IoT devices can be exposed accidentally due to lax security controls or intentionally through attacks. Users may also be susceptible to clickjacking attacks, where malicious buttons or links are overlaid on legitimate web pages, leading users to perform unintended actions. Even physical attacks, like device theft or tampering, can pose risks at the User Layer, as attackers can gain direct control over the device. The confluence of these threats and attacks at the User Layer underscores the need for robust security measures, ranging from strong authentication and encryption to ongoing user education and awareness programs.

The User Layer in industrial Internet of Things (IIoT) and operational technology (OT) environments encompasses the human elements that interact with the system, such as engineers, plant operators, and administrators. While this layer isn't always explicitly outlined in traditional IoT architecture models, its importance must be balanced, especially regarding cybersecurity. In industrial settings where systems often connect to the open Internet for various functionalities – such as remote monitoring, cloud-based analytics, or software updates – the User Layer becomes a critical point of vulnerability.

From a cybersecurity perspective, the User Layer is susceptible to a range of threats, including but not limited to phishing attacks, social engineering, and credential stuffing. The risks of unauthorized access or data leaks escalate as IIoT and OT systems become increasingly interconnected with the open Internet. Strong authentication mechanisms, such as multifactor authentication (MFA) or hardware security tokens, are often employed to ensure that only authorized users can access the system. User education and awareness programs are equally crucial, as even the most robust technical security measures can be undermined by human error or negligence.

For instance, consider a scenario where an engineer remotely monitors critical infrastructure systems, such as electrical grids or water supply networks, through a web-based interface. The interface might be accessible via the open Internet for convenience and flexibility. While this opens up the advantages of real-time monitoring and quick response, it also exposes the system to potential cyberattacks. An attacker could use phishing techniques to trick the engineer into revealing login credentials, gaining unauthorized access to critical systems. Here, robust authentication mechanisms and ongoing user training would be vital to mitigate such risks.

In another illustration, consider an industrial plant that uses cloud-based analytics for predictive maintenance. The plant operators might use mobile devices or laptops to access these analytics platforms via the open Internet. An attacker could gain access to sensitive operational data if an operator's device becomes compromised due to malware or a malicious Wi-Fi hotspot. In such cases, employing Virtual Private Networks (VPNs), secure data transmission protocols, and endpoint security measures can add extra layers of protection.

In summary, the User Layer in IIoT and OT settings is a crucial but often overlooked component in cybersecurity, especially as these systems increasingly interface with the open Internet. Ensuring robust authentication, implementing stringent access controls, and educating users about potential risks and best practices are essential to safeguarding this layer. The objective is to create a secure environment that blends technical controls and human factors, thereby minimizing the risks associated with the open Internet's inherent vulnerabilities.

Each layer presents unique vulnerabilities that attackers can exploit, making implementing a multilayered security approach in IoT environments crucial. By understanding the specific threats and examples of attacks that can occur at each layer, security measures can be more effectively tailored to mitigate these risks.

Trust, Confidentiality, and Privacy of IoT

In the Internet of Things (IoT) ecosystem, trust, data confidentiality, and privacy are critical components that span the various layers of the IoT architecture. These layers typically include the Perception Layer, Network Layer, Middleware Layer, and Application Layer.

Starting with the Perception Layer, responsible for data collection through sensors, trust is essential to ensure that the sensors are legitimate and not compromised. Data confidentiality is equally critical at this layer to encrypt the data at the point of collection, making it unreadable to unauthorized users. Privacy concerns arise when these sensors collect personal or sensitive information, such as health metrics or location data, which must be securely transmitted and stored.

The Network Layer is responsible for the transmission of data. Trust in this layer is crucial to ensure the data packets are routed through secure and reliable pathways. Data confidentiality is maintained through secure transmission protocols like TLS/SSL, ensuring that the data is encrypted during transit. Privacy controls can be implemented in this layer by anonymizing the data or using Virtual Private Networks (VPNs) to hide the origin and destination of the data.

The Middleware Layer serves as the intermediary that processes and stores the data. Trust in this layer is essential for secure data storage and access control. Data confidentiality can be maintained by encrypting the data before storing it in databases or other storage solutions. Privacy is ensured by implementing strict access controls and permissions, ensuring that only authorized users can access sensitive or personal information.

The Application Layer, where the data is made helpful through various applications, has its challenges. Trust here involves ensuring the applications are secure and free from vulnerabilities that could compromise data. Data confidentiality remains essential, especially when the data is displayed or exported. Privacy measures can be implemented through user consent dialogs and fine-grained control over what data is shared and how it is used.

The User Layer of IoT architecture concerns trust, confidentiality, and privacy. However, these factors are often the most vulnerable because of human factors. Users need to trust the IoT devices they interact with to be secure and reliable and the system to verify their legitimacy. By ensuring that only authorized users have access, robust authentication mechanisms, such as multifactor authentication, can help build this trust. Confidentiality at the User Layer involves safeguarding sensitive information that users may input into the system, such as passwords, personal data, or control commands. Techniques like end-to-end encryption can maintain data confidentiality by encrypting the data at the point of entry and only decrypting it when it reaches the intended destination. Privacy is a significant concern at the User Layer due to the large volume of personal data that IoT devices can collect. Ensuring privacy involves technical measures, like strong encryption and access controls, and policy measures, such as transparent data usage policies and obtaining explicit user consent for data collection and sharing.

As part of their participation in the IoT ecosystem, users must be informed about what types of data will be collected, how it will be used, and with whom it will be shared. IoT's User Layer must be secure and reliable by combining technical controls, policy frameworks, and user education that uphold the principles of trust, confidentiality, and privacy.

In summary, trust, data confidentiality, and privacy are intertwined across all layers of the IoT architecture. Each layer has specific challenges and solutions, but the overarching goal is to create a secure, reliable, and privacy-preserving IoT ecosystem.

Microsoft IoT Cybersecurity Solution

The Internet of Things (IoT) offers vast economic prospects across various sectors, paving the way for innovations from childcare to eldercare, healthcare to energy, manufacturing to transportation. The multifaceted nature of IoT in smart environments – including features like remote monitoring, predictive maintenance, smart spaces, integrated products, and user-friendly technologies such as mobile apps – can streamline operations, cut expenses, and hasten product launches.

As experts and industry observers forecast a broader integration of IoT devices and applications in the coming years, coupled with the constant emergence of new devices, services, and applications connected to IoT, businesses are keen to capitalize on these potential gains. Yet it's understandable that many firms tread carefully when exploring the advantages of IoT due to genuine security concerns related to IoT. These IoT initiatives introduce global security, privacy, and regulatory challenges for companies.

Unlike conventional cybersecurity, which focuses on software and its deployment, IoT security is more intricate as it bridges the digital and physical realms. Many operational and maintenance tasks within the IoT domain depend on seamless device connectivity, enabling users and services to engage, authenticate, diagnose, transmit, or gather data. While businesses may wish to leverage IoT-driven benefits, such as predictive maintenance, it's crucial to understand and adhere to established IoT security protocols. After all, operational technology (OT) holds too much significance to be jeopardized by breaches, catastrophes, or other potential hazards.

The following are the key factors that Microsoft observes as driving factors for IoT cybersecurity:

- IT and OT Convergence for Business Support: Information technology (IT) and operational technology (OT) are increasingly converging to support various business objectives, ranging from operational efficiency to data-driven decision-making. While IT traditionally focuses on data management and information flow, OT is geared toward controlling physical devices and processes. This convergence enhances organizational agility and innovation but also introduces unique cybersecurity challenges, as the security models for IT and OT have historically been quite different.

- Obsolescence of "Security by Obscurity" and "Air-Gap" Concepts: The traditional approaches of "security by obscurity" and "air-gapping" are no longer sufficient in the modern interconnected world. While these methods may have been effective in isolated OT environments, the convergence with IT and the growing need for real-time data and remote access have made them outdated. Relying solely on these approaches exposes enterprises to significant risks, including unauthorized access and data breaches.

- Insufficiency of Perimeter Security: Perimeter security measures, like firewalls and intrusion detection systems, are inadequate to address modern threats. Sophisticated malware, targeted attacks, and malicious insiders often bypass these defenses, requiring a more layered and nuanced approach to security, including technical and human-centric measures.

- Limitations of IoT Devices in Supporting Security Controls: Many IoT devices are not designed to support traditional security controls like agents, primarily due to their limited processing power and storage. This lack of built-in security measures makes these devices particularly vulnerable to attacks, requiring alternative security strategies such as network segmentation and real-time monitoring for anomaly detection.

- Increased Attack Surface Due to IoT Devices: The proliferation of IoT devices in enterprise environments has dramatically increased the attack surface. Each new device added to the network represents a potential entry point for attackers, making securing enterprise networks increasingly complex and challenging.

- Lack of Visibility by IT Security Teams: One of the significant challenges in modern enterprise environments is IT security teams' lack of visibility into the OT and IoT landscape. This lack of visibility hampers the ability to identify vulnerabilities, monitor for threats, and respond to incidents effectively, thereby increasing the organization's risk profile.

- Uncertainty About Connected Devices in Plants: Industrial settings often lack detailed inventories of connected devices and their configurations. This lack of awareness about which devices are connected – and how they are connected – complicates securing industrial networks and makes them vulnerable to external and internal threats.

- Uncontrolled Deployment and Connection of IoT Devices: IoT devices are often deployed and connected to enterprise networks without security controls. This ad hoc approach to IoT deployment exacerbates security risks, including unauthorized access and data leakage.

- Complex and Insecure Industrial Networks: Industrial networks are typically complex, heterogeneous, and insecure by design. They often include a mix of non-IT protocols and nonstandard devices like Programmable Logic Controllers (PLCs) and Distribution Control Units (DCUs), making them difficult to secure using traditional IT security solutions.

- Presence of Legacy Systems and Insecure Protocols: Many industrial environments still operate legacy systems running on unpatched Windows or using insecure protocols with weak authentication mechanisms. These legacy elements are particularly vulnerable to exploitation and pose significant security risks.

- Shortage of Qualified ICS Security Personnel: There is a notable shortage of personnel qualified in industrial control systems (ICS) security. This lack of expertise often results in inadequate security measures and a reactive approach to cybersecurity challenges.

- Need for External Expertise: Given the complexity and unique challenges of securing modern IT-OT converged environments, there is a growing need to supplement in-house teams with external expertise. Third-party consultants and specialized cybersecurity firms can provide the technical skills and insights needed to secure these complex environments effectively.

Modern landscape of IT-OT convergence and IoT proliferation presents various cybersecurity challenges that traditional security measures are ill-equipped to handle. Enterprises must adopt a multilayered, integrated approach to security that addresses this evolving landscape's unique vulnerabilities and complexities.

Digital Transformation and the IoT/OT Security Challenge

With the rise of digital transformation, organizations rely more on intelligent devices, leading to a security challenge. CISOs are anticipated to secure an attack surface three times larger than a few years ago. Many of these devices, crucial for optimizing efficiency, must be managed, unpatched, misconfigured, and unmonitored, making them susceptible to cyber threats. The business risks encompass production downtime, IP theft, and potential safety and environmental incidents.

Even if IoT devices appear minor or highly specialized, they pose genuine threats. They are network-linked, multipurpose computers vulnerable to cyberattacks, leading to concerns beyond IoT security. A seemingly harmless device can turn perilous if hacked online – from unauthorized access to baby monitor footage to critical medical equipment function disruptions. Once cybercriminals gain access, they can swipe data, hinder services, or engage in any malicious activity typical of compromised computers. Breaches in IoT systems can lead to more than just data leaks and erratic operations; they can cause tangible damage to infrastructure and, more alarmingly, pose threats to individuals dependent on or working with these systems.

To safeguard staff, clients, vital operational technologies, and business assets, it's imperative to enhance IoT infrastructure security through a comprehensive strategy, employing the appropriate IoT tools and standards. Leading IoT cybersecurity firms advocate for a tri-fold approach to safeguard data, devices, and networks:

- Ensure secure device setup.

- Maintain secure links between devices and the cloud.

- Implement security measures for data in the cloud during processing and storage.

Microsoft classify IoT into five primary categories: spoofing, tampering, information disclosure, Denial of Service, and elevation of privilege. Let's delve deeper into each category and its associated risks:

- Spoofing and Information Disclosure: Cyber attackers can exploit the vulnerability of specific IoT devices, particularly those with generalized security measures like password or PIN protection or those dependent on shared network key protections. For instance, a malicious actor might manipulate a device's status without revealing their identity or intercept broadcasts to impersonate the original sender, a tactic commonly called a Man-in-the-Middle (MitM) attack. Additionally, suppose a device's shared secret (be it a PIN, password, or network key) becomes known. In that case, it allows the attacker to control the device or monitor the data it emits.

- Unauthorized Network Changes: One of the most common alerts involves detecting unauthorized changes to the network configuration. This could be an unauthorized device connecting to the network, an unauthorized connection being established to the Internet, or even unauthorized remote access. Such alerts are critical for preventing potential breaches and unauthorized data transfers.

- Operational Events Requiring Attention: Defender for IoT also monitors for specific operational events that could indicate malicious activity or system failures. For example, alerts for "PLC Stop" commands or unauthorized changes to firmware versions can flag potentially harmful or disruptive actions. Unauthorized PLC programming, another alert-triggering event, could indicate that an attacker is attempting to manipulate the behavior of industrial machinery.

- Device Disconnection: Another critical operational alert involves flagging when a device is suspected of being disconnected. In an industrial setting, the sudden disconnection of a critical device could have immediate operational implications, from halted production lines to safety risks.

- Malicious or Anomalous Events: The platform is also adept at detecting more overtly malicious activities. For instance, it can alert administrators when a network scanning operation is detected, which could be a precursor to a more serious attack. Known malware signatures, such as WannaCry or EternalBlue, trigger immediate alerts, allowing for rapid containment and remediation measures.

- Unauthorized Login Attempts: Unauthorized SMB (Server Message Block) login attempts are also flagged in real time. Such attempts could indicate a brute-force attack on network shares or even an insider threat, and immediate action is often required to prevent data compromise.

- Network Protocol Abnormalities: On a more technical level, Defender for IoT can identify abnormalities in various network protocols specific to industrial environments. Alerts can be generated for events like Ethernet/IP CIP (Common Industrial Protocol) service request failures, BACnet operation failures, illegal DNP3 operations, or master-slave authentication errors. These alerts are precious for identifying and diagnosing issues that could disrupt industrial processes or compromise the integrity of control systems.

- Information Disclosure: Attackers can also secretly listen in on broadcasts to extract unauthorized information or deliberately disrupt the signal to prevent the dissemination of information. In some cases, broadcasts can be intercepted and altered to disseminate false data.

- Tampering: The physical integrity of IoT devices is also at risk. Attackers can exploit vulnerabilities, ranging from draining the device's battery to executing random number generator (RNG) attacks by freezing devices to decrease their entropy. Furthermore, the software on a device can be partially or entirely replaced. If the replaced software has access to key materials or cryptographic facilities holding these materials, it might misuse the device's legitimate identity.

- Denial of Service: Devices can be hindered by interrupting their radio frequencies or severing their connections. For instance, a purposely disabled surveillance camera, either by cutting its power or network connection, cannot transmit data.

- Elevation of Privilege: Devices designed for specific tasks can be manipulated to perform unintended functions. For example, a valve programmed to open partially might be deceived into opening fully, potentially leading to unforeseen consequences.

Microsoft's Solution

Microsoft Defender for IoT offers an agentless solution, focusing on unified asset discovery and security monitoring across various unmanaged devices. These include the following:

- Enterprise IoT Devices: Devices like VoIP phones, conferencing systems, printers, and building automation systems.

- Operational Technology (OT) Devices: These are used in vital sectors such as manufacturing, energy utilities, and oil and gas. Examples include PLCs, DCUs, HMIs, engineering workstations, historians, and legacy Windows systems.

Seamless Data Sharing Across Platforms

Defender for IoT ensures effortless sharing of IoT/OT asset and threat data across different platforms. Some of the platforms integrated with Defender for IoT include the following:

- Microsoft Sentinel (SIEM/SOAR): A cloud-native platform offering a comprehensive view of attack chains across the enterprise. It leverages machine learning to analyze logs and alerts from various sources, including threat feeds, network security tools, and applications like SAP.

- Microsoft 365 Defender (XDR Platform): A platform aimed at detecting and preventing attacks across various points like endpoints, identities, email, and applications.

- Microsoft Defender for Cloud: This focuses on hybrid cloud workload protection and security posture management across different environments, including Azure, other cloud platforms, and on-premises infrastructure such as VMs and containers.

Microsoft Defender for IoT

Let us now get an overview of Microsoft Defender for IoT.

Microsoft Defender for IoT is an enterprise-grade security solution that provides comprehensive protection for Internet of Things (IoT) and operational technology (OT) environments. Developed by Microsoft, this platform aims to address the unique security challenges presented by the increasing interconnectivity of industrial systems, smart devices, and cloud-based services. Defender for IoT is part of Microsoft's broader security ecosystem, including other Defender services for endpoints, identities, and cloud resources, offering an integrated approach to cybersecurity across different layers of an organization's infrastructure.

One of the standout features of Microsoft Defender for IoT is its ability to provide real-time monitoring and threat detection without requiring any changes to your existing infrastructure. The platform can be deployed in multiple ways, including as a network sensor that passively monitors traffic or as an agent-based solution installed directly on IoT and OT devices. This flexibility enables organizations to tailor their security measures according to their specific needs and existing configurations, minimizing disruptions to regular operations.

Another significant advantage is the platform's ability to deliver detailed asset inventory and vulnerability management. It automatically identifies and catalogs all connected devices in your IoT/OT environment, providing insights into each device's function, communication patterns, and potential vulnerabilities. This asset inventory is invaluable for organizations to understand their attack surface and to prioritize security measures based on the criticality of different assets.

Microsoft Defender for IoT also leverages advanced analytics and machine learning to detect anomalies and potential threats. It continuously analyzes network traffic and device behavior to identify suspicious activities that could indicate a security incident, such as unauthorized data transfers, unexpected changes in device configurations, or attempts to exploit known vulnerabilities. These analytics capabilities can be particularly beneficial in industrial settings where early detection of anomalies can prevent data breaches, operational disruptions, and safety incidents.

The platform integrates with Microsoft's Azure Sentinel, a cloud-native Security Information and Event Management (SIEM) solution. This integration allows organizations to correlate IoT security alerts with other security data across the enterprise, providing a unified view of the organization's security posture. Automated workflows can be configured to respond to specific alerts, reducing the time required for incident response and limiting the impact of security breaches.

Furthermore, Microsoft Defender for IoT supports compliance with various industry standards and regulations, such as the NIST Cybersecurity Framework, ISA/IEC 62443 for industrial automation, and GDPR for data protection. Its reporting features can help organizations demonstrate compliance during audits, which is increasingly important as regulatory bodies pay more attention to the cybersecurity risks associated with IoT and OT systems.

81

In summary, Microsoft Defender for IoT offers a robust, scalable, and flexible security solution tailored to the unique challenges of IoT and OT environments. It provides a comprehensive set of tools to protect interconnected devices and systems, from asset inventory and vulnerability management to advanced threat detection and incident response. Its integration with other Microsoft security solutions and compliance-supporting features makes it a strong choice for organizations looking to secure their IoT and OT assets while aligning with broader cybersecurity strategies.

Microsoft Defender for IoT from Cybersecurity Domain

Microsoft Defender for IoT is a purpose-built operational technology (OT) security platform designed to address the unique challenges of industrial IoT networks. Recognizing that OT environments often comprise a diverse range of specialized protocols and devices, the platform boasts a deep knowledge of OT-specific communication protocols. It is compatible with devices from various OT suppliers, including GE, Rockwell, Schneider, Emerson, Siemens, ABB, Yokogawa, and more. This wide-ranging compatibility ensures that enterprises can secure their entire industrial ecosystem, irrespective of the mix of devices and suppliers they rely on.

A standout feature of Defender for IoT is its infusion with IoT/OT-specific threat intelligence. This enables the platform to recognize and respond to a broad spectrum of known and emerging threats tailored to IoT and OT environments. This continuously updated threat intelligence provides real-time defense against the ever-evolving landscape of cybersecurity threats targeting industrial systems.

One of the key advantages of Defender for IoT is its rapid deployment capabilities. The platform can be up and running in minutes, offering immediate enhancements to an organization's security posture. Importantly, its deployment has zero impact on network performance, ensuring that critical industrial processes are not disrupted. By default, the platform operates in a 100% passive mode, monitoring network traffic and device behavior without interfering with their operation. It is ideal for sensitive industrial environments where system uptime is paramount.

Another critical benefit is its native integration with existing IT security stacks. Whether an organization uses Azure Sentinel for Security Information and Event Management (SIEM), Splunk for data analytics, or ServiceNow for incident management, Defender for IoT seamlessly integrates with these platforms. This integration simplifies the task of correlating IoT/OT security data with other enterprise security metrics and enables a unified approach to incident response and threat mitigation across both IT and OT domains.

Microsoft Defender for IoT offers a comprehensive, specialized, and easily deployable security solution for industrial IoT networks. Its deep knowledge of OT protocols and devices, specialized threat intelligence, quick and non-intrusive deployment, and seamless integration with existing IT security stacks make it a robust choice for organizations looking to secure their increasingly interconnected industrial systems.

Here are the different cybersecurity domains that Microsoft Defender for IoT emphasizes:

> Real-Time Monitoring and Threat Detection: One of the primary ways Microsoft Defender for IoT helps in IIoT/OT enterprise environments is through its real-time monitoring and threat detection capabilities. Real-time monitoring is crucial in an industrial setting where even a minor disruption can lead to significant operational downtime or safety risks. Defender for IoT's ability to continuously scan network traffic and device behavior allows for the immediate identification of irregularities or potential threats, providing the first line of defense in a multilayered security strategy.

> Asset Inventory and Vulnerability Management: Understanding the devices and assets that comprise an IIoT/OT environment is fundamental for adequate security. Microsoft Defender for IoT automatically identifies and catalogs all connected devices and systems, providing organizations with a detailed asset inventory. This not only aids in vulnerability management but also helps in compliance reporting, another critical aspect of enterprise security.

> Integrated Security Architecture: Microsoft Defender for IoT integrates with other Microsoft security solutions like Azure Sentinel, providing a unified security architecture. In an enterprise environment, correlating data from various security domains – such as endpoints, networks, identity, and applications – is essential for comprehensive threat detection and response. This integrated approach enhances situational awareness and helps in faster incident resolution.

Advanced Analytics and Machine Learning: The platform utilizes machine learning algorithms and advanced analytics to go beyond simple rule-based security measures. In an enterprise with multiple security domains, this capability enables Defender for IoT to detect complex threats that may span across different parts of the organization, such as multi-stage attacks that exploit vulnerabilities in both IT and OT systems.

Compliance and Governance: Regulatory compliance is a significant concern for enterprises, especially those operating in highly regulated industries like healthcare, energy, or manufacturing. Microsoft Defender for IoT supports compliance with various industry standards and regulations. Its detailed reporting features can be invaluable during audits, helping organizations meet compliance requirements while improving their security posture.

Scalability and Flexibility: As enterprises grow, so do their security needs. Microsoft Defender for IoT is designed to scale along with the organization. Whether deployed as a network sensor for passive monitoring or as an agent-based solution for more extensive coverage, its flexibility allows enterprises to adapt their security measures according to evolving needs and challenges.

User Training and Awareness: While not a direct feature of the Defender for IoT platform, its integration with broader Microsoft security ecosystems provides avenues for user training and awareness programs. Through alerting and reporting features, organizations can identify potential areas of weakness in their human interaction points, enabling targeted cybersecurity training to minimize risks further.

Data Security and Privacy: In an era where data is often considered the most valuable asset, Microsoft Defender for IoT ensures that data at rest and in transit is securely encrypted. This is particularly important in multi-domain enterprise environments where sensitive data may be transmitted between various departments or geographical locations.

In summary, Microsoft Defender for IoT offers a multifaceted approach to security that addresses various domains within an IIoT/OT enterprise environment. From real-time monitoring to compliance support, its features are designed to provide a comprehensive security solution that can adapt and scale according to large organizations' complex and evolving needs.

How Microsoft Defender for IoT Works

Let us start with the fundamental components and capabilities of Azure IoT and how they integrate into a comprehensive solution.

Choosing Defender for IoT

When determining the suitability of Defender for IoT for your organization, consider the following business needs and corresponding scenarios:

> Device Discovery: If your organization requires comprehensive device discovery, Defender for IoT offers valuable tools. The sensor console provides access to the Device Inventory page and Device Map page, allowing you to delve into detailed information regarding OT/IoT devices within your network, including their interconnections.

> Managing Network Risks and Vulnerabilities: To effectively manage network risks and vulnerabilities, Defender for IoT supplies risk assessment reports accessible from each sensor console. These reports play a pivotal role in identifying network vulnerabilities. Report findings include unauthorized devices, unpatched systems, unauthorized Internet connections, and devices with unused open ports.

> Staying Current with Threat Intelligence: To keep well informed about the latest threat intelligence, ensure that sensors within your network have the most up-to-date threat intelligence (TI) packages installed. These packages, curated by the Defender for IoT research team, provide insights into recent incidents, common vulnerabilities and exposures, and new asset profiles.

Managing Sites and Sensors: In fully on-premises environments, streamlined management of OT sensors in bulk is achievable through an on-premises management console. Alternatively, you can onboard OT sensors to the cloud and efficiently manage them via the Azure portal's Sites and Sensors page.

Conducting Guided Investigations: Defender for IoT offers valuable support for security operations center (SOC) teams. Microsoft Sentinel workbooks, integrated into the IoT/OT Threat Monitoring with Defender for IoT solution, enable guided investigations based on open incidents, alert notifications, and activities related to OT assets. These workbooks also facilitate a comprehensive hunting experience within the MITRE ATT&CK framework for ICS, empowering analysts, security engineers, and Managed Security Service Providers (MSSPs) to gain deeper situational awareness of the OT security landscape.

Automating Remediation Actions: Leveraging the Microsoft Sentinel playbooks included with the IoT/OT Threat Monitoring using Defender for IoT solution, organizations can automate remediation actions as part of their routine security practices. This automation enhances efficiency and responsiveness in addressing potential threats and vulnerabilities.

Azure IoT (Internet of Things) is a comprehensive platform offered by Microsoft that enables organizations to build, deploy, and manage IoT solutions. It provides various services and tools to connect, monitor, and manage IoT devices and the data they generate. Here's an overview of how Azure IoT works, depicted in Figure 2-1.

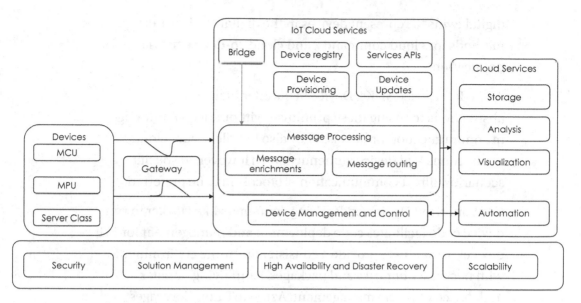

Figure 2-1. *Microsoft Defender for IOT logical view*

Device Development: In Azure IoT, developers create code for the devices within the solution. This code typically performs various tasks, such as establishing secure connections to cloud endpoints, sending telemetry data from attached sensors to the cloud, managing device state, responding to cloud commands, enabling software and firmware updates, and ensuring device functionality even when disconnected from the cloud.

Device Types: IoT devices are broadly categorized into microcontrollers (MCUs) and microprocessors (MPUs). MCUs are cost-effective and more straightforward to operate, often integrating essential functions on the chip, while MPUs rely on components in supporting chips. MCUs typically use real-time operating systems (RTOS) or run without an operating system for deterministic responses, while MPUs run general-purpose OSes like Windows, Linux, or macOS.

Primitives: Azure IoT devices utilize several primitives to interact with the cloud, including device-to-cloud messages for telemetry, file uploads for media, device twins for state synchronization, digital twins to represent devices in the digital world, direct methods for cloud commands, and cloud-to-device messages for notifications.

Azure IoT Device SDKs: Device SDKs offer high-level abstractions for using these primitives without deep knowledge of communication protocols. They also handle secure cloud connections and device authentication. However, in specific scenarios, direct communication protocols may be preferred.

Containerized Device Code: Using containers like Docker to run device code facilitates code deployment and management for IoT devices. Containers provide a consistent runtime environment with necessary libraries and packages, simplifying updates and device life cycle management. Azure IoT Edge leverages containers to deploy code modules to devices.

Device Connectivity: Devices can securely connect to an IoT Hub in two ways: directly by providing a connection string with the hostname or indirectly through the Device Provisioning Service (DPS), which assigns devices to specific IoT Hubs. DPS eliminates the need to configure individual devices with specific connection strings.

Authentication and Authorization: Azure IoT devices use TLS for verifying the authenticity of the IoT Hub or DPS endpoint. They can authenticate using shared access signature (SAS) tokens or X.509 certificates, with certificates being recommended for production environments.

Protocols: IoT devices can use various network protocols to connect to IoT Hub or DPS, including MQTT, MQTT over WebSockets, AMQP, AMQP over WebSockets, HTTPS, and OPC UA for industrial IoT scenarios.

Connection Patterns: IoT devices utilize two main connection patterns: persistent connections for command and control scenarios, which require maintaining a continuous network connection, and temporary connections for sending telemetry data, where the connection is established only when necessary.

Field Gateways: Field gateways, or edge gateways, are deployed near IoT devices and handle communication with the cloud. They can translate protocols, manage offline scenarios, filter, compress, aggregate telemetry, and run logic at the edge. Azure IoT Edge supports deploying field gateways and offers modules for common gateway scenarios.

Bridges: Device bridges enable devices connected to third-party clouds to integrate into your IoT solution, allowing seamless communication between cloud environments.

Device Management and Control: This involves processes for sending commands to devices, device registration, provisioning, deployment, updates, and monitoring. Device management ensures that devices are correctly registered, provisioned, and maintained throughout their life cycle.

Process and Route Messages: IoT solutions use message processing to route and enrich device telemetry messages. This includes routing messages to downstream services, enhancing messages with additional data, and processing messages at the edge before sending them to the cloud.

Extend Your IoT Solution: Extensibility in Azure IoT involves adding custom functionality to the built-in services. You can integrate analysis, visualization, and other systems into your IoT solution. Mechanisms for extension include service APIs, routing, rules, data export, and more.

Analyze and Visualize Your IoT Data: Analysis and visualization services enable you to derive insights from IoT data. This can involve machine learning models, data exploration, and visualization tools like Power BI and Azure Maps.

Manage Your Solution: An IoT solution uses tools like the Azure portal, PowerShell, and ARM templates to monitor and control resources and configurations.

Secure Your Solution: Security in IoT solutions encompasses device security, connection security, and cloud security. Protecting devices in the field, securing data transmission, and safeguarding data storage in the cloud are vital aspects of IoT security.

Scalability: IoT solutions often need to support a large number of devices. Scalability is achieved through services like Device Provisioning Service (DPS), Device Update for IoT Hub, IoT Hub scaling, and Azure IoT Edge, which enables edge analytics and scalability.

In summary, Azure IoT offers a comprehensive ecosystem for building scalable and secure IoT solutions, from device development and connectivity to data processing, analysis, and management. These components and capabilities can be customized and extended to meet specific IoT requirements.

Now, let us move forward with Azure Defender for IOT.

The Internet of Things (IoT) encompasses countless interconnected devices, bridging operational technology (OT) and IoT networks. IoT/OT devices and networks typically rely on specialized protocols and prioritize operational considerations over security.

In cases where traditional security monitoring systems are inadequate for safeguarding IoT/OT devices, each wave of innovation amplifies the potential risks and expands the attack surfaces within these IoT devices and OT networks.

Microsoft Defender for IoT represents a comprehensive security solution to identify IoT and OT devices, vulnerabilities, and threats. Leveraging Defender for IoT ensures the protection of your entire IoT/OT ecosystem, including preexisting devices that lack built-in security agents.

Defender for IoT offers agentless monitoring at the Network Layer and seamlessly integrates with industrial equipment and security operations center (SOC) tools.

Agentless Monitoring

Agentless device monitoring is crucial for ensuring the security of IoT and OT devices that lack embedded security agents. With this monitoring, these devices may be protected, with the potential for being left unpatched, misconfigured, and invisible to IT and security teams. Such unmonitored devices become prime targets for threat actors seeking to infiltrate corporate networks more deeply.

Microsoft Defender for IoT employs agentless monitoring to offer comprehensive visibility and security throughout your network. It excels at identifying specialized protocols, devices, and machine-to-machine (M2M) behaviors. By leveraging this capability, you can discover IoT/OT devices within your network, delve into their specifics, and gain insights into their communication patterns. This data is collected from various sources, including network sensors, Microsoft Defender for Endpoint, and third-party inputs.

The platform conducts risk assessments and manages vulnerabilities using advanced technologies like machine learning, threat intelligence, and behavioral analytics. For example, it can identify unpatched devices, open ports, unauthorized applications, unauthorized connections, changes in device configurations, PLC code alterations, firmware updates, and more. Additionally, it allows you to conduct in-depth searches within historical network traffic across various dimensions and protocols, with access to full-fidelity PCAPs for further investigation.

Defender for IoT extends its capabilities to detect sophisticated threats that may have eluded traditional static indicators of compromise (IOCs). These threats include zero-day malware, fileless malware, and tactics that operate stealthily within the system.

Regarding response, the platform integrates seamlessly with Microsoft services such as Microsoft Sentinel and other partner systems and APIs. This integration extends to a wide range of security-related services, including Security Information and Event Management (SIEM), security orchestration, automation, and response (SOAR), extended detection and response (XDR), and more.

Defender for IoT offers a centralized user experience within the Azure portal, enabling security and OT monitoring teams to visualize and secure all their IT, IoT, and OT devices, regardless of their physical locations. This centralized approach streamlines monitoring and security efforts, providing a comprehensive view of the entire ecosystem.

Flexible Deployment Options

Defender for IoT offers versatile support, catering to cloud, on-premises, and hybrid OT networks. This flexibility allows you to integrate the solution into your preferred network environment seamlessly.

Strategically Placed OT Network Sensors

To maximize visibility and coverage, deploy OT network sensors on-premises at strategic locations within your network infrastructure. These strategically placed sensors play a pivotal role in detecting devices across your entire OT environment.

Defender for IoT offers versatile deployment solutions to meet your specific needs:

- Cloud Deployments: IoT sensors, whether physical or virtual, can connect to Defender for IoT within the Azure portal. This enables you to manage your sensors and sensor data efficiently while integrating seamlessly with other Microsoft services like Microsoft Sentinel.

- Air-Gapped Networks: You can deploy Defender for IoT entirely on-premises, connecting it to an on-premises Security Information and Event Management (SIEM) system. This setup allows integration with Microsoft Sentinel directly or with a range of partner SOC tools such as Splunk, IBM QRadar, and ServiceNow.

- Hybrid Deployments: In a hybrid environment, you can manage on-premises sensors locally while maintaining connectivity to a cloud-based SIEM like Microsoft Sentinel.

Defender for IoT Sensors

Defender for IoT sensors is deployed on-premises as either virtual or physical appliances. These sensors discover and continuously monitor network devices while collecting industrial control system (ICS) network traffic.

The sensors utilize passive, agentless monitoring techniques for IoT/OT devices. They connect to a SPAN port or network TAP to perform deep-packet inspection on IoT/OT network traffic.

Data collection, processing, analysis, and alerting occur directly on the sensor machine. This approach is particularly suitable for locations with limited bandwidth or high-latency connections, as only metadata is transmitted to the Azure portal for management.

Figure 2-2 displays a sample Alerts page on a sensor console, showcasing alerts triggered by the devices connected to this sensor.

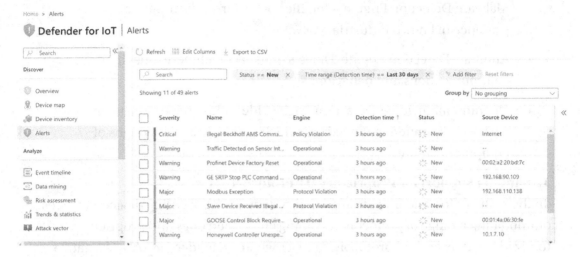

Figure 2-2. *Sample alerts page on Microsoft Defender for IOT – sensor console*

Defender for IoT Machine Learning Engines

Defender for IoT employs self-learning, machine-learning, and analytics engines, eliminating the need for constant signature updates or rule definitions. These engines utilize ICS-specific behavioral analytics and data science to analyze OT network traffic for

- Anomalies

- Malware

- Operational issues

- Protocol violations

- Deviations in baseline network activity

Defender for IoT sensors also incorporates five analytics detection engines that generate alerts based on real-time and prerecorded traffic analysis:

- Policy Violation Detection Engine: Utilizes machine learning to alert on deviations from baseline behavior, such as unauthorized usage of specific function codes, access to particular objects, or changes in device configuration

- Protocol Violation Detection Engine: Identifies the use of packet structures and field values that contravene ICS protocol specifications

93

- Malware Detection Engine: Identifies behaviors indicating the presence of known industrial malware

- Anomaly Detection Engine: Detects unusual machine-to-machine communications and behaviors

- Operational Incident Detection Engine: Identifies operational issues such as intermittent connectivity, which may indicate early signs of equipment failure

Expanding Support for Proprietary OT Protocols

In the realm of IoT and industrial control systems (ICS), securing devices involves accommodating a range of protocols, including embedded ones and proprietary, customized, or nonstandard protocols. In cases where Defender for IoT lacks native support for your particular protocols, you can leverage the Horizon Open Development Environment (ODE) SDK. This toolkit empowers you to create dissector plug-ins tailored to decode network traffic associated with your unique protocols.

By developing these custom plug-ins, you enable your network to be effectively monitored and protected. You can also establish custom alerts through these plug-ins, allowing you to precisely identify specific network activities. For instance, you can configure alerts to trigger when the sensor detects actions such as a write command to a memory register at a specific IP address and Ethernet destination, or any access to a designated IP address. These alerts serve to enhance your security posture and facilitate seamless communication among your security, IT, and operational teams.

Design Framework for IoT Cybersecurity Solution

Adopting an IoT cybersecurity framework is of paramount importance in the design of IoT security solutions. IoT, with its interconnected devices and vast data flows, introduces complex and multifaceted security challenges. Here are five key reasons why embracing a cybersecurity framework is crucial:

Proactive Threat Mitigation

Adopting an IoT cybersecurity framework enables organizations to take a proactive stance against emerging security threats. It promotes a systematic approach to identifying vulnerabilities and implementing robust security measures from the initial design phase.

This approach reduces the likelihood of cyberattacks, data breaches, and the associated consequences.

Comprehensive Security

A cybersecurity framework addresses security concerns at every level of an IoT system, from device authentication to data encryption and access control. It ensures that security is an integral part of the system's architecture, leaving fewer security gaps and vulnerabilities. By considering security comprehensively, organizations can safeguard their IoT devices, networks, and the sensitive data they handle.

Regulatory Compliance

IoT deployments often deal with sensitive data, and many industries and regions have established regulations and standards governing IoT cybersecurity. Adhering to a cybersecurity framework helps organizations maintain compliance, ensuring they meet the legal requirements. This not only protects organizations from potential legal consequences but also enhances their reputation as responsible custodians of sensitive data.

Risk Management and Mitigation

IoT devices are frequently deployed in mission-critical applications such as healthcare, transportation, and industrial processes. A cybersecurity framework enables organizations to identify, assess, and manage risks effectively. By prioritizing security measures based on potential dangers, organizations can allocate resources more efficiently and mitigate the impact of security breaches, which can be devastating in critical applications.

Continuous Improvement

Cybersecurity is an ever-evolving field, with new threats and vulnerabilities emerging regularly. A cybersecurity framework encourages continuous improvement by periodically assessing and updating security measures. It supports ongoing monitoring for anomalies and potential security breaches, ensuring that IoT systems remain resilient despite evolving threats.

Adopting an IoT cybersecurity framework is not merely a best practice; it's necessary in today's interconnected world. IoT devices and networks are prime targets for cyberattacks, and their vulnerabilities can have far-reaching consequences. By embracing a cybersecurity framework, organizations can fortify their IoT ecosystems, protect sensitive data, meet regulatory requirements, and proactively defend against emerging threats. It's an essential step to realize the full potential of IoT technology while maintaining the integrity and security of connected systems.

Designing a comprehensive framework for IoT security is crucial to protecting IoT devices and networks from potential threats and vulnerabilities. Figure 2-3 depicts the framework and essential elements of cybersecurity framework.

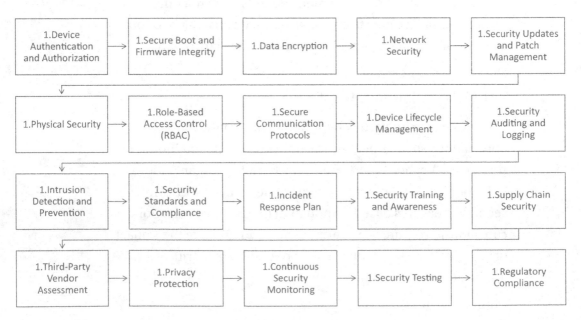

Figure 2-3. *Internet of Things security framework*

Here's a framework for IoT security component explanation laid out.

Device Authentication and Authorization

- Implement strong authentication to ensure only authorized devices can connect to the network.

- Use identity and access management (IAM) to control device permissions.

Secure Boot and Firmware Integrity

- Enable secure boot processes to ensure only trusted firmware can run on IoT devices.

- Regularly verify the integrity of firmware and software updates.

Data Encryption

- Encrypt data both in transit and at rest using robust encryption algorithms.

- Implement end-to-end encryption to protect data from the device to the cloud.

Network Security

- Segment IoT devices into isolated networks to limit the lateral movement of attackers.

- Use firewalls, intrusion detection systems (IDS), and intrusion prevention systems (IPS) to monitor and protect IoT network traffic.

Security Updates and Patch Management

- Develop a process for delivering and installing security updates and patches to IoT devices.

- Prioritize critical security updates and ensure the ability to perform over-the-air (OTA) updates.

Physical Security

- Secure IoT devices physically to prevent tampering and unauthorized access.

- Implement tamper-evident seals and enclosures where necessary.

Role-Based Access Control (RBAC)

- Implement RBAC to control and limit access to IoT devices and systems.

- Define roles and permissions for users and devices.

Secure Communication Protocols

- Choose secure communication protocols that encrypt and authenticate, such as TLS for web traffic.

- Disable unnecessary or insecure protocols.

Device Lifecycle Management

- Track and manage the entire life cycle of IoT devices, including provisioning, decommissioning, and disposal.

- Ensure that decommissioned devices do not pose security risks.

Security Auditing and Logging

- Enable logging and auditing of all device and network activities.

- Analyze logs to detect anomalies and potential security incidents.

Intrusion Detection and Prevention

- Deploy intrusion detection systems (IDS) and intrusion prevention systems (IPS) to identify and mitigate threats.

- Use anomaly detection and signature-based methods.

Security Standards and Compliance

- Adhere to industry security standards and regulations relevant to IoT, such as the IoT Cybersecurity Improvement Act, NIST guidelines, and GDPR.

Incident Response Plan

- Develop a comprehensive incident response plan to address security breaches and vulnerabilities.

- Test and regularly update the plan.

Security Training and Awareness

- Educate employees and stakeholders about IoT security best practices.

- Promote a culture of security awareness.

Supply Chain Security

- Verify the security of components and software used in IoT devices, as vulnerabilities can be introduced at the supply chain level.

Third-Party Vendor Assessment

- Assess the security practices of third-party vendors and service providers in your IoT ecosystem.

- Ensure they meet your security requirements.

Privacy Protection

- Implement privacy protection measures to handle sensitive data, especially in compliance with data protection laws.

- Use anonymization and data minimization techniques.

Continuous Security Monitoring

- Continuously monitor the security of your IoT devices and networks for emerging threats and vulnerabilities.

- Implement automated threat intelligence feeds.

Security Testing

- Conduct regular security assessments, penetration testing, and vulnerability scanning.

- Address identified vulnerabilities promptly.

Regulatory Compliance

- Ensure that your IoT security framework complies with applicable industry regulations and standards.

- Remember that IoT security is an ongoing process, and it's essential to adapt and improve your security measures as new threats and vulnerabilities emerge.

Design Principles for IoT Cybersecurity Solution

IoT solutions face the intricate task of safeguarding diverse and heterogeneous device-based workloads, often with minimal direct interaction. This responsibility is shared among IoT device manufacturers, IoT application developers, and IoT solution operators, who must collectively ensure security throughout the entire life cycle of an IoT solution. Therefore, it is imperative to incorporate security considerations from the outset of the solution's design. Understanding potential threats is paramount, and a robust defense-in-depth strategy should be integral to the solution's architecture.

The foundation of security planning lies in creating a threat model. This model enables a comprehensive understanding of how potential attackers could compromise the system and, in turn, helps implement suitable countermeasures right from the beginning. The most significant value of threat modeling is realized when it is seamlessly integrated into the design phase. As part of this process, it is possible to deconstruct a typical IoT architecture into distinct components or zones, such as devices, device gateways, cloud gateways, and services. Each zone can have unique authentication, authorization, and data handling requirements. This zoning approach serves to contain potential damage and mitigate the impact of low-trust zones on higher-trust ones.

The subsequent security guidance for IoT workloads delineates crucial considerations and offers recommendations for design and implementation.

The IoT workload design methodology is anchored in five pillars of architectural excellence. These pillars act as guiding beacons for shaping subsequent design choices across critical areas of IoT design. The ensuing design principles extend the quality pillar within the Azure Well-Architected Framework, focusing on security.

Establishing security design principles plays a pivotal role in elucidating the factors necessary to ensure that your IoT workload satisfies the stipulated criteria across the foundational layers of IoT architecture.

It's crucial to acknowledge that all these architectural layers are susceptible to diverse threats that can be systematically categorized according to the STRIDE categories: spoofing, tampering, repudiation, information disclosure, Denial of Service, and elevation of privilege. As a best practice, adhering to the Microsoft Security Development Lifecycle (SDL) is imperative when embarking on the design and construction of IoT architectures. Figure 2-4 depicts the IoT Cybersecurity Solution to Internet of Things – design principle.

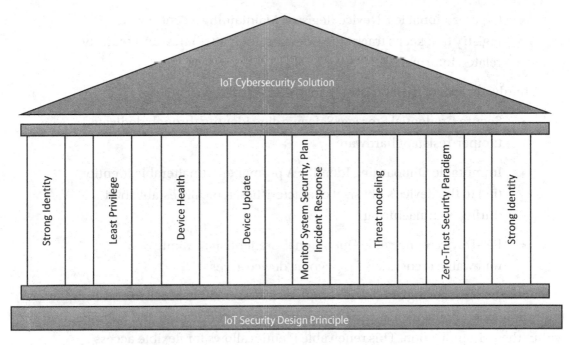

Figure 2-4. *Internet of Things – design principle*

Design Principle: Strong Identity

Considerations: Employ a robust identity framework to validate both devices and users. Establish a hardware root of trust for a secure identity foundation, register devices, issue renewable credentials, and implement advanced authentication methods like passwordless or multifactor authentication (MFA). It is essential to review broader Azure identity and access management considerations.

Seamless Integration of IoT Device Capabilities

The cohesive integration of IoT devices and services is vital in establishing a robust device identity. This integration encompasses several essential components:

- Hardware Root of Trust: The foundation of secure identity, consisting of tamper-resistant hardware with secure credential storage that verifies the device's identity

- Strong Authentication: Utilizing certificates, multifactor authentication (MFA), or passwordless authentication to ensure robust and verified user and device access

- Renewable Credentials: Providing unique, renewable operational credentials for regular device access, enhancing security over time

101

- Organizational IoT Device Registry: Maintaining a centralized registry that keeps track of IoT devices, their attributes, and security-related information

A hardware root of trust boasts the following attributes:

- Secure Credential Storage: Safeguarding identity through dedicated, tamper-resistant hardware

- Immutable Onboarding Identity: A permanent, unalterable identity tied to the device's physical characteristics, typically established during manufacturing

- Per-Device Renewable Operational Credentials: Unique and renewable credentials for ongoing device access

Once the onboarding process is complete, it's essential to provision and employ renewable operational identity and credentials for authentication and authorization within the IoT application. This renewable identity allows for flexible access management, and policies such as device integrity and health attestation can be enforced during renewal.

The hardware root of trust is also instrumental in ensuring devices adhere to security specifications and comply with necessary standards. Protecting the hardware root of trust and other device components within the supply chain is paramount to prevent potential attacks that could compromise device integrity.

Passwordless authentication, which often involves standard x509 certificates to validate a device's identity, offers more protection than traditional methods involving passwords and shared symmetric tokens. Managing certificates efficiently involves the following:

- Provisioning operational certificates from a trusted public key infrastructure (PKI)

- Establishing a renewal time frame suitable for business requirements, management efficiency, and cost considerations

- Automating the renewal process to minimize potential disruptions to access

- Implementing contemporary cryptography techniques, such as certificate signing requests (CSR), instead of transmitting private keys

- Granting device access based on their operational identity and supporting credential revocation through mechanisms like certificate revocation lists (CRL) to swiftly revoke access in response to compromises or theft

For legacy or resource-constrained IoT devices that can only partially implement strong identity and authentication practices, using IoT gateways as intermediaries is a viable solution. These gateways locally interface with less-capable devices, enabling them to access IoT services while adhering to strong identity patterns, ultimately facilitating the adoption of a zero-trust approach.

In cases where virtual machines (VMs), containers, or services incorporate IoT clients but lack hardware root of trust support, available capabilities such as passwordless authentication and renewable credentials can be utilized. Employing a defense-in-depth strategy helps address security gaps by adding redundancies where feasible. For example, VMs and containers can be located in physically secure environments like data centers compared to IoT devices deployed in the field.

Using a centralized organizational IoT device registry plays a pivotal role in managing the entire life cycle of IoT devices within an organization. This approach aligns with the principles of zero-trust security, similar to securing the user identities of a workforce. A cloud-based identity registry provides the scalability, management, and security required for a comprehensive IoT solution.

IoT device registry data serves various purposes, including the following:

- Inventory Management: Viewing and maintaining an inventory of an organization's IoT devices, tracking their health, patch status, and security condition

- Operational Efficiency: Querying and grouping devices to facilitate scaled operations, management, workload deployment, and access control

- Unmanaged Device Awareness: Utilizing network sensors to detect and inventory unmanaged IoT devices that do not connect to Azure IoT services, enhancing awareness and monitoring capabilities

Design Principle: Least Privilege

Considerations: Implement automated systems that enforce the principle of least privilege for access control. This approach minimizes the impact of compromised devices, identities, or unapproved workloads.

Implementing Least-Privileged Access Control for IoT Security

Least-privileged access control is a vital measure to mitigate the potential consequences of authenticated identities being compromised or unauthorized workloads running. In IoT scenarios, the following strategies are employed to grant access to operators, devices, and workloads:

- Device and Workload Access Control: Provide access exclusively to specific, scoped workloads on the device.

- Just-in-Time Access: Grant access precisely when needed.

- Strong Authentication Methods: Utilize robust authentication mechanisms like multifactor authentication (MFA) and passwordless authentication.

- Conditional Access: Apply access conditions based on the device's context, including IP address, GPS location, system configuration, uniqueness, time of day, or network traffic patterns. Services can also use device context to make conditional workload deployments.

To implement effective least-privileged access:

- Configure IoT Cloud Gateway Access Management: Tailor access permissions for the back end's functional requirements, ensuring access is limited to the necessary functionality.

- Minimize Access Points: Reduce access points to IoT devices and cloud applications by enforcing stringent access controls on ports.

- Tampering Prevention and Detection: Develop mechanisms to deter and detect physical tampering of devices.

- User Access Management: Manage user access through an appropriate access control model, such as role-based or attribute-based access control, to ensure the principle of least privilege is upheld.

- Network Segmentation: Apply network segmentation to layer least-privileged access for IoT devices, enhancing security through controlled isolation.

The design and configuration of your network offer valuable opportunities to establish a comprehensive defense strategy, employing segmentation based on IoT device traffic patterns and their vulnerability to risks. This segmentation strategy limits compromised devices' potential fallout and adversaries' efforts to pivot toward higher-value assets. Typically, next-generation firewalls are the linchpin of network segmentation.

Network micro-segmentation takes this further by isolating less-capable devices at the network level, either positioning them behind a gateway or placing them on dedicated network segments. By skillfully grouping IoT devices through network segmentation and complementing this with endpoint protection, you fortify your defenses against potential compromises.

Establishing a holistic firewall rule strategy is imperative, granting network access to devices when needed and promptly blocking access when it's not authorized. For organizations seeking an elevated level of security through a defense-in-depth approach, consider implementing micro-segmentation policies at various tiers of the Purdue model. Additionally, when necessary, introduce firewalls on the devices to impose stringent network access controls.

By embracing these practices, your IoT ecosystem gains a multilayered defense mechanism, considerably enhancing its resilience to potential threats.

By adhering to these practices, IoT environments can maintain a strong security posture while minimizing risks associated with access control.

Design Principle: Device Health

Considerations: Prioritize device health assessment as a gatekeeper for device access. This involves evaluating security configurations, identifying vulnerabilities, addressing insecure passwords, monitoring for potential threats and anomalies, and constructing continuous risk profiles.

Prioritizing Device Health in the Zero-Trust Paradigm

Within the framework of zero trust, the health of a device emerges as a pivotal determinant in ascertaining its risk profile and trustworthiness. This risk profile, in turn, functions as a gateway for access, ensuring that only devices in robust health can connect with IoT applications and services. Simultaneously, it helps to flag devices exhibiting questionable health for necessary remediation.

By industry standards, the evaluation of device health should encompass the following elements:

- Security Configuration Assessment and Attestation: Verification that the device maintains a secure configuration.

- Vulnerability Assessment: Identification of potential vulnerabilities, including outdated software or known security weaknesses within the device.

- Insecure Credential Assessment: Evaluation of device credentials, including certificates, and assessment of protocols such as Transport Layer Security (TLS) 1.2 and higher.

- Active Threat Detection and Alerting: Continuous monitoring for emerging threats and timely alerting.

- Detection of Anomalous Behavior: This covers alerts for deviations in network patterns and usage that may indicate suspicious or unexpected device behavior.

By integrating these health evaluation criteria into your zero-trust approach, you construct a robust security framework that safeguards your IoT ecosystem from compromised or questionable devices.

Design Principle: Device Update

Considerations: Embrace a strategy of continuous updates to maintain the health of devices. Implement a centralized configuration and compliance management solution and a robust update mechanism to ensure that devices remain up to date and healthy.

To regulate device access based on their health status, it is imperative to take proactive measures to ensure that production devices consistently maintain a functional and healthy state. To achieve this, update mechanisms should possess the following attributes:

- Remote Deployment Capabilities: The ability to remotely deploy device updates, enabling swift and efficient distribution of necessary improvements

- Resilience to Environmental Changes: Resilience against environmental variations, shifts in operating conditions, and alterations in authentication mechanisms, including scenarios such as certificate changes due to expiration or revocation

- Support for Update Rollout Verification: The capacity to support verification processes during the rollout of updates, ensuring their effectiveness and integrity

- Integration with Security Monitoring: Seamless integration with comprehensive security monitoring systems facilitates scheduled updates to enhance security measures

It is also advisable to have the flexibility to postpone updates that disrupt essential business operations. Still, these updates should be completed within a predefined time frame after detecting vulnerabilities. Devices that remain unpatched should be identified as unhealthy, highlighting the need for immediate attention.

Design Principle: Monitor System Security and Plan Incident Response

Considerations: Take a proactive stance toward system security by continually monitoring for unauthorized or compromised devices. Be prepared to respond swiftly to emerging threats, ensuring the overall security of the IoT ecosystem.

An IoT solution must be capable of conducting comprehensive, large-scale monitoring and remediation for all its connected devices. As part of a defense-in-depth strategy, monitoring serves as an additional layer of protection for well-managed, newly implemented devices while also acting as a compensating control for legacy, unmanaged devices within the existing infrastructure that lack support for agents and cannot be remotely patched or configured.

In this context, the decision-making process should involve the following:

- Establishing specific logging levels

- Determining the types of activities that warrant monitoring

- Defining appropriate responses for generated alerts

It is essential that logs are securely stored and do not contain sensitive security details.

Following guidelines provided by the Cybersecurity and Infrastructure Security Agency (CISA), a robust security monitoring program should encompass the following:

- Asset and Network Discovery: Creating an up-to-date asset inventory and network map encompassing all IoT and OT devices

- Protocol Identification: Identifying and documenting all communication protocols utilized across IoT and OT networks

- External Connection Documentation: Cataloging all external connections to and from these networks

- Vulnerability Assessment: Identifying vulnerabilities in IoT and OT devices and employing a risk-based approach to mitigate them

- Anomaly Detection: Implementing vigilant monitoring with anomaly detection capabilities to identify malicious activities, including tactics like "living off the land" within IoT systems

Many IoT attacks adhere to a kill chain pattern, wherein adversaries establish an initial foothold, elevate their privileges, and move laterally across the network. Frequently, attackers utilize privileged credentials to circumvent barriers, such as next-generation firewalls enforcing network segmentation across subnets. Rapidly detecting and responding to these multistage attacks necessitates a unified view encompassing IT, IoT, and OT networks supported by automation, machine learning, and threat intelligence.

Gathering data from the entire ecosystem, covering users, devices, applications, and infrastructure, whether on-premises or in various cloud environments, is crucial. Analyzing this data within centralized Security Information and Event Management (SIEM) and extended detection and response (XDR) platforms enables security operations center (SOC) analysts to hunt for and uncover previously unknown threats.

Finally, security orchestration, automation, and response (SOAR) platforms can rapidly respond to incidents and mitigate attacks before significantly impacting the organization. Playbooks can be defined to trigger automated responses when specific incidents are detected, including actions such as blocking or quarantining compromised devices to prevent them from infecting other systems.

Design Principle: Threat Modeling

Designing threat models is crucial in IoT (Internet of Things) and OT (operational technology) security design principles for several compelling reasons:

- Complex and Interconnected Systems: IoT and OT environments are characterized by intricate, interconnected systems involving various devices, sensors, networks, and data flows. Threat modeling helps comprehensively understand these complexities and their associated risks, allowing for effective security measures.

- Risk Identification: Threat modeling enables the proactive identification of potential security risks and vulnerabilities within the IoT and OT ecosystem. By anticipating these risks, security measures can be designed to mitigate them, reducing the likelihood of security breaches and their associated consequences.

- Tailored Security Measures: IoT and OT systems often have unique security requirements due to resource-constrained devices, legacy equipment, and specific communication protocols. Threat modeling helps customize security solutions to address these distinctive challenges, ensuring a more effective and efficient security posture.

- Data Protection: IoT and OT systems typically handle sensitive data, and maintaining this data's privacy and integrity is paramount. Threat modeling helps identify potential points of data exposure or manipulation, allowing for robust data protection mechanisms.

- Compliance and Regulation: Many industries have stringent regulatory requirements for IoT and OT security. Threat modeling assists in identifying compliance gaps and ensuring that security measures align with these regulations.

- Cost-Effective Security: Threat modeling supports the allocation of security resources cost-effectively. By identifying the most critical threats and vulnerabilities, organizations can prioritize their security investments where they are needed most.

- Security Awareness: Creating threat models fosters security awareness and a deeper understanding of potential risks within the organization. This heightened awareness can lead to a security-conscious culture and better decision-making at all levels.

- Adaptive Security: Threat modeling is not a one-time activity but an iterative process that adapts to evolving threats and system changes. It ensures that security remains effective despite new vulnerabilities and attack techniques.

In summary, threat modeling is a fundamental component of IoT and OT security design principles, enabling organizations to understand, assess, and proactively address security risks and vulnerabilities in complex and dynamic environments.

The STRIDE model is used in computer security and threat modeling to categorize and analyze potential threats and vulnerabilities associated with software systems and applications. STRIDE is an acronym that stands for six different types of threats:

- Spoofing: This threat involves attackers assuming false identities to gain unauthorized access to a system or resource. It can include impersonating a legitimate user, device, or component.

- Tampering: Tampering threats involve unauthorized alterations or modifications to data, software, or hardware components. Attackers may tamper with data integrity, software code, or system configurations.

- Repudiation: Repudiation threats deal with the ability of entities (users, devices, etc.) to deny that they performed a particular action or transaction. These threats, such as maintaining a reliable audit trail, are especially relevant for non-repudiation requirements.

- Information Disclosure: This threat encompasses the unauthorized exposure of sensitive information. It can occur through data leaks, eavesdropping, or other means, leading to the disclosure of confidential or personal data.

- Denial of Service (DoS): Denial of Service threats aim to disrupt or degrade the availability and functionality of a system. Attackers often flood a target system with excessive traffic or requests, rendering it inaccessible or unusable.

- Elevation of Privilege: Privilege threats involve attackers gaining unauthorized access to higher system privileges or rights. This can allow them to perform actions or access typically restricted resources.

Security professionals and software developers use the STRIDE model as a tool for identifying and analyzing potential threats and vulnerabilities during the software design and development process. By considering these categories of threats, they can proactively implement security controls and safeguards to protect against these risks, ensuring that software and systems are more resilient and secure.

The core elements of a threat model focus on processes, communication, and storage.

Processes threats are classified according to the STRIDE model as follows:

- Spoofing: In this threat scenario, an attacker gains access to cryptographic keys, either through software or hardware exploitation, and uses these keys to impersonate the original device from a different physical or virtual device.

- Denial of Service: This threat involves rendering a device nonfunctional or disrupting its communication by interfering with radio frequencies or physically tampering with it. For example, a surveillance camera losing power or network connectivity would be unable to transmit any data.

- Tampering: Tampering encompasses various attack vectors. An attacker may wholly or partially replace a device's software, potentially compromising its cryptographic keys and allowing unauthorized access. Tampering can also involve manipulating the device to provide false or manipulated information, even if it is technically secure.

- Information Disclosure: Devices running manipulated software may unintentionally leak data to unauthorized parties. Additionally, attackers with access to cryptographic keys can inject code into the communication path between the device and gateways, enabling the interception of sensitive information.

- Elevation of Privilege: In this scenario, an attacker manipulates a device initially designed for a specific function to perform another unintended action. For example, tricking a valve programmed to open halfway into opening fully.

- Repudiation: With consumer remote controls, which are often inadequately secured, attackers can anonymously manipulate a device's state, leading to potential spoofing, tampering, and repudiation threats.

Communication threats are classified based on the STRIDE model as follows:

- Denial of Service: Constrained devices are particularly susceptible to DoS threats when actively listening for inbound connections or unsolicited datagrams on a network. Attackers can open numerous links in parallel, either not servicing them or doing so slowly or flooding the device with unsolicited traffic. In both scenarios, the device can be effectively incapacitated on the network.

- Information Disclosure: Constrained and specialized devices often rely on simplistic security measures like passwords or PINs. Sometimes, they place complete trust in the network and grant access to any device on the same network. If the network's shared key is compromised, an attacker could take control of the device or intercept the data it transmits.

- Spoofing: Attackers may intercept or partially override broadcast signals and impersonate the legitimate source.

- Tampering: Attackers may intercept or partially override broadcast signals and transmit false information.

- Information Disclosure: Attackers may eavesdrop on broadcast communications and obtain information without proper authorization.

- Denial of Service: In this threat scenario, attackers may jam the broadcast signal, preventing the distribution of information.

Storage threats are classified based on the STRIDE model as follows:

- For device storage, implementing encryption and log signing helps mitigate the risks associated with reading data, tampering with telemetry data, or altering cached command control data. Additional protection includes using encryption, message authentication codes (MAC), digital signatures, and strong access control measures such as resource access control lists (ACLs) or permissions.

- In the case of the device OS image, the primary concern is tampering with or replacing OS components. Measures like a read-only OS partition, a signed OS image, and encryption are recommended to address this.

- Field gateway storage, particularly data queuing, benefits from storage encryption and log signing to protect against unauthorized data access and tampering. Tampering with cached or queued command control data and configuration or firmware update packages can lead to OS and system component compromise. Implementing BitLocker is an effective solution.

- Regarding the field gateway OS image, the focus is on preventing tampering or replacing OS components. This is achieved through a read-only OS partition, a signed OS image, and encryption.

Design Principle: Zero-Trust Security Paradigm

Unauthorized intrusion into IoT systems can result in severe consequences, including extensive data exposure like factory production records leakage or the unauthorized elevation of privileges, potentially enabling control over cyber-physical systems, leading to actions such as halting a factory production line. Adopting a zero-trust security model is instrumental in curtailing the potential impact of users acquiring unauthorized entry to cloud or on-premises IoT services and their associated data.

Rather than presuming everything located behind a corporate firewall is inherently secure, the zero-trust approach mandates rigorous verification, authorization, and encryption for every access request before granting permission. Securing IoT solutions through a zero-trust framework initiates with the implementation of fundamental security practices concerning identity, devices, and access. This encompasses techniques like explicit user verification, scrutinizing devices within the network, and deploying real-time risk detection to make dynamic access determinations.

To align with the principles of zero trust, IoT devices should exhibit the following key attributes:

- Hardware Root of Trust: To establish a robust and unassailable device identity, each device must incorporate a hardware root of trust.

- Renewable Credentials: Employ renewable credentials for routine device operation and access, ensuring continuous security.

- Least-Privileged Access Control: Enforce strict least-privileged access control measures, limiting local access to device resources like cameras, storage, and sensors.

- Device Health Signals: Devices should emit accurate and timely signals related to their health, facilitating the enforcement of conditional access based on their state.

- Sustainable Software Updates: Provide update agents and corresponding software updates throughout the device's usable lifetime, enabling the application of crucial security updates.

- Device Management Capabilities: Inclusion of device management capabilities that allow cloud-driven device configuration and automated security responses.

- Security Agents: Run security agents seamlessly integrating with security monitoring, detection, and response systems.

- Minimal Attack Surface: Minimize the physical attack footprint of devices by turning off unnecessary features like USB or UART ports and Wi-Fi or Bluetooth connectivity. Utilize physical removal, covering, or blocking when needed.

- Data Protection: Safeguard data stored on devices using standard encryption algorithms for data at rest.

Microsoft Azure offers various products and services to enhance IoT device security:

- Azure Sphere Guardian Modules: These modules facilitate the connection of critical legacy devices to IoT services while employing zero-trust measures, including robust identity verification, end-to-end encryption, and regular security updates.

- Azure IoT Edge: It provides an edge runtime connection to IoT Hub and other Azure services, supporting certificates for strong device identities. IoT Edge is also compatible with the PKCS#11 standard for device manufacturing identities and secrets stored on a Trusted Platform Module (TPM) or Hardware Security Module (HSM).

- Azure IoT Hub SDKs: This comprehensive set of device client libraries and tools incorporates multiple security features like encryption and authentication to aid in developing resilient and secure device applications.

- Azure RTOS: Designed as a real-time operating system, it offers a range of C language libraries suitable for deployment across diverse embedded IoT device platforms. Azure RTOS includes a complete TCP/IP stack with support for TLS 1.2 and 1.3 and basic X.509 capabilities. It integrates seamlessly with Azure IoT Hub, Azure Device Provisioning Service (DPS), and Microsoft Defender, ensuring secure network communication through features like X.509 mutual authentication and modern TLS cipher suites such as ECDHE and AES-GCM.

Azure RTOS further accommodates zero-trust design for microcontroller platforms featuring hardware security capabilities like Arm TrustZone and is compatible with secure element devices such as the STSAFE-A110 from STMicroelectronics.

- Azure Certified Device Program: This program simplifies the differentiation and promotion of IoT devices by device partners. It aids solution builders and customers in identifying devices equipped with zero-trust-compatible features.

- Edge Secured-Core Program (Preview): Designed to validate devices for adherence to security requirements concerning device identity, secure boot, operating system hardening, device updates, data protection, and vulnerability disclosures. These requirements are distilled from various industry standards and security engineering perspectives.

The Edge Secured-Core Program empowers Azure services like the Azure Attestation Service to make conditional decisions based on device posture, thereby enabling the zero-trust model. Devices seeking certification must encompass a hardware root of trust, secure boot, and firmware protection attributes that can be measured by the attestation service and used for conditional access to sensitive resources downstream.

Zero-Trust Prerequisites for IoT Services

When considering IoT services, prioritize those that encompass the following essential zero-trust capabilities:

- Robust User Access Control: Ensure the IoT services provide comprehensive support for zero-trust user access control. This encompasses strong user identities, multifactor authentication (MFA), and the establishment of conditional user access.

- Integration with User Access Control Systems: Seek integration capabilities with access control systems that enable least-privileged access and conditional controls.

- Centralized Device Registry: Employ a centralized device registry offering comprehensive inventory and efficient device management.

- Mutual Authentication: Emphasize mutual authentication, which involves the provision of renewable device credentials coupled with robust identity verification mechanisms.

- Least-Privileged Device Access Control: Implement least-privileged device access controls and employ conditional access policies. This ensures that only devices meeting specific criteria, such as health status or known location, can establish connections.

- Over-the-Air (OTA) Updates: Enable OTA updates to maintain the health and security of devices by ensuring they remain up to date.

- Security Monitoring: Facilitate continuous security monitoring for IoT services and interconnected IoT devices, enhancing threat detection and response capabilities.

- Comprehensive Endpoint Security: Extend monitoring and access control to encompass all public endpoints, with rigorous authentication and authorization mechanisms in place for any interactions with these endpoints.

Design Principle: Design of Microsoft Defender for IoT

Microsoft Defender for IoT is a comprehensive security solution tailored to safeguard IoT and OT devices and networks. Notably, it employs an agentless device monitoring approach, eliminating the need for additional security agents on devices

116

to ensure protection. Leveraging advanced technologies like machine learning, threat intelligence, and behavioral analytics, Defender for IoT excels in the detection of IoT and OT devices, vulnerabilities, and potential threats, all while providing network-wide visibility and security. This solution seamlessly integrates with cloud, on-premises, and hybrid OT networks, and it can be customized to interact with proprietary OT protocols through the Horizon Open Development Environment (ODE) SDK. Moreover, it offers extension possibilities to enterprise IoT devices via Microsoft Defender for Endpoint or an enterprise IoT network sensor. Through a unified and user-friendly interface within the Azure portal, both security and OT monitoring teams gain the capability to oversee and fortify the security of all IT, IoT, and OT devices from a centralized vantage point.

With the ongoing transformation of critical industries, as they evolve their operational technology (OT) systems into digital IT infrastructures, the responsibilities of security operations center (SOC) teams and chief information security officers (CISOs) are expanding to encompass the realm of threats originating from OT networks.

Simultaneously, these new responsibilities come with a set of unique challenges that SOC teams must navigate. These challenges include the following:

- Lack of OT Expertise: Existing SOC teams often lack the requisite expertise and knowledge pertaining to OT alerts, industrial equipment, communication protocols, and network behavior. Consequently, this knowledge gap may result in a limited understanding of OT incidents and their potential impact on business operations.

- Communication and Process Silos: Inefficient communication and disjointed processes between OT and SOC entities can hinder the smooth flow of information and coordination in responding to threats.

- Limited Technology and Tools: The absence of advanced technology and tools tailored for OT network security, including visibility and automated remediation capabilities, poses a significant hurdle. Integrating such tools with existing SOC solutions can also be a costly endeavor.

However, the absence of adequate OT telemetry, contextual information, and seamless integration with existing SOC tools and workflows could potentially lead to inadequate handling of OT security and operational threats, potentially allowing them to go undetected or improperly addressed. It is imperative to address these challenges in order to ensure the robust security and operational integrity of OT networks in this evolving landscape.

Microsoft Sentinel and Defender for IoT Should Be Integrated

Leveraging the integration between Microsoft Defender for IoT and Microsoft Sentinel, SOC teams gain access to a scalable cloud service designed for Security Information and Event Management (SIEM) and security orchestration, automation, and response (SOAR). This integration empowers SOC teams to seamlessly collect data from diverse networks, detect, investigate, and proactively respond to security threats and incidents.

Within the Microsoft Sentinel platform, the Defender for IoT data connector and solution offers ready-made security content, providing SOC teams with a comprehensive toolkit for viewing, analyzing, and addressing security alerts specific to operational technology (OT). This includes a deeper understanding of the generated incidents within the broader context of organizational threat landscapes.

To harness this integration, begin by installing the Defender for IoT data connector, enabling the streaming of OT network alerts directly to Microsoft Sentinel. Additionally, deploying the Microsoft Defender for IoT solution brings added value by introducing IoT/OT-specific analytics rules, pre-configured workbooks, and security orchestration, automation, and response (SOAR) playbooks. These resources are complemented by incident mappings aligned with MITRE ATT&CK for industrial control systems (ICS) techniques. This integrated approach enhances the capabilities of SOC teams, facilitating a more robust and responsive security posture in the face of evolving threats.

Streamline Detection and Response for IoT/OT

The collaborative approach between the OT team utilizing Defender for IoT and the SOC team leveraging Microsoft Sentinel enables swift threat detection and response throughout the attack timeline.

In this integrated process:

1. OT Alert Triggered: High-confidence OT alerts, driven by Defender for IoT's Section 52 security research group, are initiated based on the data ingested into Defender for IoT.

   - OT Incident Created: Analytics rules are automatically triggered, opening relevant incidents and avoiding alert fatigue in the OT environment.

2. SOC Teams Map Business Impact: The SOC team assesses business impact, including data regarding the affected site, production line, compromised assets, and OT owners.

   - OT Incident Business Impact Mapping: In parallel, this information is used to map the business impact within the OT incident context.

3. SOC Teams Investigate: SOC teams escalate incidents to the Active status, initiating investigations. They utilize network connections, event data, workbooks, and the OT device entity page.

   - OT Incident Investigation: Correspondingly, alerts are escalated to the Active status, prompting OT teams to conduct investigations using PCAP data, detailed reports, and device-specific details.

4. SOC Teams Respond: SOC teams employ OT playbooks and notebooks to respond to incidents, taking appropriate actions in line with security best practices.

   - OT Incident Response: Similarly, OT teams act based on the investigation's findings, either suppressing the alert or gaining insights for future incidents.

5. Incident Closure: After successfully mitigating the threat, SOC teams conclude their incident, marking it closed.

   - OT Incident Closure: In tandem, OT teams resolve the alert after effectively addressing the threat.

Alert Status Synchronization

It's essential to note that alert status changes are synchronized exclusively from Microsoft Sentinel to Defender for IoT, not vice versa. To ensure a cohesive approach, when integrating Defender for IoT with Microsoft Sentinel, it is advisable to manage alert statuses alongside the associated incidents within Microsoft Sentinel. This synchronization ensures that the alert level in Defender for IoT aligns with the overall incident management in Microsoft Sentinel for enhanced threat response and resolution.

Design Elements of Microsoft Defender for IoT

In this section, let us get started by understanding key design elements of Microsoft Defender for IoT.

The Internet of Things (IoT) has ushered in an era of billions of connected devices, spanning operational technology (OT) and IoT networks. These networks often rely on specialized protocols and may focus more on operational functionality than security. This creates a challenge, as traditional security systems may need to be equipped to protect these IoT/OT devices. As a result, each new wave of technological innovation expands these networks' potential risks and vulnerabilities.

Microsoft Defender for IoT offers a specialized approach to securing network environments by providing passive, agentless monitoring. This solution is specifically designed to discover and protect IoT and OT devices within your business-critical networks. Unlike traditional signature-based security measures, Defender for IoT employs behavioral analytics and threat intelligence tailored for IoT and OT environments. This enables it to detect sophisticated threats that might otherwise go unnoticed, such as zero-day malware or stealthy "living-off-the-land" tactics.

The system is a valuable asset for both OT and IT teams by automatically identifying unmanaged devices, connections, and critical vulnerabilities in the network. This allows Defender for IoT to flag anomalous or unauthorized activities without compromising the stability or performance of your IoT and OT systems. Overall, Defender for IoT delivers an advanced level of security tailored to the unique challenges of interconnected environments.

To address these security gaps, Microsoft Defender for IoT offers a tailored solution specifically designed to identify and protect IoT and OT devices and detect vulnerabilities and threats. It is a comprehensive security layer for your entire IoT/OT landscape, even for devices lacking built-in security features. What sets Defender for IoT apart is its agentless approach to monitoring at the Network Layer, allowing for seamless integration with both industrial equipment and security operations center (SOC) tools. This ensures that your network remains secure without compromising on operational efficiency.

Microsoft Defender for IoT is designed to keep a close eye on your network by pulling in data from various sources. Imagine it as a central hub where information from network sensors and other third-party tools come together to give you a complete picture of your IoT and operational technology (OT) security.

You can access Defender for IoT through the Azure portal, where you'll find features like device inventories, checks for security weaknesses, and ongoing monitoring for potential threats. The system works with both cloud-based and local (on-premises) setups, and it's designed to handle large networks spread across different locations.

Here's a quick rundown of its main parts:

- Azure Portal: This is your cloud-based dashboard where you can manage everything and connect to other Microsoft services like Microsoft Sentinel.

- Network Sensors: These sensors scan your operational technology (OT) or broader enterprise IoT network to identify devices. You can install these sensors on a virtual or physical machine. Plus, you can choose whether these sensors send data to the cloud or only work locally.

- Local Management Console: For networks not connected to the Internet (known as air-gapped environments), an on-site management console lets you oversee your OT sensors.

So whether you have a small setup or a vast, global network, Microsoft Defender for IoT adapts to meet your security needs.

Sensors for OT and Enterprise IoT Networks

Microsoft Defender for IoT network sensors is crucial in monitoring and securing both operational technology (OT) and enterprise IoT networks. These sensors are specifically designed for these types of networks and can be easily connected to a SPAN port or network TAP. Remarkably, they can start providing insights into potential risks within minutes of being connected. Utilizing advanced analytics engines that are aware of OT/IoT nuances and Layer-6 Deep Packet Inspection (DPI), these sensors can identify a range of threats, including fileless malware, based on unusual or unauthorized activities on the network.

What sets these network sensors apart is their capability for on-device data handling. All the processes, from data collection and analysis to threat alerting, happen directly on the sensor. This feature is particularly beneficial for environments with limited bandwidth or those that experience high-latency issues, as only essential telemetry data and insights are forwarded for further management. These summarized findings can be sent to the cloud-based Azure portal or a local on-premises management console, depending on your setup and needs.

121

Sensors Connected to the Cloud vs. Sensors Located Locally

Cloud-connected sensors and locally managed sensors in the Defender for IoT system serve similar purposes but have distinct functionalities and management approaches.

With agentless device monitoring, if your IoT and OT devices lack built-in security features, they can become vulnerable to threats and often go unnoticed by IT and security teams. These unprotected devices can be easy entry points for attackers seeking to infiltrate corporate networks. Microsoft Defender for IoT addresses this gap with its agentless monitoring system, which offers comprehensive visibility and security across your entire network. It identifies specialized protocols, devices, and machine-to-machine (M2M) behaviors, pulling data from network sensors, Microsoft Defender for Endpoint, and various third-party sources.

With Defender for IoT, you can assess risks and manage vulnerabilities using a combination of machine learning, threat intelligence, and behavioral analytics. For instance, the system can identify devices that haven't been updated, detect open ports, flag unauthorized applications and connections, and even spot changes to device configurations, PLC code, and firmware. It allows you to search historical traffic data across different dimensions and protocols, offering full-fidelity packet capture (PCAP) for deeper investigation.

Moreover, Defender for IoT is adept at detecting sophisticated threats that may evade traditional indicators of compromise (IOCs), such as zero-day and fileless malware. It enhances your response capabilities by integrating seamlessly with other Microsoft services like Microsoft Sentinel, as well as with third-party Security Information and Event Management (SIEM), security orchestration, automation, and response (SOAR), and extended detection and response (XDR) services.

The Azure portal's centralized user interface allows security and OT monitoring teams to visualize and secure all their IT, IoT, and OT devices, irrespective of their physical locations. This makes Defender for IoT a robust and versatile solution for managing the security challenges posed by today's interconnected environments.

When you use a cloud-connected OT network sensor, all the data it captures is shown in the sensor console. However, alerts are also sent to Azure for further analysis and integration with other Azure services. Another advantage of cloud-connected sensors is that they automatically receive Microsoft's threat intelligence updates. Additionally, the name you give to the sensor during its initial setup is what you'll see displayed in the sensor console, and this name is read-only, meaning you can't change it from the console itself.

On the other hand, locally managed sensors offer a more hands-on approach. All the sensor data can be viewed directly from the sensor console. You must use an on-premises management console if you want a consolidated view of data from multiple sensors. Unlike cloud-connected sensors, you'll have to upload threat intelligence packages to these locally managed units manually. Also, you can change the sensor names directly from the sensor console.

In summary, cloud-connected sensors offer seamless integration with Azure and automated updates, while locally managed sensors provide more control and are better suited for environments that require manual oversight.

IoT Analytics Engines with Microsoft Defender

Defender for IoT employs a range of sophisticated analytics engines to scrutinize data ingested from network sensors. These engines generate alerts based on real-time and pre-recorded network traffic. They incorporate machine learning, profile analytics, risk assessment, a comprehensive device database, threat intelligence, and behavioral analytics to form a robust security framework.

One notable feature is the policy violation detection engine, which is particularly adept at modeling industrial control systems (ICS) networks. This engine uses Behavioral Anomaly Detection (BAD) as specified in NISTIR 8219 to identify deviations from established baseline behaviors. These baselines are created by understanding regular network activities, such as standard traffic patterns and user actions. Any divergence from this baseline, such as unauthorized code functions or changes in device configurations, is flagged as a policy violation.

Importantly, these analytics engines are tailored for operational technology (OT) networks instead of information technology (IT) networks. This specialization allows for a more rapid learning curve for detecting new threats in ICS environments.

The primary analytics engines in Defender for IoT include the following:

- Protocol Violation Detection Engine: This engine identifies any deviations in packet structures and field values from ICS protocol specifications. For example, an alert may be triggered for an "Illegal MODBUS Operation" if a primary device sends an incorrect request to a secondary device.

- Policy Violation Engine: Flags deviations from learned or manually configured baseline behaviors. An example alert might be an "Unauthorized HTTP User Agent," indicating the use of an unapproved web browser or application on a device.

- Industrial Malware Detection Engine: This engine detects malicious activities from known malware strains like Conficker, Black Energy, and Stuxnet. For instance, if the sensor detects activities related to Stuxnet malware, a "Suspicion of Malicious Activity" alert will be triggered.

- Anomaly Detection Engine: Specialized in identifying unusual machine-to-machine (M2M) communications, this engine benefits from a shorter learning period due to its focus on ICS networks. Alerts could include "Periodic Behavior in Communication Channel," which is common in industrial setups.

- Operational Incident Detection Engine: This engine is designed to detect operational issues like intermittent connectivity, which can be early indicators of equipment failure. For example, a "Device is Suspected to be Disconnected" alert could signify a device shutdown or malfunction.

In summary, Defender for IoT offers a robust set of analytics engines that are highly specialized for OT and ICS networks, providing a nuanced and practical approach to network security and operational reliability.

Options for Managing IoT Devices with Defender

Defender for IoT offers versatile management options to accommodate hybrid networks, including cloud-based and on-premises components. One option is the Azure portal, which serves as a centralized dashboard for viewing all data collected by your cloud-connected network sensors. The portal displays the raw data and enhances it with various features such as workbooks, connections to Microsoft Sentinel, and security recommendations. It is also your go-to place for obtaining new appliances, software updates, and threat intelligence packages.

Another management interface is the OT sensor console. This console allows you to monitor data specific to each OT sensor in your network. You can view a network map of detected devices, follow a timeline of events related to that sensor, and even forward sensor information to other systems for further analysis.

For networks that are not connected to the Internet, often referred to as air-gapped environments, Defender for IoT provides an on-premises management console. This console gives you a centralized view of all your sensor data and provides additional maintenance tools and reporting features. It's important to note that the software version on your on-premises console should match that of your most current sensor version for compatibility. Although the on-premises console is backward compatible with older sensor versions, it cannot connect to sensors with newer software versions.

In summary, whether you're operating in the cloud, on-premises, or a hybrid environment, Defender for IoT offers a range of management options to suit your specific needs, each with its features and advantages.

Monitored Devices by Defender for IoT

Defender for IoT can identify various devices across different settings, be it IT, OT, or IoT environments. These devices appear in the Defender for IoT Device Inventory pages, uniquely identified by a combination of their IP and MAC addresses.

When it comes to counting devices, there are some specifics to note. Devices with one or more Network Interface Cards (NICs) – which could include networking hardware like switches and routers – are considered individual devices. Even if a device has additional modules or components, such as racks or slots, it is still counted as a single, unique device.

On the flip side, there are elements that Defender for IoT does not count as individual devices. These include public Internet IP addresses, multicast groups, and broadcast groups. Such items do not impact your OT site license or enterprise IoT pricing plan. Additionally, devices are marked as "inactive" if no network activity is detected for an extended period: more than 60 days for OT networks and more than 30 days for enterprise IoT networks.

For those using Microsoft Defender for Endpoint Plan 2, it's worth noting that endpoints already managed by this service are not counted again by Defender for IoT. This ensures that you're not double-counting devices in your network.

Microsoft Defender for IoT is an integral component of Microsoft Defender for Cloud's comprehensive cloud workload protection (CWP) suite. This offering provides advanced and intelligent protection for Azure and hybrid resources and workloads.

Microsoft Defender for IoT Features

Microsoft Defender for IoT offers two distinct sets of capabilities tailored to suit different environments: one for "end-user organizations" and another for "device builders."

For end-user organizations operating within IoT/OT environments, Microsoft Defender for IoT delivers agentless, network-level monitoring that boasts the following attributes:

- Rapid deployment

- Seamless integration with various industrial equipment and SOC (security operations center) tools

- Flexibility to deploy fully on-premises or in Azure-connected and hybrid environments

For IoT device builders and IoT solutions centered around Azure IoT Hub, Microsoft Defender for IoT also provides a lightweight micro agent compatible with standard IoT operating systems like Linux and RTOS. This Microsoft Defender device builder agent ensures that security is an integral part of your IoT/OT initiatives, spanning from the edge to the cloud, and includes source code for adaptable deployment.

The agent-based option of Microsoft Defender for IoT encompasses the following components:

- IoT Hub integration.

- Device agents (optional).

- Send security message SDK.

- Analytics pipeline.

The Architecture of Microsoft Defender for IoT Agent-Based Solutions

Defender for IoT security agents offer advanced security features, including monitoring of best practices in operating system configurations. With one service, you can protect devices from threats while maintaining a secure network environment.

These security agents effectively gather raw events from the device operating system, aggregate events to optimize cost, and configure settings through a device module twin. Security messages are transmitted via your IoT Hub to the Defender for IoT analytics services.

The architecture of the Microsoft Defender for IoT agent-based solutions is depicted in Figure 2-5.

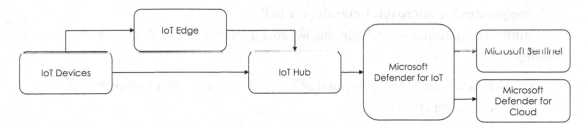

Figure 2-5. High-level overview of Microsoft Defender for IOT

It's important to note that Microsoft Sentinel enables organizations to swiftly detect multi-stage attacks that often traverse IT and OT (operational technology) domains. Additionally, integrating Defender for IoT with Microsoft Sentinel's security orchestration, automation, and response (SOAR) capabilities allows for automated response and prevention using specialized OT-optimized playbooks. However, further details about Microsoft Sentinel should be explored in this course.

Critical Components of Microsoft Defender for IoT

IoT Hub Built-In Security

- Enabled by default in every new IoT Hub created

- Provides real-time monitoring, recommendations, and alerts

- Does not require agent installation on devices

- Utilizes advanced analytics on IoT Hub metadata for device and IoT Hub protection

Defender for IoT Micro Agent

- Offers in-depth security protection and visibility into device behavior

- Collects, aggregates, and analyzes raw security events from devices, including IP connections, process creation, user logins, and other security-related information

- Provides event aggregation to manage network throughput

- Offers high customization, allowing tailored usage for specific tasks

Prerequisites for Microsoft Defender for IoT

Minimum requirements for deploying Microsoft Defender for IoT include the following:

- Network switches supporting traffic monitoring via a SPAN (Switched Port Analyzer) port

- Hardware appliances for NTA (Network Traffic Analysis) sensors

- Azure Subscription Contributor role (for onboarding and defining committed devices and connecting to Microsoft Sentinel in agentless solutions)

- Azure IoT Hub (Free or Standard tier) Contributor role for cloud-connected management

- Compatibility with a growing list of devices and platforms for device-level security module support

Using Microsoft Defender for IoT Service

Microsoft Defender for IoT is enabled by default in every new IoT Hub, and its insights and reporting can be accessed directly through the Azure portal within the IoT Hub user interface.

Supported Service Regions

Microsoft Defender for IoT is nonregional and does not depend on a specific Azure region. It routes traffic from all European regions to the West Europe regional data center and traffic from all other regions to the Central US regional data center.

Verifying IoT Hub Location

Before getting started, it's essential to verify your IoT Hub location to ensure service availability. You can do this by

- Opening your IoT Hub

- Clicking on "Overview"

- Confirming that the listed location matches one of the supported service regions

Supported Platforms for Agents

Microsoft Defender for IoT agents support a growing range of devices and platforms, including Linux versions for C-based agents and both Linux and Windows versions for C#-based agents.

128

Reference Architecture for IoT

In IoT solutions, events play a pivotal role in generating valuable insights. These insights, in turn, catalyze actions aimed at refining business processes. The cloud-hosted services and applications discern which actions are appropriate in response to the events relayed by devices. At the inception, devices are responsible for producing these events and transmitting them to applications situated in the cloud. Upon receiving this data, applications meticulously evaluate these device events to derive pertinent insights. Informed by these insights, the applications spring into action, executing various processes and workflows. Moreover, these applications can transmit specific commands back to the originating devices, further exemplifying the symbiotic relationship between devices and cloud-based applications in the IoT landscape.

Figure 2-6 illustrates how events can lead to insights that can be used to inform actions in IoT solutions.

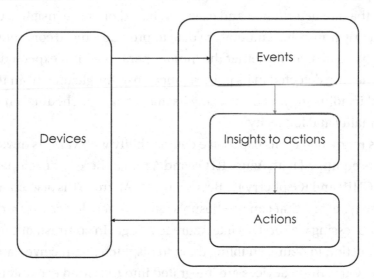

Figure 2-6. *Internet of Things – insights to inform actions*

Using cloud-based applications, Internet of Things (IoT) solutions leverage a multifaceted blend of technologies to establish connections between devices, events, and subsequent actions. The specific technologies and services that one might opt for are largely determined by the unique requirements associated with developing, deploying, and managing the scenario in question.

Azure IoT solutions encompass a multi-tiered approach to device management and data analysis.

Firstly, at the core of these solutions are "Things." These are typically devices that are tasked with the generation of data. A prime example would be a motor that transmits temperature readings.

Next, we move to the "Insights" phase. The data procured from these devices is meticulously analyzed to form conclusions. Using the previous example, one would assess the temperature data from the motor to determine its performance metrics.

Lastly, based on these insights, appropriate "Actions" are devised. For instance, if the data indicates that the motor is not performing optimally, the insights would lead one to re-evaluate and prioritize its maintenance schedule to ensure optimal functionality.

Taking Azure IoT solutions as an illustrative example, they generally encompass three primary components. The first is "Things," which usually refers to devices responsible for generating data. The second component is the "Insights" derived from these devices' data. These insights are crucial as they offer a deeper understanding of the underlying patterns or anomalies present in the data. The third and final component is the "Actions" that are determined and executed based on these insights. Consider a motor that regularly transmits temperature data to provide a more concrete example. This data is analyzed to assess whether the motor operates within expected parameters. If any irregularities are detected in its performance, insights gleaned from the data can be instrumental in adjusting and prioritizing its maintenance schedule, ensuring its optimal functionality and longevity.

Azure IoT is renowned for its expansive compatibility with various devices, from microcontrollers equipped with Azure RTOS and Azure Sphere to developer-centric boards like MXCHIP and Raspberry Pi. Beyond these, Azure IoT is also compatible with intelligent server gateways that can run bespoke code. Some devices are structured to conduct local processing via services like Azure IoT Edge. In contrast, others might opt for a direct connection to Azure, enabling them to dispatch and receive data within the IoT solution. Once these devices are integrated into the cloud ecosystem, several services, such as Azure IoT Hub, facilitate data ingestion. The IoT Hub serves as a cloud gateway, ensuring a secure connection and efficient management of devices. Furthermore, the Azure IoT Hub Device Provisioning Service (DPS) streamlines the process of securely registering many devices, while Azure Digital Twins offers virtual representations of tangible systems.

Upon establishing a connection to the cloud, the data from these devices can be processed and examined, resulting in tailored insights about the encompassing environment. There are three distinct pathways for data processing: the hot, warm, and cold paths. These paths are differentiated based on their latency requirements and data accessibility. The hot path, for instance, necessitates real-time data analysis using engines like Azure Stream Analytics or Azure HDInsight. Meanwhile, the warm path is more lenient, permitting longer processing times, with Azure Data Explorer as an ideal data storage and examination tool. Conversely, the cold path engages in batch processing at extensive intervals, storing large data volumes in Azure Data Lake Storage and leveraging tools like Azure Machine Learning or Azure Databricks for analysis.

With these insights, actions can be formulated to optimize the surrounding environment. Such actions can manifest as storing informational messages, triggering alarms, dispatching emails or SMS notifications, or even integrating with enterprise applications like CRM and ERP. Azure offers a suite of services to facilitate these integrations, such as Power BI for data visualization and collaboration, Azure Maps for geospatial applications, Azure Cognitive Search for comprehensive content searches, Azure API Management for API consolidation, and Azure App Service for scalable web applications. Additional tools like Dynamics 365, which merges CRM and ERP functionalities, Microsoft Power Automate, Azure Logic Apps, and Azure Mobile Apps further enhance operational capabilities. Lastly, to ensure the security and monitoring of the entire IoT solution, Azure proffers diagnostic tools like Azure Monitor and robust security services, including Azure Active Directory (Azure AD) and Microsoft Defender for IoT.

Azure Well-Architected Framework

Cloud computing has ushered in a transformative era, fundamentally altering businesses' methodologies to address their challenges. This innovation extends beyond merely shifting workloads and reshaping how security frameworks are constructed and deployed. The role of a solution architect has evolved in tandem. Today, an architect is more than just tasked with translating business needs into application functionalities. There's an added layer of complexity: ensuring that the solution not only fulfills its primary function but also stands up to the demands of scalability, resilience, efficiency, and security.

A robust and comprehensive framework becomes paramount when we delve into the Internet of Things (IoT). An ideal IoT solution is expected to be a paragon of service provision, ensuring availability, flexibility, recoverability, and performance that cater to the nuanced demands of cloud consumers. While crafting such solutions, there are pivotal design principles that one must adhere to in the IoT design.

The term "architecture" in the technological context encapsulates a broad spectrum of activities, from planning and designing to implementing and refining technological systems. Good system architecture is akin to a well-oiled machine – it seamlessly integrates business needs with the technical prowess necessary to materialize them. This intricate design process necessitates a reasonable balance among risk, cost, and capability, ensuring that each system component harmoniously aligns with the others.

Figure 2-7 illustrates Internet of Things – Azure Well-Architected Framework that has to be adopted while designing IoT solution.

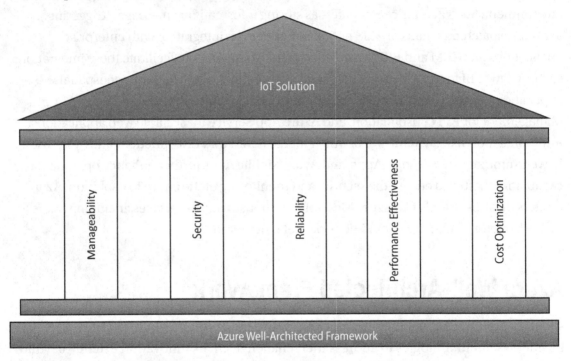

Figure 2-7. *Internet of Things – Azure well-architected framework*

With its well-architected framework, Azure simplifies the process of crafting top-tier solutions. Understanding that architecture isn't a monolithic entity with a standard template is crucial. Each solution is as unique as the problem it aims to solve. Nevertheless, there exist overarching principles, universal in their applicability, irrespective of the cloud provider in question, the architecture's specifics, or the technology employed. While these concepts are incomplete, emphasizing them ensures that IoT solution architects lay down a foundation that's not just solid but also malleable to future needs.

It's these very principles that IoT architects and engineers emphasize, focusing on the core tenets of reliability, availability, flexibility, recoverability, and performance. Such characteristics aren't merely surface-level considerations; they're deeply ingrained in the fabric of the design, ensuring that each layer of the IoT solution adheres to these guiding principles, ultimately delivering a solution that stands the test of time and demand.

Cloud computing has significantly transformed how businesses address challenges and approach workload management and security design. A solution architect's role in this paradigm extends beyond translating business requirements into application functionalities. The design must ensure the solution is scalable, resilient, efficient, and secure.

Manageability

Azure Digital Twins offers a unique way to control and monitor connected environments. A digital twin represents a virtual physical environment model driven by data from business systems and IoT devices. Such models are pivotal for businesses and organizations as they facilitate actionable insights. For instance, industries can leverage digital twin solutions for predictive maintenance in manufacturing, enhancing supply chain transparency, implementing smart shelves for real-time inventory management, and developing connected homes and smart buildings.

Reliability

Reliability is the cornerstone of any application. It guarantees that the application can uphold the promises made to its users. A resilient IoT solution strongly emphasizes business continuity and disaster recovery. Designing with high availability (HA) and disaster recovery (DR) in mind is crucial to ascertain the desired uptime for a solution. Azure offers various services, each with unique redundancy and failover options, to achieve specific uptime goals. Selecting an appropriate HA/DR option necessitates evaluating the required level of resiliency, the intricacies of implementation and maintenance, and the impact on the Cost of Goods Sold (COGS).

Security

Security is paramount. It safeguards against intentional attacks and potential misuse of valuable data and systems. One of the forefront security models adopted today is the zero-trust model. This approach assumes that breaches are inevitable and views every access attempt as potentially malicious. Implementing zero trust involves

- Ensuring strong device authentication

- Adhering to the principle of least privilege

- Monitoring device health

- Updating devices regularly

- Maintaining vigilance against emerging threats

Communication security is equally essential. All device interactions must be trustworthy, encrypted, and supported by robust cryptographic capabilities. Firmware and application software should also be regularly updated to address security vulnerabilities. Physical tamper-proofing of devices, such as using Trusted Platform Modules and intrusion detection sensors, adds an extra layer of security.

The zero-trust security model operates on a foundational belief that security breaches are not just possible but inevitable. Under this model, every access attempt to a network is treated with caution, as if originating from an unsecured network, regardless of its source. This approach assumes that basic security measures, such as identity protection and restricted access, have been established. At its core, this means verifying users and maintaining visibility into the devices they use. This allows for dynamic decisions on access based on real-time risk evaluations. Once these foundational measures are ensured, the focus shifts to more stringent requirements for IoT solutions. This includes using robust authentication methods, limiting access to essential functions, continuous monitoring of device health, regular updates to ensure device functionality, and vigilant monitoring to identify and counteract emerging threats.

Communication security is equally pivotal. Every piece of information that a device sends or receives must be inherently trustworthy. If a device lacks certain cryptographic capabilities, it should be limited to local network communication. Such cryptographic capabilities encompass data encryption, digital signatures based on reliable symmetric-key encryption algorithms, support for specific communication protocols like TLS 1.2 or DTLS 1.2, and the ability to handle certificates like X.509. However, there's flexibility in replacing X.509 with more efficient modes for TLS and supported cryptographic algorithms like AES and SHA-2. A paramount feature is that each device should have a unique identifier stored securely, which can be updated regularly or during emergencies.

Additionally, the device's firmware and software should be amenable to updates to rectify any identified security vulnerabilities. A field gateway is recommended for devices that are constrained in meeting these security standards. This gateway facilitates secure device-to-cloud communication.

Physical security must be noticed. A well-designed device should resist physical tampering, ensuring the system's overall safety and trustworthiness. This can be achieved by opting for microcontrollers or other hardware components that offer secure storage for cryptographic keys, preferably integrated with trusted platforms like TPM. This ensures a secure boot-up process and software loading. Moreover, devices should be equipped with sensors to detect unauthorized intrusions or manipulations, alerting the system and possibly initiating a "digital self-destruction" to safeguard data and functionality.

Cost Optimization

Cost optimization focuses on curtailing unnecessary expenditures and enhancing operational efficiency. Using tools like the Azure pricing calculator can offer insights into potential costs.

Performance Efficiency

Performance efficiency deals with a workload's capability to scale based on user demands efficiently. Building globally scalable solutions involves constructing IoT applications with distinct services that can independently scale. Scalability considerations extend to Azure services, including IoT Hub, Azure Functions, and Stream Analytics. Each service has unique scaling factors and best practices to ensure optimal performance.

The IoT Hub is a critical component in managing device communication. Every IoT Hub is set up with a designated number of units within a specific pricing and scale tier. This combination defines the maximum daily message quota devices can relay to the hub. Notably, scaling up the hub keeps ongoing operations intact. When considering the scalability of the IoT Hub, several factors come into play. These include the daily message quota, the quota for connected devices per instance, the speed at which the IoT Hub ingests messages (ingestion throughput), and how swiftly these incoming messages are processed (processing throughput). Another unique feature of the IoT Hub is its automatic partitioning of device messages based on the device ID. This ensures that messages from a specific device consistently land in the same partition, even though a partition might house messages from several devices. Consequently, the partition ID determines the core unit for parallel processing.

Shifting the focus to Azure Functions, when they access an Azure Event Hubs endpoint, there's a cap on the number of function instances for each event hub partition. The pinnacle of processing capability is gauged by the speed of a single function instance in handling events from one partition. The function should handle messages in grouped batches for efficiency.

Lastly, Stream Analytics optimally scales when it operates in parallel throughout its entire pipeline, from data input and querying to the final output. Such a similar configuration empowers Stream Analytics to distribute tasks across several computational nodes, maximizing efficiency and speed.

Best Practices for IOT Design to Be Applied

Designing Microsoft Defender for IoT with robust cybersecurity practices is essential in safeguarding the growing Internet of Things (IoT) ecosystem. IoT devices often possess limited resources and, as such, can be more susceptible to security threats.

Figure 2-8 illustrates the constituent elements of IoT cybersecurity design best practices.

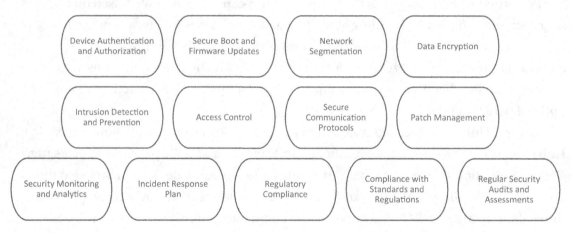

Figure 2-8. *Components of best practices for IoT cybersecurity design*

Here, we delve into comprehensive insights for each best practice.

Device Authentication and Authorization

Strong device authentication is a fundamental security measure. Devices should be uniquely identified and authorized before connecting to the network. Utilize digital certificates, hardware-based authentication, or biometric methods for a multilayered approach. This ensures that only trusted devices can access the IoT ecosystem.

Secure Boot and Firmware Updates

Secure boot processes verify the integrity of device firmware and operating systems during startup, preventing unauthorized modifications. Furthermore, supporting over-the-air (OTA) firmware updates is crucial to patch vulnerabilities and improve security over time. These updates should be encrypted to ensure they cannot be tampered with during transmission.

Network Segmentation

IoT networks should be segmented into different zones based on their functions and security requirements. This segmentation isolates critical systems and sensitive data from less critical components, limiting the lateral movement of attackers. It can also help contain potential breaches and reduce the blast radius of security incidents.

Data Encryption

End-to-end encryption is vital for protecting data privacy and integrity. It ensures that data is secured both in transit and at rest. Strong encryption algorithms should be used to safeguard data from eavesdropping and tampering. Protocols such as TLS for secure communication and encryption at rest are essential components.

Intrusion Detection and Prevention

Intrusion detection and prevention systems (IDPS) continuously monitor network traffic for signs of suspicious activity. They can trigger alerts and automated responses when anomalies are detected. These systems are critical in identifying and mitigating potential threats in real time, reducing the risk of successful attacks.

Access Control

Access control mechanisms should be deployed to restrict permissions and privileges on a need-to-know basis. Role-based access control (RBAC) effectively ensures that users and devices only have access to the resources and functions necessary for their roles. This minimizes the potential attack surface and reduces the risk of unauthorized access.

Secure Communication Protocols

IoT devices communicate using various protocols, and it's essential to choose secure options. Protocols like MQTT-TLS, HTTPS, and CoAP with DTLS (Datagram Transport Layer Security) offer encryption and data integrity, protecting information from being intercepted or altered during transmission.

Patch Management

Implement a proactive approach to patch management. Security vulnerabilities in IoT devices and software should be identified and addressed promptly. Automate patch deployment to minimize the window of exposure to known threats. Regularly update and patch not only device firmware but also underlying software and libraries.

Security Monitoring and Analytics

Effective security monitoring and analytics are indispensable. Advanced tools and technologies, including machine learning and artificial intelligence, should be used to analyze network traffic, system logs, and behavior patterns for anomalies and potential threats. These solutions enhance threat detection capabilities, allowing timely responses to security incidents.

Incident Response Plan

An incident response plan should be comprehensive and well documented. It outlines procedures for identifying, reporting, and responding to security incidents. The plan should cover containment, investigation, mitigation, recovery, and lessons learned to improve security practices continuously.

Compliance with Standards and Regulations

Ensure that your IoT ecosystem complies with relevant cybersecurity standards and regulations. This may include following the NIST Cybersecurity Framework, adhering to GDPR data protection regulations, or meeting industry-specific guidelines such as HIPAA for healthcare IoT.

Regular Security Audits and Assessments

Regular security audits and assessments are critical for identifying vulnerabilities and weaknesses within the IoT infrastructure. These evaluations help in maintaining the security posture of IoT devices and networks. It's essential to conduct penetration testing, vulnerability scanning, and code reviews to identify and address potential security risks.

By adopting these detailed cybersecurity best practices in the design of Microsoft Defender for IoT, you can create a resilient and secure environment for IoT devices, protecting them from evolving threats and vulnerabilities. This comprehensive approach ensures that IoT ecosystems remain safeguarded, data remains private, and the system's integrity remains intact.

Microsoft Security Recommendations

Microsoft has developed a comprehensive set of security guidelines for individuals and corporations working with IoT solutions.

Microsoft has provided a comprehensive set of guidelines to bolster the security of IoT (Internet of Things) solutions. Adhering to these recommendations ensures that IoT systems remain resilient against potential vulnerabilities and threats.

Microsoft guidelines align with the shared responsibility model proposed by Microsoft, emphasizing the joint duty of Microsoft and its users to ensure security. A significant portion of these guidelines can be seamlessly overseen by Microsoft Defender for Cloud (formerly Azure Security Center and Azure Defender). This tool stands as a vanguard in safeguarding Azure resources. It conducts periodic security assessments of Azure resources, pinpointing potential vulnerabilities and offering actionable advice to rectify them.

Among the general recommendations, Microsoft advocates for staying updated with the most recent versions of platforms, languages, protocols, and frameworks. Emphasis is also placed on safeguarding authentication keys, particularly post-deployment, to thwart malicious entities from impersonating registered devices. Leveraging device SDKs is encouraged since they encapsulate essential security functions like encryption and authentication. With Microsoft's consistent improvements to SDKs, users are poised to reap the benefits of emerging security enhancements.

In identity and access management, it's crucial to delineate access controls for the IoT Hub, ensuring each component's access aligns with its function. Furthermore, backend services like Cosmos DB, Stream Analytics, and Blob Storage that consume data from the IoT Hub should have clearly defined access permissions.

Regarding data protection, devices should communicate securely with the IoT Hub. This can be achieved using unique identity keys, security tokens, or on-device X.509 certificates. The IoT Hub employs the TLS standard for device connections, recommending TLS 1.2 for optimal security. Moreover, when the data is transmitted to backend services, it's imperative to employ robust encryption and protection mechanisms.

On the networking front, devices should be designed to minimize hardware ports, reducing the risk of unauthorized access. Features that detect or deter physical tampering should be incorporated. The device's architecture should prioritize security, with elements like encrypted storage and a Trusted Platform Module (TPM). Keeping the device's software updated and including antivirus capabilities are also advocated.

Lastly, monitoring plays a crucial role. Regularly checking for unauthorized device access using built-in logging features is recommended. The overall health of the IoT Hub solution can be assessed using Azure Monitor metrics. Furthermore, setting up diagnostics by logging solution-specific events and channeling them to Azure Monitor can provide invaluable insights into performance and potential issues.

Review Security Fundamentals

The Internet of Things (IoT) introduces distinct security, privacy, and compliance challenges. Unlike conventional digital technology, IoT blends cyber and physical realms, making its security parameters unique. Ensuring the protection of IoT solutions demands secure device provisioning, fortified connectivity between devices and cloud services, and safeguarding data during cloud processing and storage. Factors like resource-limited devices, widespread deployments, and the sheer volume of devices within a given solution magnify these challenges.

Microsoft Azure steps in as a robust solution to these challenges. Offering a continually expanding suite of integrated cloud services, from analytics and machine learning to storage and security, Azure stands out with its unwavering dedication to data protection and privacy. The platform's inbuilt systems offer continuous intrusion detection, service attack prevention, and regular penetration tests. Multifactor authentication enhances security for end users, while for the application and host providers, Azure provides a plethora of tools ranging from access control and monitoring to vulnerability scanning and configuration management.

The Azure IoT Hub stands as a pivotal component in this ecosystem. This fully managed service ensures consistent and secure two-way communication between IoT devices and Azure services, employing per-device security credentials and access control. For a device to securely integrate with the IoT infrastructure, providing it with a unique identity key is essential. This key, combined with a user-selected device ID, forms the foundation for all communication between the device and the Azure IoT Hub.

Physical security of devices is also paramount. Devices are designed to deny unsolicited network connections, establishing connections in an outbound-only manner. Furthermore, they connect exclusively with recognized services, and system-level authorization employs per-device identities for enhanced security.

Azure IoT Hub employs industry-standard protocols like HTTPS, AMQP, and MQTT on the connectivity front. It guarantees message durability between devices and the cloud, caching messages for up to seven days for telemetry and two days for commands. This robust design ensures even intermittently connecting devices can receive commands. Security is further enhanced with the Transport Layer Security (TLS) protocol, with the Azure IoT Hub authenticated via the X.509 protocol.

Secure processing and storage in the cloud are achieved using Azure Active Directory for user authentication. With Azure, users can define and control the security levels, monitoring and auditing all data access to prevent unauthorized intrusions.

Additionally, Azure offers options for both IP filtering and virtual networks to bolster security when accessing Azure resources, ensuring that IoT solutions remain resilient in an ever-evolving digital landscape.

Analyze the Foundational Aspects of IoT Security Infrastructure

The Internet of Things (IoT) presents distinct challenges related to security, privacy, and compliance for businesses worldwide. Unlike traditional cybersecurity, which focuses primarily on software and its implementation, IoT concerns the convergence of the digital and physical worlds. Safeguarding IoT solutions necessitates ensuring the secure setup of devices, establishing secure connections between these devices and the cloud, and implementing secure data protection within the cloud during data processing and storage. However, several factors work against achieving these objectives, including resource-constrained devices, widespread geographic deployments, and the presence of a large number of devices within a single solution.

Microsoft Azure – A Secure IoT Infrastructure for Your Business

Microsoft Azure provides a comprehensive cloud solution that combines an ever-expanding suite of integrated cloud services, encompassing analytics, machine learning, storage, security, networking, and web services, with a steadfast commitment to data protection and privacy.

Microsoft's systems incorporate continuous intrusion detection and prevention, prevention of service attacks, regular penetration testing, and forensic tools to identify and mitigate threats. Multifactor authentication adds an extra layer of security for end users seeking access to the network. For application and host providers, Microsoft offers access control, monitoring, anti-malware measures, vulnerability scanning, patch management, and configuration control.

Azure IoT Hub, part of the Microsoft Azure ecosystem, delivers a fully managed service facilitating reliable and secure two-way communication between IoT devices and Azure services such as Azure Machine Learning and Azure Stream Analytics. It employs per-device security credentials and access control for this purpose.

Ensuring Secure Device Provisioning and Authentication

Secure device provisioning involves assigning a unique identity key to each device, which the IoT infrastructure uses to communicate with the device during its operation. The generated key, coupled with a user-selected device ID, forms the basis for a token used in all communications between the device and Azure IoT Hub.

Device IDs can be associated with a device during manufacturing (e.g., embedded in a hardware trust module) or use an existing fixed identity as a proxy (e.g., CPU serial numbers). Given the complexity of altering this identifying information in the device, it is crucial to introduce logical device IDs to account for changes in the underlying hardware while retaining the same logical device. In some cases, device identity association may occur during deployment, with an authenticated field engineer configuring a new device while communicating with the solution backend. The Azure IoT Hub identity registry securely stores device identities and security keys, allowing for granular control over device access through allowlists and blocklists.

Azure IoT Hub access control policies in the cloud enable activation and deactivation of any device identity, offering a means to disassociate a device from an IoT deployment when necessary. This association and disassociation of devices are tied to each device's identity.

Additional device security features include the following:

- Devices only establish outbound connections and do not accept unsolicited network connections.

- Devices exclusively connect to well-known, peered services, such as Azure IoT Hub.

- Per-device identities are used for system-level authorization and authentication, making access credentials and permissions revocable with minimal delay.

Secure Connectivity

Azure IoT Hub supports secure connectivity through established protocols, including HTTPS, AMQP, and MQTT. The durability of messaging between the cloud and devices is maintained through acknowledgment mechanisms in response to messages. Additional messaging durability is achieved by caching messages in the IoT Hub for up to seven days for telemetry and two days for commands, enabling devices with sporadic connections to receive commands. Azure IoT Hub maintains a per-device queue for each device.

Scalability necessitates the secure interoperability of a wide range of devices, which Azure IoT Hub enables through secure connections to IP-enabled and non-IP-enabled devices, utilizing an IoT Edge device as a gateway where needed.

Other Features Related to Connection Security

Communication between devices and Azure IoT Hub, as well as between gateways and Azure IoT Hub, is secured using industry-standard Transport Layer Security (TLS) with Azure IoT Hub authenticated via the X.509 protocol.

142

Azure IoT Hub does not initiate unsolicited inbound connections to protect devices, with devices responsible for creating all connections. Azure IoT Hub durably stores messages for devices, ensuring they are accessible for two days, accommodating devices with sporadic connections due to power or connectivity issues. Azure IoT Hub maintains a per-device queue for each device.

Secure Processing and Storage in the Cloud

Azure IoT Hub, through Microsoft Entra ID for user authentication and authorization, implements a policy-based authorization model for cloud data. This model facilitates flexible access management that is audit-ready. Once data resides in the cloud, it can be processed and stored within user-defined workflows. Microsoft Entra ID controls access to data segments, depending on the storage service employed.

All keys used by the IoT infrastructure are securely stored in the cloud, with the ability to roll over keys when needed. Data can be stored in Azure Cosmos DB or SQL databases, providing the flexibility to define the desired level of security. Furthermore, Azure offers monitoring and auditing capabilities to alert users of any unauthorized access or intrusions.

Secure Networks

By default, IoT Hub's hostnames map to a public endpoint with publicly routable IP addresses accessible online. This configuration allows multiple customers to share the same IoT Hub public endpoint, ensuring that IoT devices connecting over wide-area networks and on-premises networks can access the hub. However, for situations requiring restricted access to Azure resources, Azure IoT solutions support IP filtering and virtual networks to enhance security when necessary.

Microsoft-Recommended Approach to Design Security for IoT Cybersecurity Solution

Microsoft recommends security within an IoT solution can be categorized into three distinct areas, each addressing critical aspects of safeguarding the system:

- Device security, which focuses on protecting IoT devices while they operate in the real world.

- Connection security guarantees that all data exchanged between IoT devices and cloud services remains confidential and immune to tampering.

- Cloud security is essential for safeguarding data as it traverses through cloud networks and resides in storage, providing a comprehensive security framework encompassing the entire IoT ecosystem.

In ensuring robust security for an IoT solution, several key practices and principles must be followed, spanning three essential areas: device security, connection security, and cloud security.

Device Security

Device security begins with carefully scoping the hardware to include only the minimum features necessary for device functionality, reducing exposure to potential vulnerabilities. Selecting tamper-proof hardware with built-in mechanisms to detect physical tampering further reinforces security. Devices should ideally incorporate secure features such as encrypted storage and secure boot functionality based on a Trusted Platform Module (TPM) to protect data and ensure the device's integrity. Secure firmware upgrades with cryptographic assurance are essential for maintaining security during and after upgrades. A secure software development methodology should be followed from project inception to deployment. Device SDKs that implement security features like encryption and authentication should be used whenever possible. When utilizing open source software, it's critical to consider the activity level of the open source community, ensuring ongoing support and issue resolution. Secure hardware deployment is necessary, especially in unsecured locations, with tamper-proof measures, such as covering USB ports. Authentication keys must be kept physically safe, even post-deployment, to prevent malicious devices from masquerading as existing ones. Keeping the device's operating systems and drivers up to date and implementing antivirus and anti-malware capabilities where permitted are further steps in bolstering device security. Regular auditing and compliance with device manufacturer security and deployment best practices are also essential. For legacy or constrained devices, a modern and secure field gateway can be used to aggregate data and provide security features.

Connection Security

In connection security, X.509 certificates are recommended for device authentication to IoT Hub or IoT Central, offering robust security in production environments. Transport Layer Security (TLS) 1.2 should be used to secure connections from devices, as it provides superior security to legacy TLS versions. Ensuring a means to update TLS root certificates on devices is essential to maintain secure connections over time. Azure Private Link can be considered to block access to public device-facing endpoints, enhancing security further.

Cloud Security

Cloud security is a critical component that starts with following a secure software development methodology, emphasizing security considerations from project inception to deployment. The careful selection of open source software with an active community ensures ongoing support and issue resolution. The integration of software components should be performed with care, paying attention to potential security flaws at the boundaries of libraries and APIs. Protecting cloud credentials is paramount, with best practices including changing passwords frequently and avoiding using these credentials on public machines. Access controls for IoT Hubs, IoT Central applications, and backend services must be well defined and configured based on specific requirements. Ongoing monitoring from the cloud using IoT Hub metrics in Azure Monitor and setting up diagnostics for logging and event tracking further enhance cloud security.

By meticulously following these security practices across device, connection, and cloud security domains, IoT solutions can be effectively safeguarded from potential threats and vulnerabilities, ensuring their reliability and integrity.

Summary

This chapter focused on establishing a robust security strategy for the Internet of Things (IoT) and operational technology (OT) environments, leveraging the capabilities of Microsoft Defender for IoT. It delved into various facets, providing a comprehensive guide to fortify the cybersecurity landscape of IoT and OT systems.

IoT's Cybersecurity

The chapter began with a thorough exploration of the cybersecurity challenges inherent to IoT ecosystems. It illuminates the unique vulnerabilities associated with interconnected devices, emphasizing the need for a proactive and adaptive security approach.

How Microsoft Defender for IoT Works

Readers were introduced to the workings of Microsoft Defender for IoT, shedding light on the sophisticated mechanisms employed by the solution. This section offered insights into threat detection, incident response, and the overall protective measures incorporated to safeguard IoT and OT environments.

Design Framework for IoT Cybersecurity Solution

A pivotal aspect of the chapter involves presenting a comprehensive design framework for building a robust IoT cybersecurity solution. This framework is a road map for architects and security professionals, guiding them through the essential elements necessary to create a secure and resilient IoT infrastructure.

Design Principle for IoT Cybersecurity Solution

Building on the framework, the chapter outlined critical design principles that underpin an effective IoT cybersecurity solution. These principles encompass risk assessment, continuous monitoring, and adaptive defense strategies to ensure a proactive stance against evolving cyber threats.

Design Elements of Microsoft Defender for IoT

The discussion was narrowed down to the specific design elements of Microsoft Defender for IoT. Readers gained insights into the features and functionalities that empower the solution, enhancing their understanding of how these elements contribute to a holistic cybersecurity strategy.

Microsoft-Recommended Approach to Design Security for IoT Cybersecurity Solution

The chapter concluded by consolidating the information into a recommended approach endorsed by Microsoft for designing security in IoT environments. This approach encapsulates best practices, industry standards, and the innovative features of Defender for IoT, providing readers with a comprehensive guide to fortifying their IoT and OT landscapes.

In summary, this chapter is an indispensable resource for organizations and professionals seeking to establish a robust security posture for their IoT and OT ecosystems. By leveraging Microsoft Defender for IoT and adhering to the recommended strategies, readers can fortify their systems against the ever-evolving landscape of cybersecurity threats.

In the next chapter, you will read about the method of planning deployment and implementation defender for IoT.

CHAPTER 3

Plan Microsoft Defender for IoT

Planning a comprehensive plan for Microsoft Defender for IoT is paramount due to the unique security challenges associated with Internet of Things (IoT) devices. Unlike traditional computing devices, IoT devices often operate in diverse and distributed environments, making them susceptible to various threats. A well-structured plan is necessary to address these challenges and ensure the security and integrity of the IoT ecosystem.

Firstly, the plan involves conducting a thorough assessment of the IoT environment. Identifying all IoT devices, categorizing them based on their function, and assessing their criticality help understand the scope of potential security risks. Regular scanning and assessment of vulnerabilities, along with prioritized patching and firmware updates, are critical to safeguard against known exploits.

Network segmentation is another crucial element in the plan. Organizations can contain potential breaches and limit unauthorized access by isolating critical IoT devices from the rest of the network. Defining access controls and authentication mechanisms ensures only authorized entities can interact with the IoT devices, reducing the attack surface. The plan's threat detection and response aspect involve real-time monitoring, behavioral analytics, and anomaly detection. Incident response procedures specific to IoT security incidents should be well defined to minimize the impact of any breaches.

Integration with existing security infrastructure is crucial for seamless operations. Ensuring that Microsoft Defender for IoT integrates with other security tools and solutions allows for a more holistic and coordinated response to threats. Regular audits and assessments and adjustments to the security plan based on findings contribute to the plan's ongoing effectiveness. Compliance with regulations and industry standards is also addressed to ensure that the organization meets legal requirements and maintains high security.

© Puthiyavan Udayakumar and Dr. R. Anandan 2024
P. Udayakumar and Dr. R. Anandan, *Design and Deploy Microsoft Defender for IoT*,
https://doi.org/10.1007/979-8-8688-0239-3_3

In summary, a well-structured plan for Microsoft Defender for IoT is essential to address the unique security challenges posed by IoT devices. The plan encompasses vulnerability management, network segmentation, policy enforcement, threat detection and response, and integration with existing infrastructure. This comprehensive approach is crucial for maintaining the integrity and security of IoT ecosystems in today's interconnected world.

By the end of this chapter, you should be able to understand the following:

- Plan Microsoft Defender for IoT deployment

- Prepare for Microsoft Defender for IoT deployment

- Plan Microsoft Defender for IoT licenses

- Plan Microsoft Defender for IoT roles and permissions

- Plan Microsoft Defender for IoT with cybersecurity

Plan Microsoft Defender for IoT Deployment

Microsoft Defender for IoT is compatible with proprietary embedded OT devices and legacy Windows systems frequently encountered in OT environments. This solution facilitates inventorying all IoT devices, conducts vulnerability assessments, offers risk-based mitigation recommendations, and ensures continuous monitoring for anomalous or unauthorized device behavior.

Microsoft Defender for IoT employs IoT-aware behavioral analytics for ongoing monitoring of network traffic, enabling the identification of unauthorized or compromised components.

Microsoft Defender for IoT delivers robust threat detection capabilities tailored for IoT/OT environments, offering flexibility through various deployment options, including cloud-connected, fully on-premises, or hybrid configurations. This chapter outlines the key steps at a high level to guide the planning process for deploying Defender for IoT in operational technology (OT) monitoring scenarios.

Implementing a robust security strategy for your Internet of Things (IoT) landscape is paramount in today's digital landscape. In this context, planning for Microsoft Defender for IoT becomes crucial to fortifying your IoT ecosystem against evolving cyber threats. Microsoft Defender for IoT is a comprehensive security solution designed to protect and monitor IoT devices, ensuring sensitive data integrity, confidentiality, and availability. This planning process involves meticulously examining your IoT environment, encompassing device categorization, risk assessment, network architecture, access controls, and incident response planning. By adhering to best practices and integrating seamlessly with other Microsoft Defender solutions, this strategic deployment enhances your organization's overall resilience, providing a robust defense mechanism for IoT's dynamic and interconnected world.

Planning for Microsoft Defender for IoT requires a meticulous and comprehensive approach to safeguard your Internet of Things (IoT) ecosystem. Commence by creating a thorough inventory of all IoT devices, categorizing them based on their roles, and assessing the associated risks. Develop robust security policies aligned with industry standards, addressing encryption, secure communication, and access controls. Design a resilient network architecture, incorporating VLANs and firewalls to segment and protect IoT devices from critical infrastructure, minimizing the impact of potential breaches. Implement robust authentication mechanisms and role-based access controls to prevent unauthorized access. Establish a disciplined update and patch management plan, ensuring regular maintenance to address vulnerabilities. Continuous monitoring and anomaly detection are critical; configure Microsoft Defender for IoT to scrutinize network traffic and device behavior, setting up alerts for deviations.

Integration with Microsoft Defender for Endpoint enhances threat detection and response capabilities, providing a holistic security solution. Equip your team with a well-defined incident response plan, conducting regular drills and simulations to ensure readiness. Foster a culture of security awareness through employee training, emphasizing IoT security best practices. Regular audits, assessments, and penetration testing should be routine, enabling the adaptation of security policies to evolving threats. This comprehensive strategy, encompassing device management, network security, access controls, and continuous improvement, forms the foundation for a robust Microsoft Defender for IoT deployment.

Table 3-1 describes business needs and scenarios that may make Defender for IoT a good choice for your company.

Table 3-1. *Business Needs of Defender for IoT*

Business Needs	Description
Device Discovery	The Defender for IoT sensor console offers a comprehensive Device Inventory page and a Device Map page, providing detailed insights into each OT/IoT device in the network and their interconnections.
Manage Network Risks and Vulnerabilities	Defender for IoT facilitates risk assessment through detailed reports accessible from each sensor console. These reports identify vulnerabilities, including unauthorized devices, unpatched systems, and unused open ports.
Keep Up to Date with Recent Threat Intelligence	Ensure sensors in the network have the latest threat intelligence (TI) packages from the Defender for IoT research team. These packages include recent incidents, common vulnerabilities and exposures (CVEs), and updated asset profiles.
Manage Sites and Sensors	In fully on-premises environments, bulk manage OT sensors using an on-premises management console. Alternatively, onboard OT sensors to the cloud and manage them through the Azure portal on the Sites and Sensors page.
Run Guided Investigations for OT Entities	Security operations center (SOC) teams can utilize Microsoft Sentinel workbooks provided with the IoT/OT Threat Monitoring solution. These workbooks aid in investigations based on incidents, alerts, and activities for OT assets, offering a hunting experience across the MITRE ATT&CK framework for ICS.
Automate Remediation Actions	Leverage Microsoft Sentinel playbooks associated with the IoT/OT Threat Monitoring solution to automate routine remediation actions. These playbooks enhance the efficiency of security teams by automating responses to incidents identified by Defender for IoT.

Planning for Microsoft Defender for IoT requires a comprehensive approach encompassing various critical elements depicted in Figure 3-1. Initiating the inventory and categorizing IoT devices are essential to understand the ecosystem. Subsequently, conducting a thorough risk assessment and formulating robust security policies become imperative for preemptive threat mitigation. Addressing network architecture and segmentation ensures a resilient defense strategy, followed by robust authentication and access controls. An effective update and patch management plan safeguards against vulnerabilities. The integration with Microsoft Defender for Endpoint enhances overall security capabilities. To bolster the defense further, incorporating monitoring and anomaly detection mechanisms is crucial, alongside incident response planning for swift and effective counteractions. Regular audits and assessments uphold ongoing security standards, while employee training and awareness programs foster a proactive security culture within the organization. This holistic approach ensures a robust and adaptive security framework for IoT environments.

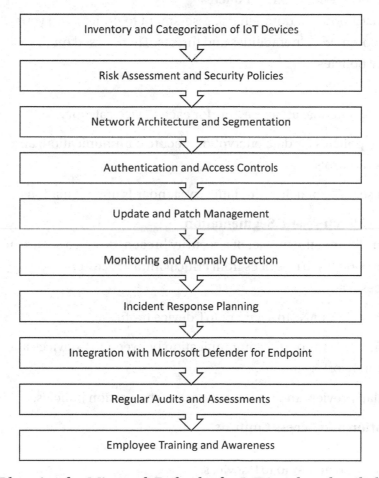

Figure 3-1. Planning for Microsoft Defender for IoT involves detailed steps and considerations

Here's a comprehensive component with clear explanations and best practices.

Inventory and Categorization of IoT Devices

Explanation: Start by creating an inventory of all IoT devices in your network. Categorize them based on functionality, criticality, and the data type they handle.

Best Practices

- Maintain a central repository with detailed information about each device.

- Classify devices based on their role in the system (e.g., sensors, actuators, gateways).

- Assess the risk associated with each device type.

Risk Assessment and Security Policies

Explanation: Conduct a thorough risk assessment to understand your IoT environment's potential vulnerabilities and threats. Then, based on the assessment, develop security policies.

Best Practices

- Identify potential attack vectors for each device category.

- Define policies for data encryption, secure communication, and access controls.

- Align security policies with industry standards and regulations.

Network Architecture and Segmentation

Explanation: To limit the impact of a security breach, design a secure network architecture that isolates IoT devices from critical infrastructure.

Best Practices

- Implement VLANs to segment IoT device traffic.

- Use firewalls to control communication between IoT devices and other network segments.

- Regularly review and update network segmentation policies.

Authentication and Access Controls

Explanation: Implement robust authentication mechanisms and access controls to prevent unauthorized access to IoT devices.

Best Practices

- Enforce solid and unique passwords for device access.

- Implement multifactor authentication (MFA) where possible.

- Use role-based access control (RBAC) to restrict permissions based on user roles.

Update and Patch Management

Explanation: Develop a comprehensive plan for updating and patching IoT devices to address vulnerabilities and improve security.

Best Practices

- Establish a regular schedule for applying updates and patches.

- Test updates in a controlled environment before deploying them to production.

- Monitor vendor releases for security patches and updates.

Monitoring and Anomaly Detection

Explanation: Set up continuous monitoring to detect unusual activities or deviations from normal behavior within the IoT environment.

Best Practices

- Configure Microsoft Defender for IoT to monitor network traffic and device behavior.

- Establish baseline behavior for devices and set up alerts for anomalies.

- Conduct regular reviews of alerts to identify and respond to potential threats.

Incident Response Planning

Explanation: Develop a well-defined incident response plan specific to IoT security incidents.

Best Practices

- Clearly define roles and responsibilities for incident response team members.

- Conduct regular drills and simulations to ensure the effectiveness of the plan.

- Establish communication channels and procedures for reporting and responding to incidents.

Integration with Microsoft Defender for Endpoint

Explanation: Integrate Microsoft Defender for IoT with Microsoft Defender for Endpoint for a unified security approach.

Best Practices

- Leverage the combined capabilities for comprehensive threat detection and response.

- Ensure seamless communication between the two solutions.

- Monitor alerts and events from both platforms for a holistic view of security.

Regular Audits and Assessments

Explanation: Conduct regular audits and assessments to evaluate the effectiveness of your security measures.

Best Practices

- Perform penetration testing to identify vulnerabilities.

- Regularly review and update security policies based on the findings.

- Engage third-party security experts for independent assessments.

Employee Training and Awareness

Explanation: Educate employees about IoT security best practices and raise awareness about potential risks.

Best Practices

- Provide regular training sessions on recognizing and reporting security threats.

- Promote a culture of security awareness among all staff members.

- Share real-world examples to illustrate the importance of IoT security.

In summary, planning for Microsoft Defender for IoT involves a holistic approach that addresses device inventory, risk assessment, network architecture, access controls, monitoring, incident response, and ongoing evaluation. Regularly update your strategy to adapt to emerging threats and technology advancements. Integration with other Microsoft Defender solutions enhances the overall security posture of your IoT environment.

Enterprise Plan for Operation Technology

The Enterprise Plan for operation technology (OT) is a comprehensive strategy that involves meticulous planning across various essential aspects to ensure OT environments' secure and efficient operation. Organizations must meticulously plan OT sites and zones, strategically grouping devices based on geographical and functional criteria. Simultaneously, developing a plan for OT users involves defining access controls, user roles, and authentication mechanisms tailored to the specific requirements of OT operations. Additionally, planning the connections between OT sensors and management consoles is crucial for seamless data flow and effective monitoring.

Furthermore, the Enterprise Plan encompasses a detailed strategy for Azure connectivity methods, ensuring a secure and reliable connection between on-premises OT environments and the Azure cloud. This involves considering network architecture, encryption, and data transfer protocols to optimize connectivity and data protection.

The Enterprise Plan for operation technology is a holistic approach that integrates site and user planning, sensor and management connections, and Azure connectivity methods to establish a robust and secure foundation for OT operations within an organization. This strategic framework ensures the efficient functioning of OT environments while adhering to the highest security and operational standards.

Plan Operation Technology Sites and Zones

Persist in applying the foundational principles of zero trust to your operational technology (OT) networks, maintaining consistency with established practices in traditional IT networks. However, adapt these principles with necessary logistical modifications. Identify and manage all connections between networks and devices to prevent untracked interdependencies and mitigate unexpected downtime during maintenance. Given that specific OT systems may not fully support requisite security practices, Microsoft recommends restricting connections by utilizing a limited number of jump hosts. These jump hosts, equipped with robust security measures, including multifactor authentication and Privileged Access Management systems, can initiate secure remote sessions with other devices.

Implement network segmentation to restrict data access, ensuring encrypted and secure communication between devices and segments. This prevents lateral movement between systems, with pre-authorized and secured devices adhering to organizational policies. While trusting communication within industrial control and safety information systems (ICS and SIS), further network segmentation into manageable areas facilitates effective monitoring for security and maintenance purposes.

Leverage device location, health, and behavior signals to gate access or trigger remediation actions. Enforce prerequisites for device access, requiring devices to be up to date, and employ analytics for enhanced visibility, scaling defenses with automated responses.

Continuous monitoring of security metrics, including authorized devices and network traffic baselines, is essential to uphold the integrity of your security perimeter amidst organizational changes. Adapt segments and access policies in response to evolving landscapes involving people, devices, and systems, ensuring the sustained efficacy of your security posture over time.

Implement Microsoft Defender for IoT network sensors strategically across your operational technology (OT) networks to discern devices and oversee traffic. This solution evaluates devices for vulnerabilities, offers risk-based mitigation measures, and maintains continuous vigilance for anomalous or unauthorized behavior. When deploying sensors for OT networks, employ the concept of sites and zones for effective network segmentation.

In this context, sites represent clusters of devices in specific locations, such as an office at a designated address. Meanwhile, zones define logical segments within a site, delineating functional areas like a specific production line. To optimize monitoring capabilities, associate each OT sensor with a particular site and zone, ensuring that each sensor covers a designated network area. Segmentation across sites and zones facilitates vigilant tracking of traffic flow between segments, allowing the enforcement of tailored security policies for each zone.

Additionally, establish site-based access policies to grant least-privileged access to Defender for IoT data and activities. This approach ensures a finely tuned security framework, aligning with Microsoft's recommendation for network segmentation in OT environments.

Multiple sensors can be accommodated within each zone, especially when deploying Defender for IoT at a larger scale. In such scenarios, individual sensors may capture distinct facets of the same device. Defender for IoT seamlessly amalgamates devices detected within the same zone, sharing identical logical combinations of device characteristics, such as IP and MAC addresses.

In cases where you manage multiple networks and encounter unique devices with resembling characteristics, such as recurring IP address ranges, it is advisable to allocate each sensor to a distinct zone. This ensures that Defender for IoT can effectively distinguish between devices and uniquely identify each one, enhancing the precision of device detection and facilitating more accurate monitoring and management across diverse network environments.

This approach aligns with the principles of the zero-trust security model, reinforcing the notion that trust should not be assumed for any device, user, or network, thereby enhancing security posture. By implementing this strategy, organizations can achieve heightened monitoring and reporting granularity, allowing for a more nuanced understanding of network activities and potential security threats within specific areas of the network architecture. This meticulous segmentation contributes to a robust security framework, aligning with Microsoft's recommendation for organizations operating in OT environments.

Plan Operation Technology Users

Thoroughly strategize the user management aspect of deploying Defender for IoT by understanding the individuals within your organization who will interact with the system and identifying their specific use cases. While the security operations center (SOC) and IT personnel are anticipated to be the primary users, it's essential to recognize that other stakeholders within your organization may also require read access to resources, whether in Azure or on local platforms.

In the Azure environment, user assignments are intricately linked to their Microsoft Enterprise ID and roles within the role-based access control (RBAC) framework. Particularly, when segmenting your network into multiple sites, careful consideration should be given to defining and applying specific permissions per site tailoring access levels to the requirements of distinct organizational units or functional areas.

Flexibility of OT network sensors extends to accommodating local users and those synchronized with Active Directory. In instances where Active Directory integration is part of your user management strategy, ensuring that you possess the necessary access details for the Active Directory server becomes imperative. This meticulous approach to user planning establishes a foundation for efficient and secure access management within the Defender for IoT deployment, aligning with best practices recommended by Microsoft.

Plan Operation Technology Sensor and Management Connections

When dealing with cloud-connected sensors, establish a clear strategy for connecting each operational technology (OT) sensor to Defender for IoT within the Azure cloud. This entails deciding on the type of proxy necessary to facilitate these connections.

In scenarios where an air-gapped or hybrid environment is in play, and you're managing multiple OT network sensors locally, it is prudent to plan the deployment of an on-premises management console. This console serves as a centralized tool, enabling the configuration of settings and the visualization of data from a central location. This planning approach ensures seamless connectivity and efficient management, catering to the diverse deployment scenarios encountered in different network environments.

Identify which certificates you'll use for each OT sensor, which tools you'll use to generate them, and which attributes you'll include in each certificate.

Plan Azure Connectivity Method

Azure connectivity refers to establishing and maintaining network connections between various components and services within the Microsoft Azure cloud platform. Azure provides a range of networking features and services that enable organizations to connect their on-premises infrastructure, data centers, and remote locations to resources hosted in the Azure cloud.

Azure connectivity services and features provide the flexibility and scalability needed for organizations to build and manage complex, hybrid, and multi-cloud environments. They enable secure, reliable, and efficient communication between on-premises infrastructure and resources hosted in the Azure cloud.

Network sensors establish connections to Azure to deliver a comprehensive array of data, encompassing information about detected devices, alerts, and the health status of the sensors themselves. This connection serves various purposes, from data provision to accessing threat intelligence packages and engaging with connected Azure services. Among these services are prominent platforms like IoT Hub, Blob Storage, Event Hubs, Aria, and the Microsoft Download Center.

Regardless of the specific Azure service employed, all connection methods share common characteristics designed to enhance security, efficiency, and scalability. One notable feature is the intrinsic improvement in security, eliminating the need for additional security configurations. The connection to Azure is established through specific and secure endpoints, mitigating risks associated with wildcard configurations.

Furthermore, robust encryption mechanisms are implemented to ensure the confidentiality and integrity of communication between the sensor and Azure resources. Utilizing Transport Layer Security (TLS 1.2) and Advanced Encryption Standard (AES-256), the connection facilitates encrypted data transmission, providing an added layer of protection against potential security threats.

Deploying network sensors in conjunction with Azure ensures scalability, particularly for new features exclusively supported in the cloud. This integration bolsters the security posture and seamlessly positions the infrastructure to embrace advancements and innovations in the cloud-based environment.

Consider the specific requirements outlined in this section to determine the most suitable connection method for your cloud-connected Microsoft Defender for IoT sensors. If your scenario requires private connectivity between the sensor and Azure, if your site establishes connectivity via ExpressRoute, or if a VPN is the chosen connection method to link your site with Azure, then the recommended approach is to opt for proxy connections facilitated by an Azure proxy.

Alternatively, if your sensor necessitates a proxy to bridge the gap from the operational technology (OT) network to the cloud, or if the objective is to have multiple sensors converge and connect to Azure through a centralized point, the recommended method is proxy connections with proxy chaining.

The straightforward option for scenarios where a direct connection between your sensor and Azure is desired, without the intermediary of a proxy, is to employ direct connections. This is preferred when you intend to establish a direct and unmediated link between your sensor and the Azure cloud.

In cases where sensors are distributed across multiple public clouds, opting for multi-cloud connections becomes crucial. This approach ensures seamless integration and communication between sensors hosted in diverse public cloud environments, contributing to a cohesive and interconnected Defender for IoT network architecture.

Establishing Connections Through an Azure Proxy for Proxy Functionality

Figure 3-2 depicts a proxy connection facilitated by an Azure proxy. The illustration shows how to link your sensors to the Defender for IoT portal in Azure via an Azure VNET proxy. This setup guarantees the confidentiality of all interactions between your sensors and Azure.

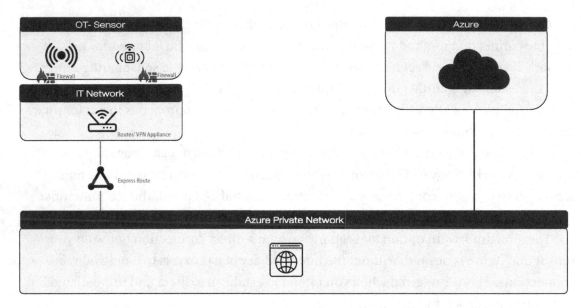

Figure 3-2. *Establishing connections through an Azure proxy for proxy functionality*

Access to the VNET can be achieved through either a VPN connection or an ExpressRoute connection, depending on your network configuration.

In this approach, a proxy server is employed within Azure. The proxy is set up for automatic scaling behind a load balancer to manage load balancing and ensure failover capabilities.

Establishing Connections Through Proxy Chaining for Enhanced Proxy Functionality

Establishing connections through proxy chaining for enhanced proxy functionality approach enables the connection of your sensors via direct Internet access, private VPN, or ExpressRoute. The sensor establishes an SSL-encrypted tunnel to transfer data from the sensor to the service endpoint through multiple proxy servers. The proxy server does not conduct data inspection, analysis, or caching.

The customer is responsible for setting up and maintaining third-party proxy services with proxy chaining; Microsoft does not offer support.

Figure 3-3 depicts a proxy connection utilizing proxy chaining. The illustration demonstrates how to link your sensors to the Defender for IoT portal in Azure through a series of proxies, incorporating various tiers of the Purdue model and the enterprise network hierarchy.

Figure 3-3. *Establishing connections through proxy chaining for enhanced proxy functionality*

Establishing Direct Connection to Azure

Figure 3-4 depicts a direct connection to Azure. The illustration outlines the process of establishing a direct connection from remote sites to the Defender for IoT portal in Azure, bypassing the enterprise network.

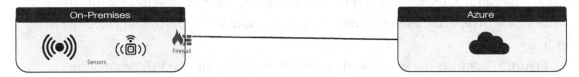

Figure 3-4. *Establishing direct connection to Azure*

Key features of direct connections include the following:

- Sensors connected directly to Azure data centers over the Internet or through Azure ExpressRoute benefit from a secure and encrypted link to the Azure data centers. The use of Transport Layer Security (TLS 1.2/AES-256) ensures constant and secure communication between the sensor and Azure resources.

- The sensor initiates all connections to the Azure portal. This approach safeguards internal network devices from unsolicited inbound connections and eliminates the need to configure inbound firewall rules.

Establishing Connections Across Multiple Clouds

Azure Hybrid Connections enables you to connect Azure App Service (web apps, mobile apps, etc.) to on-premises resources securely without exposing them to the public Internet.

You are presented with the choice to connect your sensors to the Defender for IoT portal in Azure, enabling the monitoring of OT/IoT management processes across various public clouds. The method of establishing connections depends on your environmental configuration, offering flexibility through options such as ExpressRoute with customer-managed routing, ExpressRoute with a cloud exchange provider, or a site-to-site VPN over the Internet.

Prepare for Microsoft Defender for IoT Deployment

Let us get started with understanding Microsoft Defender for IoT components.

Defender for IoT boasts a robust connectivity framework that integrates with cloud-based and on-premises elements. It was explicitly designed to ensure scalability within expansive and widely distributed environments. This sophisticated system encompasses various operational technology (OT) security monitoring components to fortify its capabilities. Diverse data sources are covered and analyzed by Microsoft Defender for IoT.

Figure 3-5 depicts the seamless flow of data into Defender for IoT, originating from network sensors and external third-party sources. This integration culminates in creating a cohesive and comprehensive overview of IoT/OT security. Within the Azure portal, Defender for IoT emerges as a centralized hub offering extensive functionalities, including the provision of asset inventories, the execution of vulnerability assessments, and the continuous monitoring of potential threats. Through this unified approach, Defender for IoT in the Azure portal aggregates data and serves as a powerful tool for holistic management and vigilance in IoT/OT security.

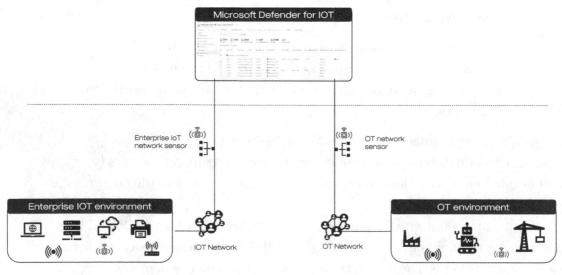

Figure 3-5. *Microsoft Defender for IOT – key components*

At the forefront is the Azure portal, a versatile interface facilitating cloud management and seamless integration with an array of Microsoft services, including the powerful Microsoft Sentinel. This strategic linkage enhances Defender's overall efficiency and responsiveness for IoT by tapping into the expansive Microsoft ecosystem.

Additionally, Defender for IoT incorporates cutting-edge operational technology (OT) and enterprise Internet of Things (IoT) network sensors. These sensors play a pivotal role in detecting devices spanning your network landscape. Deployment flexibility is a crucial feature, with these network sensors capable of being installed on virtual machines or physical appliances. Furthermore, users can configure OT sensors as either cloud-connected or fully on-premises, locally managed sensors. This adaptability ensures optimal customization to suit diverse organizational preferences and requirements.

To further augment its utility, Defender for IoT introduces an on-premises management console, offering centralized oversight for administering and monitoring OT sensors. This console is a crucial hub, particularly in local, air-gapped environments where centralized control is paramount. The comprehensive suite of features provided by Defender for IoT underscores its commitment to providing a versatile, secure, and seamlessly integrated solution for the intricate demands of contemporary IoT and OT security.

OT and Enterprise IoT Network Sensors

Defender for IoT network sensors excel in uncovering and perpetually monitoring network traffic coursing through your network devices. These specialized sensors are meticulously crafted for the intricacies of operational technology (OT) and Internet of Things (IoT) networks, establishing connections through SPAN ports or network TAPs. Notably agile, Defender for IoT network sensors swiftly unravels the intricacies of potential risks within minutes of integration into the network.

The efficacy of these network sensors lies in their adept utilization of OT/IoT-aware analytics engines and Layer-6 Deep Packet Inspection (DPI) techniques. Their advanced capabilities empower them to discern and pinpoint threats, such as fileless malware, predicated on indicators of anomalous or unauthorized activities within the network environment.

To ensure swift and secure responses, the entire gamut of data-related processes – including collection, processing, analysis, and alerting – transpires directly on the sensor itself.

This proves particularly advantageous in locations with low bandwidth or high-latency connectivity, as it minimizes dependence on external resources. In this streamlined process, only the essential telemetry and insights are transmitted for management purposes, directed either to the Azure portal or an on-premises management console. This approach underscores Defender for IoT's commitment to operational efficiency, real-time threat detection, and the seamless orchestration of security measures across diverse network landscapes.

Sensors Connected to the Cloud vs. Sensors Located Locally

Cloud-connected sensors, when integrated with Defender for IoT in Azure, present distinct features compared to their locally managed counterparts.

In the context of a cloud-connected OT network sensor, all detected data is not only showcased in the sensor console but also concurrently transmitted to Azure, enabling comprehensive analysis and collaboration with other Azure services. Furthermore, automatic dissemination of Microsoft threat intelligence packages to cloud-connected sensors streamlines the reinforcement of security measures. In this configuration, the sensor name established during onboarding remains immutable within the sensor interface, functioning in a read-only capacity from the sensor console.

Conversely, the approach with locally managed sensors offers a nuanced perspective. Here, users can exclusively view data for a specific sensor through the sensor console, while a consolidated overview of information gathered by multiple sensors necessitates the utilization of an on-premises management console. Notably, the process of updating sensor names is a flexible undertaking within the sensor console. Additionally, in the locally managed sensor scenario, manual uploading of threat intelligence packages becomes a requisite step for enhancing security protocols. This demarcation underscores the nuanced functionalities and management processes associated with cloud-connected and locally managed sensors within the Defender for IoT ecosystem.

Analyzer of Defender for IoT

Defender for IoT network sensors meticulously scrutinize ingested data through their integrated analytics engines, which, in turn, initiate alerts based on a combination of real-time and pre-recorded traffic parameters. These advanced analytics engines encompass an array of functionalities, offering machine learning capabilities, profile analytics, risk analysis, a comprehensive device database, insights generation, threat intelligence integration, and behavioral analytics.

For instance, this framework's policy violation detection engine adopts a sophisticated approach, modeling industrial control systems (ICS) networks to identify deviations from the anticipated "baseline" behavior. This process leverages Behavioral

Anomaly Detection (BAD), a methodology outlined in NISTIR 8219. Establishing this baseline involves a comprehensive understanding of routine activities within the network, encompassing normal traffic patterns, user actions, and interactions with the ICS network. Subsequently, the BAD system vigilantly monitors the network for any aberrations from the expected behavior, promptly flagging instances of policy violations. Examples of baseline deviations encompass unauthorized utilization of function codes, access to specific objects, or modifications to the configuration of a device.

Incorporating this specialized baseline for ICS networks is particularly noteworthy, as many detection algorithms were originally designed for information technology (IT) rather than operational technology (OT) networks. Addition baseline listed in Table 3-2 significantly accelerates the system's learning curve when adapting to new detection parameters, thereby enhancing the overall efficacy of Defender for IoT in safeguarding OT environments.

Table 3-2. *Key Capabilities of Defender for IOT*

Name	Description	Examples
Protocol Violation Detection Engine	Identifies noncompliant packet structures and field values in ICS protocols	Alert: "Illegal MODBUS Operation (Function Code Zero)" – indicates an unauthorized request violating protocol specifications
Policy Violation	Flags deviations from baseline behavior, highlighting unauthorized usage	Alert: "Unauthorized HTTP User Agent" – indicates unauthorized application use as an HTTP client on a device
Industrial Malware Detection Engine	Identifies behaviors indicative of known malware for prompt threat response	Alert: "Suspicion of Malicious Activity (Stuxnet)" – signals suspicious network activity related to the Stuxnet malware
Anomaly Detection Engine	Detects unusual M2M communications, models ICS networks for faster learning	Alert: "Periodic Behavior in Communication Channel" – detects periodic data transmission, common in industrial networks Additional examples include alerts for excessive SMB sign-in attempts and detected PLC scans

(*continued*)

Table 3-2. (*continued*)

Name	Description	Examples
Operational Incident Detection	Identifies operational issues, signaling potential equipment failure	Alert: "Device is Suspected to be Disconnected (Unresponsive)" – indicates a nonresponsive device, hinting at potential issues Another example involves alerts triggered by the Siemens S7 stop PLC command, indicating potential operational incidents

Management Options for Microsoft Defender for IOT

Defender for IoT offers hybrid network support through various management options, with the Azure portal serving as a central hub for comprehensive oversight. Utilize the Azure portal as a unified interface to seamlessly visualize all data collected from your devices through cloud-connected network sensors. Beyond this consolidated view, the Azure portal delivers added value by providing features like workbooks, integration with Microsoft Sentinel, security recommendations, and more.

Azure Portal

The Azure portal is a web-based management interface provided by Microsoft Azure, Microsoft's cloud computing platform. It is a centralized hub for users to manage and monitor their Azure resources, services, and applications. Through the portal, users can access and interact with various Azure services, configure settings, deploy resources, monitor performance, and analyze data.

The Azure portal's key features include a customizable dashboard that allows users to arrange and display relevant information, a marketplace to discover and deploy Azure services, and a range of tools for monitoring and managing resources. It provides a unified and user-friendly experience for administrators, developers, and stakeholders to work with Azure cloud services.

Furthermore, leverage the Azure portal depicted in Figure 3-6 for tasks such as acquiring new appliances, accessing software updates, onboarding and maintaining sensors within Defender for IoT, and updating threat intelligence packages.

Figure 3-6. *Microsoft Defender for IOT – Azure portal*

OT Sensor Console

Explore detections for devices linked to a particular OT sensor through the sensor console, depicted in Figure 3-7. Utilize the sensor console to access a network map illustrating devices identified by that specific sensor, review a chronological timeline of all events recorded on the sensor, transmit sensor information to affiliated systems, and access additional functionalities.

Figure 3-7. *Microsoft Defender for IOT – OT sensor console*

Defender for IoT exhibits the capability to discover devices of diverse types across various environments comprehensively. The device inventory pages within Defender for IoT categorize devices based on a distinctive coupling of IP and MAC addresses, ensuring a detailed and organized representation. The identification process distinguishes individual devices into two categories: those identified as individual devices and those not identified as such. The former encompass IT, OT, or IoT devices, including network infrastructure components like switches and routers, while considering devices with modules or backplane components counted as a singular entity. Conversely, the latter category excludes certain items, such as public Internet IP addresses, multicast and broadcast groups, and inactive devices.

The status of network-monitored devices as inactive is determined by the absence of network activity within specified durations, such as 60 days for OT networks and 30 days for enterprise IoT networks. It's noteworthy that endpoints already under the management of Defender for Endpoint are not treated as separate devices within the purview of Defender for IoT, thereby streamlining device categorization.

On-Premises Management Console

The on-premises management console is a focal point in air-gapped environments, offering a consolidated perspective of data from all sensors. This console provides additional maintenance tools and reporting features for enhanced control.

It's essential to ensure parity between the software version on your on-premises management console and the latest sensor version. While each on-premises management console version maintains backward compatibility with older, supported sensor versions, it cannot establish connections with newer sensor versions. This alignment ensures seamless integration and optimal performance within your network environment.

Designing Enterprise Network

Designing network architectures in an enterprise involves careful planning and consideration of various factors to ensure a robust and efficient infrastructure that meets the organization's requirements. The design process encompasses several key elements:

- Requirements Analysis

  Understand the business needs and goals to determine the network's functional requirements.

  Identify the number of users, types of applications, data transfer needs, and security requirements.

- Topology Design

  Choose an appropriate network topology (e.g., star, bus, ring, mesh) based on the organization's size, structure, and communication needs.

  Consider redundancy and fault tolerance to ensure high availability.

- Network Layering

  Divide the network into logical layers, typically including core, distribution, and access layers.

  This layering facilitates scalability, ease of management, and modular upgrades.

- IP Addressing and Subnetting

  Plan and implement an IP addressing scheme, ensuring sufficient addresses for current and future devices.

  Subnetting helps in organizing and managing IP addresses efficiently.

- VLAN Design

  Implement virtual local area networks (VLANs) to logical segmentation, improve security, and reduce broadcast domains.

- Routing and Switching

  Choose appropriate routing protocols for communication between different network segments.

  Implement switching technologies for efficient local traffic.

- Security Measures

  Integrate security features such as firewalls, intrusion detection/prevention systems, and VPNs to safeguard the network.

  Employ role-based access controls and encryption where necessary.

- Quality of Service (QoS)

  Prioritize network traffic to ensure optimal performance for critical applications.

Manage bandwidth effectively and control network congestion.

- Scalability and Future Growth

  Design the network to accommodate growth and changes in technology.

  Consider technologies like virtualization and cloud integration for scalability.

- Wireless Network Design

  Plan and implement a secure and reliable wireless network if required.

  Ensure appropriate coverage and capacity for wireless devices.

- Monitoring and Management

  Implement network management tools for monitoring performance, troubleshooting, and ensuring proactive maintenance.

  Consider automation for routine tasks to streamline operations.

- Documentation

  Maintain thorough documentation of the network design, configurations, and any changes made over time.

  Documentation aids troubleshooting, upgrades, and knowledge transfer.

By addressing these aspects in the design process, enterprises can create a resilient, scalable, and secure network architecture that aligns with their business objectives and adapt to evolving technological demands.

Hierarchical Model of Network Design

The hierarchical model of network design, often referred to as the three-layer hierarchical model, is a structured approach to organizing and designing network architectures. This model consists of three layers: access, distribution, and core. Each layer serves a specific purpose and has distinct functionalities, contributing to the network's overall efficiency, scalability, and manageability. Here's a detailed explanation of each layer.

Access Layer

Functionality: The access layer is the entry point for end-user devices and connects them to the network. It focuses on providing network access to individual devices, such as computers, printers, and IP phones.

Characteristics

- Access layer devices include switches and access points.

- This layer is responsible for user authentication, port-based security, and VLAN assignments.

- Policies related to Quality of Service (QoS) may be implemented here to prioritize traffic.

Considerations

- Scalability and flexibility to accommodate various types of devices.

- Security measures to control access and protect against unauthorized activities.

- Implementation of VLANs for logical segmentation.

Distribution Layer

Functionality: The distribution layer acts as an intermediary between the access and core layers. It facilitates communication between different access layer devices and aggregates the traffic before forwarding it to the core. This layer is crucial for network segmentation and policy enforcement.

Characteristics

- Devices at the distribution layer include routers and Layer 3 switches.

- Routing between VLANs typically occurs at this layer.

- Aggregates multiple access layer switches and provides redundancy for network paths.

Considerations

- Efficient routing and filtering to control traffic flow

- Implementation of policies for network segmentation and security

- High availability and fault tolerance through redundancy

Core Layer

Functionality: The core layer is the network's backbone, responsible for high-speed, low-latency data forwarding between different distribution layer devices. It is designed for fast and reliable data transmission without imposing additional processing or filtering.

Characteristics

- Core layer devices include high-speed routers and switches.

- Typically, it operates at the highest speed supported by the network, often using technologies like fiber optics.

- Minimizes latency and ensures rapid packet forwarding.

Considerations

- High-speed, fault-tolerant infrastructure to support the traffic needs of the entire network

- Minimal processing and filtering to maintain high-speed data transmission

- Redundancy and load balancing to ensure network availability

Advantages of the Hierarchical Model

- Scalability: The modular design allows for easy scalability by adding or upgrading components within a specific layer.

- Manageability: Each layer has distinct management responsibilities, simplifying network administration.

- Fault Isolation: Problems in one layer are contained within that layer, reducing the impact on other network parts.

- Performance Optimization: Each layer can be optimized for its specific function, enhancing overall network performance.

By adhering to the hierarchical model, network architects can create well-organized, scalable, and efficient network architectures that meet the diverse needs of modern enterprises.

Planning an IT Network

Planning for an IT network in an enterprise involves a systematic and comprehensive approach to meet the organization's technology requirements. Here's an overview of the key steps in the planning process.

Business Needs Assessment

Understand the business goals and objectives that the IT network should support.

Identify specific requirements from different departments and stakeholders.

Current Infrastructure Analysis

Evaluate the existing IT infrastructure, including hardware, software, and network components.

Assess the performance, security, and scalability of the current network.

User and Device Inventory

Create an inventory of current users and devices connected to the network.

Anticipate future growth and technological advancements that may impact user and device counts.

Bandwidth and Performance Requirements

Determine the required bandwidth for data transfer based on the nature of applications and services used.

Consider the performance needs of critical applications and services.

Security Considerations

Assess security risks and requirements. Define access controls, encryption, firewalls, and other security measures.

Ensure compliance with industry regulations and internal security policies.

Technology Selection

Choose appropriate networking technologies, including routers, switches, and wireless solutions.

Decide on using virtualization, cloud services, and emerging technologies based on business needs.

Network Topology Design

Develop a network topology that aligns with the organization's structure and requirements.

Consider redundancy and fault tolerance for critical network components.

IP Addressing and Subnetting

Plan and allocate IP address ranges to accommodate the number of devices and facilitate efficient network management.

Implement subnetting for organizational and security purposes.

Wireless Network Planning

If applicable, plan for a secure and efficient wireless network.

Consider factors such as coverage, capacity, and security protocols.

Integration with Other Systems

Ensure integration with other IT systems, applications, and services.

Plan for interoperability and data exchange between different systems.

Disaster Recovery and Business Continuity

Develop strategies for disaster recovery and business continuity to minimize downtime in case of network failures or disasters.

Budgeting

Create a budget considering hardware, software, licensing, personnel, and ongoing maintenance costs.

Prioritize investments based on critical needs and available resources.

Implementation Plan

Develop a phased implementation plan that minimizes disruptions to ongoing operations.

Consider pilot testing in specific areas before a full-scale rollout.

Training and Documentation

Plan user training to ensure employees can effectively use the new network.

Document configurations, procedures, and troubleshooting processes for future reference.

Monitoring and Optimization

Implement network monitoring tools to track performance, detect issues, and optimize the network.

Establish regular review processes to adapt the network to changing business requirements.

By following these steps, enterprises can develop a strategic and well-documented plan for their IT network, aligning technology with business objectives and ensuring a resilient, secure, and scalable infrastructure.

Adopting Purdue Networking Model for Industrial Control System (ICS) Security in Your Planning

The Purdue model for industrial control system (ICS) security, commonly referred to as the Purdue Reference Model, is a framework that organizes the architecture of ICS environments. Developed by Purdue University, this model helps in understanding, designing, and implementing security measures for industrial control systems. The model divides the ICS architecture into hierarchical levels, each representing a specific function within the control system. The following is a detailed explanation of each layer in the Purdue model, along with its architecture:

Level 0: Process Devices and Physical Processes

- Description: This is the lowest level of the Purdue model, encompassing the physical processes and devices involved in industrial control. It includes sensors, actuators, and other devices directly interacting with the physical environment.

- Architecture: At this level, the focus is on real-time control and data acquisition. Devices communicate with the higher levels to provide real-time data and receive control commands.

Level 1: Basic Control

- Description: Level 1 consists of controllers responsible for basic control functions. These are often programmable logic controllers (PLCs) in discrete manufacturing, while process manufacturing may use distributed control systems (DCS).

- Architecture: Controllers at this level interface with Level 0 devices to execute control functions. They process sensor data, make decisions, and send commands to actuators.

Level 2: Supervisory Control

- Description: This level involves systems supervising and coordinating multiple control processes within a specific area. It includes human-machine interfaces (HMIs), process historians, and batch management systems.

- Architecture: Supervisory systems communicate with Level 1 controllers, providing a higher-level view of the processes. They also interact with operators through HMIs and manage historical data.

Level 3: Manufacturing Operations

- Description: Level 3 represents systems responsible for managing the overall manufacturing operation within a site. It includes production scheduling, detailed reporting, and overall site-level operations management.

- Architecture: This level integrates information from lower classes and communicates with enterprise-level systems. It facilitates the coordination and optimization of manufacturing processes.

Level 4: Business Planning and Logistics

- Description: At this level, business-related systems, such as enterprise resource planning (ERP), are included. It focuses on business planning, logistics, and higher-level decision-making.

- Architecture: Systems at Level 4 interact with Level 3 to gather production data and contribute to business-level decision-making processes. They often use standard IT infrastructure.

Level 5: Enterprise Business Planning

- Description: The highest level involves enterprise-wide business planning and management systems. It includes strategic decision-making and integration with corporate IT systems.

- Architecture: Systems at this level interact with lower levels for data exchange and contribute to corporate-level decision-making processes.

Each level in the Purdue model has its own set of security considerations, and the model emphasizes the importance of proper segmentation and security controls to protect critical industrial processes from cybersecurity threats.

Table 3-3 delineates each tier of the Purdue model as it pertains to devices that might be present in your network.

Table 3-3. *Level-by-Level Purdue Model*

Level	Description
Level 0: Cell and Area	Encompasses a diverse range of sensors, actuators, and devices essential for basic manufacturing processes. Functions include driving motors, measuring variables, setting outputs, and performing tasks like painting, welding, and bending.
Level 1: Process Control	Comprises embedded controllers managing the manufacturing process. In discrete manufacturing, these are typically PLCs or RTUs; in process manufacturing, it's a distributed control system (DCS).
Level 2: Supervisory	Represents systems for real-time supervision and operation of a production facility area. Includes operator interfaces (HMIs), alarm/alert systems, process historians, batch management, and control room workstations.
Levels 3 and 3.5: Site-Level and Industrial Perimeter Network	The highest-level managing site-wide functions critical to operations. Involves production reporting, plant historians, production scheduling, site-level operations management, device/material management, patch launch, file server, and industrial domain services. Communicates with production zones and shares data with enterprise systems (Level 4 and Level 5).
Levels 4 and 5: Business and Enterprise Networks	Represents the site or enterprise network containing centralized IT systems. Managed directly by the IT organization, it encompasses services, systems, and applications crucial for business operations.

Recognizing Network Traffic Nodes Part of Planning

Generally, notable points from a security standpoint involve the interfaces linking the default gateway entity with the core or distribution switch.

Recognizing these interfaces as pivotal points ensures the monitoring of traffic flowing from within the IP segment to outside the IP segment. It is essential also to consider missing traffic, referring to instances where traffic initially intended to exit the segment remains within it.

When strategizing the deployment of Defender for IoT, Microsoft suggests considering the listed components in Table 3-4 within your network traffic planning.

Table 3-4. *Planning Consideration for Network Traffic*

Planning Consideration	Description
Unique Traffic Types Inside a Network Segment	Particularly focus on the following types of traffic within a network segment: broadcast/multicast traffic, sent to any entity within the subnet, including the default gateway, and unicast traffic, forwarded directly to the destination without crossing the entire subnet. Monitor unicast traffic with Defender for IoT by placing sensors on access switches.
Monitor Bidirectional Streams of Traffic	While streaming traffic to Defender for IoT, ensure monitoring for both directions of traffic. Some vendors/products offer a directional stream, potentially causing gaps in data. Monitoring both directions provides comprehensive network conversation information and better accuracy.
Locate a Subnet's Default Gateway	Identify the default gateway for each interesting subnet, considering any connection to the entity that serves as the default gateway. Monitor traffic within the subnet that may not be covered by regular interesting points, especially on sensitive subnets.
Look for Atypical Traffic	Monitoring traffic not covered by the typical deployment may require additional streaming points and network solutions, such as RSPAN, network tappers, etc. Ensure comprehensive coverage, especially for sensitive subnets, by incorporating extra streaming points and network solutions.

Devices initiating network traffic compare the configured subnet mask and IP address with a destination IP address to determine the intended destination. The destination is identified as either the default gateway or another location within the IP segment. This comparison may also initiate an Address Resolution Protocol (ARP) process to obtain the MAC address corresponding to the destination IP address.

Table 3-5 listed that matching process, devices categorize their network traffic as either internal, occurring within the IP segment, or external, directed outside the IP segment, based on the comparison outcomes.

Table 3-5. *Planning Consideration for Network Traffic in and Out*

Traffic	Description	Example
Traffic outside of the IP segment	When the destination IP address falls outside the subnet mask's range, the device sends the traffic to the designated default gateway. The default gateway is responsible for routing the traffic to other relevant segments. Placing a Defender for IoT/OT network sensor at this point ensures monitoring and analysis of all outbound traffic.	A PC with IP 10.52.2.201 and subnet mask 255.255.255.0 sends traffic to a web server at IP 10.17.0.88. The OS calculates the destination IP's range, finding it outside the segment, and directs the traffic to the default gateway.
Traffic within the IP segment	If the destination IP falls within the subnet mask's range, the traffic stays within the segment and travels directly to the destination MAC address. This type of traffic requires an ARP resolution, involving a broadcast packet to discover the destination IP address's MAC address.	A PC with IP 10.52.2.17 and subnet mask 255.255.255.0 sends traffic to another PC at IP 10.52.2.131. The OS calculates the destination IP's range, finding it within the segment, and directs the traffic directly on the segment.

When dealing with a unidirectional gateway like Waterfall, Owl Cyber Defense, or Hirschmann, where data flows through a data diode in a single direction, you have two options for placing your OT sensors.

Outside the Network Perimeter (Recommended)

Description: Position your OT sensors outside the network perimeter in this preferred scenario. The sensor receives SPAN traffic through the diode, flowing unidirectionally from the network to the sensor's monitoring port. This method is particularly recommended for large deployments.

Inside the Network Perimeter

Description: Place your OT sensors inside the network perimeter in this scenario. The sensor sends UDP syslog alerts to targets outside the perimeter through the data diode. Note that sensors inside the network perimeter are air-gapped and must be locally managed. They cannot connect to the cloud or be managed from the Azure portal. Manual updates for these sensors, including new threat intelligence packages, are required.

Additional Note

If you are working with a unidirectional network and require cloud-connected sensors managed from the Azure portal, placing your sensors outside the network perimeter is crucial.

Choosing a traffic mirroring method hinges on your network setup and organizational requirements.

For optimal results, Microsoft suggests configuring traffic mirroring on a switch or Terminal Access Point (TAP) specifically designed to encompass only industrial ICS and SCADA traffic. This ensures that Defender for IoT analyzes only the desired traffic for monitoring purposes.

Microsoft suggests configuring traffic mirroring for all ports on your switch, even if they are not currently used. Failure to do so may leave unmonitored ports vulnerable to the connection of rogue devices, which may go undetected by Defender for IoT network sensors.

For OT networks employing broadcast or multicast messaging, it is advised to set up traffic mirroring exclusively for RX (Receive) transmissions. This approach avoids unnecessary bandwidth usage, as multicast messages will be duplicated for all pertinent active ports

Microsoft Defender for IoT supports the traffic mirroring methods listed in Table 3-6.

Table 3-6. *Planning Consideration for Network Traffic Mirroring Methods*

Method	Description	Overview
Switch SPAN port	Mirrors local traffic from interfaces on the switch to a different interface on the same switch	Set up a Remote SPAN (RSPAN) session on your switch to replicate traffic from numerous distributed source ports into a dedicated remote VLAN. Subsequently, the data within the VLAN is transmitted through trunked ports, traversing multiple switches until it reaches a designated switch housing the physical destination port. Establish a connection from the destination port to your OT network sensor for monitoring traffic with Defender for IoT.
Remote SPAN (RSPAN) port	Mirrors traffic from multiple, distributed source ports into a dedicated remote VLAN	

(continued)

Table 3-6. (*continued*)

Method	Description	Overview
Active or passive aggregation (TAP)	Installs an active/passive aggregation TAP inline to your network cable, duplicating traffic to the OT network sensor. Best for forensic monitoring	When employing active or passive aggregation for traffic mirroring, an active or passive aggregation Terminal Access Point (TAP) is inserted in line with the network cable. The TAP duplicates received and transmitted traffic to the OT network sensor, facilitating traffic monitoring using Defender for IoT. A TAP is a hardware device that enables the uninterrupted flow of network traffic between ports. It creates a precise copy of both directions of the traffic flow consistently, ensuring continuous monitoring without compromising network integrity. Defender for IoT has been tested for compatibility with the following TAP models. Other vendors and models, such as Garland P1GCCAS, IXIA TPA2-CU3, and US Robotics USR 4503, may also be suitable.
Encapsulated Remote Switched Port Analyzer (ERSPAN)	Mirrors input interfaces to your OT sensor's monitoring interface	Employ an Encapsulated Remote Switched Port Analyzer (ERSPAN) to duplicate input interfaces across an IP network to the monitoring interface of your OT sensor, particularly when securing remote networks with Defender for IoT. The sensor's monitoring interface operates promiscuously without a specifically assigned IP address. With ERSPAN support configured, the sensor can analyze traffic payloads with GRE tunnel encapsulation. ERSPAN encapsulation is recommended when there's a requirement to extend monitored traffic across Layer 3 domains. It's essential to note that ERSPAN is a Cisco proprietary feature and is available exclusively on specific routers and switches.

(*continued*)

Table 3-6. (*continued*)

Method	Description	Overview
An ESXi vSwitch	Mirrors traffic using promiscuous mode on an ESXi vSwitch	Although a virtual switch lacks native mirroring capabilities, you can employ promiscuous mode within a virtual switch environment as a workaround for configuring a monitoring port akin to a SPAN port. In a typical scenario, a SPAN port on a physical switch mirrors local traffic from interfaces on the switch to a different interface on the same switch.
A Hyper-V vSwitch	Mirrors traffic using promiscuous mode on a Hyper-V vSwitch	
		Establish a connection from the destination switch to your OT network sensor to facilitate traffic monitoring using Defender for IoT.
		Promiscuous mode operates as a mode of operation and a technique for security, monitoring, and administration, defined at the virtual switch or portgroup level. When activated, any network interfaces of virtual machines in the same portgroup can observe all network traffic passing through that virtual switch. By default, promiscuous mode is deactivated.

Network Ports for Planning

Table 3-7 lists all network communication requirements between Microsoft Defender for IoT network sensors, on-premises management consoles, and deployment workstations to ensure proper functionality of services.

Table 3-7. Network Ports Requirements

Protocol	Transport	Direction	Port	Purpose	Source	Destination
SSH	TCP	Bidirectional	22	CLI	Client	Sensor and on-premises management console
HTTPS	TCP	Bidirectional	443	Web console	Client	Sensor and on-premises management console
HTTPS	TCP	Out	443	Access to Azure	Sensor	OT network sensors connect to Azure for alert and device data, sensor health messages, access to threat intelligence packages, etc. Connected Azure services included
NTP	UDP	Bidirectional	123	Time Sync	Sensor	On-premises management console
TLS/SSL	TCP	Bidirectional	443	Give the sensor access to the on-premises management console	Sensor	On-premises management console
SMTP	TCP	Out	25	Used to open the customer's mail server to send emails for alerts and events	Sensor and on-premises management console	Email server

(continued)

Table 3-7. (*continued*)

Protocol	Transport	Direction	Port	Purpose	Source	Destination
DNS	TCP/UDP	Bidirectional	53	The DNS server port	On-premises management console	Sensor
HTTP	TCP	Out	80	The CRL download for certificate validation when uploading certificates	Sensor and on-premises management console	CRL server
WMI	TCP/UDP	Out	135, 1025-65535	Monitoring	Sensor	Relevant network element
SNMP	UDP	Out	161	Monitoring	On-premises management console and sensor	SNMP server
LDAP	TCP	Bidirectional	389	Active Directory	On-premises management console and sensor	LDAP server
Proxy	TCP/UDP	Bidirectional	443	Proxy	On-premises management console and sensor	Proxy server
Syslog	UDP	Out	514	LEEF	On-premises management console and sensor	Syslog server
LDAPS	TCP	Bidirectional	636	Active Directory	On-premises management console and sensor	LDAPS server
Tunneling	TCP	One-way	9000 (in addition to port 443)	Allows access from the sensor or end user to the on-premises management console	Endpoint, sensor	On-premises management console

Plan Microsoft Defender for IoT Licenses

Microsoft Azure is a comprehensive cloud computing platform offering various services and solutions to individuals, businesses, and enterprises. Understanding Azure cloud licensing is integral to optimizing costs and leveraging the platform's full potential. This extensive explanation delves into the core concepts, licensing models, key services, and considerations associated with Azure cloud licensing.

Azure Cloud Licensing

Azure is Microsoft's cloud computing platform that provides a broad range of services, including computing power, storage, databases, networking, artificial intelligence (AI), and more. Licensing in Azure is a multifaceted domain designed to accommodate diverse business needs, from startups to large enterprises. The structure of Azure licensing is critical for users to effectively manage resources, control costs, and align their cloud strategy with business objectives.

Azure Services Overview

Azure's services span various domains, each designed to cater to specific computing needs. These services include the following:

- Azure Virtual Machines (VMs): Offering scalable computing power in the cloud, VMs form the backbone of many applications and workloads.

- Azure Storage: Providing scalable and secure cloud storage solutions for data, documents, and other digital assets.

- Azure SQL Database: A fully managed relational database service for quickly building and deploying applications.

- Azure App Service: A platform enabling web application development, deployment, and scaling.

- Azure Kubernetes Service (AKS): Simplifying containerized applications' deployment, management, and scaling using Kubernetes.

- Azure Active Directory (AD): Delivering identity and access management services to secure user access and authentication.

- Azure Functions: Facilitating serverless code execution in response to events, allowing efficient handling of variable workloads.

- Azure Key Vault: Securely stores and manages sensitive information such as secrets, encryption keys, and certificates.

Azure Licensing Models

Azure employs diverse licensing models to accommodate different usage patterns and business requirements. The primary licensing models include the following:

- Pay-As-You-Go (PAYG): Users pay for Azure services based on hourly or per-minute usage with no upfront commitment. This model suits short-term projects, testing, or workloads with variable resource requirements.

- Reserved Instances (RIs): Users commit to a one- or three-year term for VM usage, leading to significant cost savings compared to PAYG pricing. RIs are well-suited for stable, long-term workloads.

- Azure Hybrid Benefit: Users with on-premises licenses for Windows Server or SQL Server can leverage the Azure Hybrid Benefit to achieve reduced pricing on Azure VMs.

Azure Cost Management and Billing

Managing costs effectively is a crucial aspect of Azure cloud licensing. Azure provides tools such as Azure Cost Management, Azure Advisor, and the Azure Pricing Calculator to help users monitor, analyze, and optimize spending.

- Azure Cost Management: Offers visibility into resource usage and costs, allowing users to make informed decisions about resource allocation and optimization

- Azure Advisor: Provides personalized best practices and recommendations to optimize resources and reduce costs based on the user's historical usage

- Azure Pricing Calculator: Allows users to estimate costs for Azure services based on usage patterns, helping with budgeting and planning

Core Azure Licensing Considerations

Several critical considerations shape Azure licensing decisions based on the type of services used:

- Virtual Machines and Compute Services: Azure VM sizes vary in performance characteristics and pricing. Understanding the needs of applications helps in selecting the right VM size. Licensing costs may include charges for the operating system (Windows or Linux), and the Azure Hybrid Benefit can be leveraged for Windows VMs to save costs.

- Storage Services: Azure offers different storage services, including Blob Storage, File Storage, and Disk Storage, each with its own pricing model. Understanding data access patterns is crucial for optimizing storage costs.

- Database Services: Azure provides diverse database services, such as Azure SQL Database, Azure SQL Managed Instance, Cosmos DB, MySQL, and PostgreSQL. Licensing costs vary based on factors like the type of database, performance requirements, and data storage.

- Networking Services: Azure networking services, such as Virtual Network (VNet), Azure Load Balancer, and Application Gateway, come with associated costs based on usage. Understanding data transfer costs is crucial for organizations with high network activity.

- AI and Machine Learning Services: Azure Machine Learning and Cognitive Services have specific pricing models. Users can choose between pay-as-you-go and reserved capacity pricing based on their usage patterns and requirements.

- Identity and Access Management: Azure Active Directory (Azure AD) has different licensing options, including free, Office 365, and Premium plans. Organizations should choose based on their identity and access management needs.

- Serverless Computing: Azure Functions, a serverless computing option, is billed based on the number of executions and resource consumption. This model is cost-efficient for sporadic workloads with variable resource requirements.

Azure Licensing Scenarios

Different scenarios necessitate distinct licensing approaches. Understanding these scenarios helps organizations make informed decisions:

- Development and Testing: Azure DevTest Labs can be leveraged to manage resources cost-effectively for development and testing environments.

- Production Workloads: Stable, long-term workloads benefit from evaluating reserved capacity options. The Azure Hybrid Benefit can be utilized for existing licenses.

- Hybrid Environments: Organizations with hybrid scenarios, combining on-premises and cloud resources, can maximize cost savings by leveraging the Azure Hybrid Benefit for Windows Server and SQL Server licenses.

- Startups and Small Businesses: PAYG pricing provides flexibility for startups and small businesses. As the business grows, exploring options like reserved capacity helps optimize costs.

Licensing Management and Best Practices

Effective management of Azure licenses requires adherence to best practices:

- Cost Monitoring: Regularly using Azure Cost Management tools to monitor spending, set budgets, and receive alerts for cost overruns.

- Rightsizing Resources: Rightsizing VMs and other resources based on actual utilization to avoid unnecessary costs.

- Policy Enforcement: Implementing Azure Policies to enforce resource tagging, naming conventions, and compliance, aiding in cost governance.

- Resilience and High Availability: Designing for resilience and high availability to ensure business continuity, considering the additional costs associated with redundancy.

Azure cloud licensing is a dynamic and critical aspect of adopting Microsoft's cloud platform. As organizations increasingly embrace the cloud, understanding Azure licensing becomes paramount for effectively managing costs, optimizing resource usage, and aligning cloud strategies with business objectives. Regularly reviewing and adjusting licensing strategies in response to evolving business needs is essential for success in the ever-changing landscape of the Azure cloud environment.

In the strategic planning phase of your Microsoft Defender for IoT deployment, it becomes crucial to gain a comprehensive understanding of the pricing plans and billing models associated with the Defender for IoT service, allowing you to make informed decisions and optimize your costs effectively.

Table 3-8 provides an overview of various offerings from Microsoft concerning Defender for IOT.

Table 3-8. *Defender for IOT Licensing Option*

Licensing Option	Description
Enterprise IoT Licensing Options	
Included with Microsoft 365 E5	Enterprise IoT licensing is included as part of Microsoft 365 E5, offering comprehensive security features for IoT.
Microsoft Defender for IoT – EIoT Device License (Add-on)	An add-on option for individual device licensing, allowing organizations to enhance security coverage for each IoT device. $0.85-device/month
Operational Technology (OT) Licensing Options	
Microsoft Defender for IoT – OT Site License – XS	Tailored for smaller OT environments, the XS site license provides comprehensive security measures for moderate-scale sites. $70.00-license/month (as per Microsoft, it includes up to 100 devices per site; annual subscription – auto-renews)
Microsoft Defender for IoT – OT Site License – S	The S site license is designed for small to medium-sized OT environments, offering robust security features for a broader scope of operations. $150.00-license/month (as per Microsoft, it includes up to 250 devices per site; annual subscription – auto-renews)

(continued)

Table 3-8. (*continued*)

Licensing Option	Description
Microsoft Defender for IoT – OT Site License – M	The M site license caters to medium-sized OT environments, providing scalable security measures to accommodate growing operational needs. $250.00-license/month (as per Microsoft, it includes up to 500 devices per site; annual subscription – auto-renews)
Microsoft Defender for IoT – OT Site License – L	Geared toward larger OT environments, the L site license delivers extensive security coverage for expansive and complex operational setups. $400.00-license/month (as per Microsoft, it includes up to 1000 devices per site; annual subscription – auto-renews)
Microsoft Defender for IoT – OT Site License – XL	Designed for extra-large OT environments, the XL site license offers comprehensive security measures for the most expansive and intricate operational landscapes. $1500.00-license/month (as per Microsoft, it includes up to 5000 devices per site; annual subscription – auto-renews)

For the billing structure related to OT (operational technology) monitoring, site-based licenses are employed, and each license is designated for an individual site, contingent on the site's size. A "site" is a physical location encompassing various settings such as facilities, campuses, office buildings, hospitals, rigs, etc. An arbitrary number of network sensors may be deployed within each site, each responsible for monitoring the devices identified within the connected networks.

Specifically, in enterprise IoT monitoring, the billing model supports a quota of five devices per Microsoft 365 E5 (ME5) or E5 Security license. Alternatively, it provides flexibility by offering stand-alone, per-device licenses tailored for customers subscribed to Microsoft Defender for Endpoint P2. This intricate billing structure allows adaptability and cost-effectiveness in aligning with the specific needs and scale of IoT monitoring in the enterprise environment.

Security monitoring for enterprise IoT with Defender for IoT is backed by a Microsoft 365 E5 (ME5) or E5 Security license. Additionally, stand-alone per-device licenses can be acquired as supplements to Microsoft Defender for Endpoint. For commercial customers deploying Microsoft Defender for IoT for OT monitoring, management is facilitated through a site-based license, obtainable from the Microsoft 365 admin center. Once the license is procured, it should be applied to the OT plan within the Azure portal.

Several prerequisites must be fulfilled to set up Defender for IoT for commercial users. These include having a Microsoft 365 tenant access to the Microsoft 365 admin center, where the user should hold either Global or Billing admin roles. Additionally, an Azure subscription is necessary; users can sign up for a free account if not already available. A user with a Security admin, Contributor, or Owner role for the specific Azure subscription is required to integrate with Azure. Furthermore, a clear understanding of the site size and the ability to calculate devices within the network are essential for a seamless setup process.

The entire spectrum of license management tasks, such as purchasing, canceling, renewing, enabling auto-renewal, and conducting audits, is shown through the Microsoft 365 admin center. The procedural steps to follow involve purchasing a Defender for IoT license and, subsequently, in step 2, adding an OT plan to your Azure subscription. These streamlined processes ensure comprehensive license control and efficient integration of Defender for IoT into your environment.

Enterprise customers must possess one of the following license configurations to utilize Defender for IoT effectively:

- A Microsoft 365 E5 (ME5) or E5 Security license coupled with a Microsoft Defender for Endpoint P2 license.

- Alternatively, a stand-alone Microsoft Defender for Endpoint P2 license is sufficient.

In addition to the requisite licenses, access to the Microsoft 365 Defender portal is essential, with the user holding Global administrator privileges. These specifications ensure enterprise customers have the necessary licensing and administrative access for optimal deployment and management of Defender for IoT.

Getting Started

To initiate an assessment of the capabilities of Defender for IoT, you can commence a free trial with the following steps.

For OT (operational technology) networks, take advantage of a trial license that spans 60 days. During this trial period, deploy one or more Defender for IoT sensors across your network. These sensors are crucial in monitoring network traffic, conducting data analysis, generating alerts, and providing insights into network risks and vulnerabilities. It's important to note that the OT trial specifically accommodates a large site license, allowing you to comprehensively explore the features and functionalities of Defender for IoT within the 60-day trial period.

On the other hand, for enterprise IoT networks, opt for a trial stand-alone license that extends for 90 days. This trial license functions as an add-on to Microsoft Defender for Endpoint. Within this trial period, you can support up to 100 devices. This trial setup enables you to assess and experience the integration of Defender for IoT within the broader Microsoft Defender ecosystem, offering a more extensive exploration of capabilities and performance across enterprise IoT networks.

Plan Microsoft Defender for IoT Roles and Permissions

Role-based access control (RBAC) is crucial for managing access and permissions within the Azure cloud environment. RBAC provides a flexible and secure framework for controlling who has access to what resources and actions they can perform. The importance of RBAC in Azure can be explained through several key aspects:

- Granular Access Control: RBAC allows administrators to assign specific roles to users or groups, defining precisely what actions they can perform on specific Azure resources. This granular control ensures that users have the minimum necessary permissions to carry out their tasks, reducing the risk of unauthorized access or inadvertent changes to critical resources.

- Security: RBAC enhances security by implementing the principle of least privilege. Users are granted only the permissions required to perform their designated tasks, limiting the potential impact of security breaches or accidental misconfigurations. This approach minimizes the attack surface and mitigates the risk of unauthorized access.

- Compliance: Many industries and organizations have specific regulatory compliance requirements. RBAC helps in meeting these compliance standards by enabling organizations to enforce access controls and monitor user activities. This is particularly important in healthcare, finance, and government sectors, where data privacy and security regulations are stringent.

- Efficient Resource Management: RBAC simplifies the management of Azure resources by allowing organizations to delegate administrative tasks without compromising security. Administrators can assign roles based on job responsibilities, enabling teams to work independently on their specific tasks without unnecessary access to unrelated resources.

- Auditability and Accountability: RBAC provides detailed logs and audit trails, allowing organizations to track user activities and changes made to Azure resources. This auditability enhances accountability, making investigating incidents, detecting suspicious behavior, and maintaining a comprehensive record of access events easier.

- Dynamic Scaling: RBAC adapts to changes seamlessly in dynamic cloud environments like Azure, where resources can be provisioned and de-provisioned rapidly. Administrators can adjust role assignments dynamically as users and resources evolve, ensuring that access controls remain aligned with the organization's evolving structure and needs.

- Collaboration and DevOps Practices: RBAC supports collaborative efforts and DevOps practices by allowing teams to work concurrently on different aspects of cloud deployment. Development, testing, and operations teams can be granted specific roles tailored to their responsibilities, fostering a more streamlined and efficient workflow.

In summary, RBAC in Azure is instrumental in maintaining a secure, compliant, and well-organized cloud environment. It aligns with the principles of security best practices, least privilege, and efficient resource management, contributing to the overall success of cloud-based operations.

In the context of Microsoft Defender for IoT, role-based access control (RBAC) holds particular significance for several reasons:

- Security and Threat Mitigation

  RBAC ensures that access to critical Defender for IoT resources, such as monitoring services and threat intelligence data, is tightly controlled.

By assigning roles based on responsibilities, organizations can restrict access to sensitive information, reducing the risk of unauthorized access and potential security threats.

- Protection of Operational Technology (OT) Networks

  Defender for IoT is designed to secure OT networks, which are crucial for industrial and infrastructure operations. RBAC helps secure access to OT-related data and services, preventing unauthorized interference with essential operational processes.

- Least Privilege Principle

  RBAC follows the principle of least privilege, allowing organizations to grant only the minimum necessary permissions for users to perform their tasks. This approach limits potential damage in case of a security breach or unintentional actions.

- Customization for Different User Roles

  Defender for IoT involves various tasks, from monitoring alerts to managing devices and configurations. RBAC allows organizations to customize access based on user roles, ensuring that individuals have the appropriate permissions for their responsibilities.

- Compliance and Auditing

  RBAC supports compliance efforts by providing a structured approach to managing access controls. This is critical in industries where compliance with regulatory standards is essential for data protection and operational integrity.

  The auditing capabilities of RBAC contribute to accountability, allowing organizations to track user activities and maintain compliance records.

- Efficient Incident Response

  In the event of a security incident or alert, RBAC ensures that only authorized personnel have access to the tools and information needed for an effective response. This helps contain and resolve security issues promptly.

- Collaboration in IoT Security Operations

  RBAC facilitates collaborative security efforts by allowing teams to work together on securing IoT devices and networks. With well-defined roles, security operations can be distributed among different team members, enhancing overall efficiency.

- Integration with Azure RBAC

  Since Defender for IoT is part of the broader Microsoft ecosystem, integrating RBAC with Azure RBAC provides a seamless and unified approach to access control across the entire Azure environment.

In conclusion, RBAC in Microsoft Defender for IoT is crucial in securing IoT environments, ensuring proper access controls, and supporting compliance efforts. It aligns with best practices for security, risk management, and efficient collaboration within IoT security operations.

Assign specific roles to your Azure subscription users using the portal or PowerShell based on their needs, whether viewing alert or device data or managing pricing plans and sensors.

For on-premises users in Defender for IoT, services and data are accessible through on-premises OT network sensors and the on-premises sensor management console alongside the Azure portal.

Define on-premises users on OT network sensors and the on-premises management console besides Azure. Default privileged users are installed on both the OT sensors and the management console, serving as a basis for defining additional administrators and users.

Incorporate Active Directory support for sensors and on-premises management consoles. Integrating sensors and Active Directory enables AD users to sign in or use AD groups, streamlining permissions management, especially for a large user base requiring read-only access.

Defender for IoT's Active Directory integration supports LDAP v3 and various LDAP-based authentication types:

- Full Authentication: Retrieve user details from the LDAP server, including first name, last name, email, and permissions.

- Trusted User: Retrieve only the user password, with additional details based on users defined in the sensor.

To efficiently manage on-premises Defender for IoT users, adopt a global business topology based on business units, regions, and sites. Establish user access groups to enforce global access control, defining rules for user access to specific entities within the business topology. This approach ensures streamlined access permissions across Defender for IoT on-premises resources.

Roles and Permissions for Azure Users in Defender for IoT

Microsoft Defender for IoT offers tools for managing user access across the Azure portal and on-premises resources. Utilizing Azure role-based access control (RBAC) grants access to monitoring services and data within Defender for IoT on the Azure portal.

Roles such as Azure Security Reader, Security Admin, Contributor, and Owner are pertinent for use within Defender for IoT. User management at the subscription level occurs in the Azure portal through Microsoft Entra ID and Azure RBAC. Azure subscription users may possess one or more roles, defining their access to data and actions, including those within Defender for IoT.

Reference for Roles and Permissions

Permissions are assigned to user roles throughout an entire Azure subscription or, in certain instances, specific Defender for IoT sites. Additional details can be found in resources discussing "zero trust and your OT networks" and "manage site-based access control" (Public preview).

In this system, roles such as Security Reader are designed to grant limited read access to security-related information. Security Admin roles carry the authority to manage various security-related configurations. Contributors can change resources without owning them, while Owners have full control and ownership over resources and settings. This structured RBAC framework ensures a nuanced and flexible approach to access control within the system.

Table 3-9 offers an overview of the built-in role-based access control (RBAC).

Table 3-9. *RBAC for Azure Users in Defender for IoT*

Action and Scope	Security Reader	Security Admin	Contributor	Owner
Grant permissions	-	-	-	Yes
Onboard OT/IoT sensors	-	Yes	Yes	Yes
Download sensor software	Yes	Yes	Yes	Yes
Download sensor details	Yes	Yes	Yes	Yes
Download activation files	-	Yes	Yes	Yes
View plans and pricing	Yes	Yes	Yes	Yes
Modify plans and pricing	-	Yes	Yes	Yes
View sites and sensors	Yes	Yes	Yes	Yes
Modify sites and sensors	-	Yes	Yes	Yes
Recover console passwords	-	Yes	Yes	Yes
Download threat intelligence packages	Yes	Yes	Yes	Yes
Push threat intelligence updates	-	Yes	Yes	Yes
View Azure alerts	Yes	Yes	Yes	Yes
Modify Azure alerts	-	Yes	Yes	Yes
View Azure device inventory	Yes	Yes	Yes	Yes
Manage Azure device inventory	-	Yes	Yes	Yes
View Azure workbooks	Yes	Yes	Yes	Yes
Manage Azure workbooks	-	Yes	Yes	Yes
View Defender for IoT settings	Yes	Yes	Yes	Yes
Configure Defender for IoT settings	-	Yes	Yes	Yes

Users and Roles Designated for On-Premises Operations in the Context of OT Monitoring with Defender for IoT

When engaging with OT networks, Defender for IoT services and data are accessible through on-premises OT network sensors, on-premises sensor management consoles, and Azure. Default privileged users are automatically installed with each sensor and on-premises management console. Specifically, a privileged support user is present on both, and the on-premises management console includes a default cyberx user.

These privileged support and cyberx users are equipped with advanced tools for troubleshooting and setup, including the command-line interface (CLI). When configuring a sensor or on-premises management console, Microsoft recommends initially signing in with the support user. Subsequently, create an initial user with an Admin role, using this Admin user to establish additional users with diverse roles.

In sensor software versions preceding 23.1.x, the cyberx and cyberx_host privileged users are also accessible. However, in newly installed versions 23.1.x and higher, these users are available but not enabled by default. Their passwords need to be modified to activate these additional privileged users, such as those used for the Defender for IoT CLI. During the initial deployment of an OT monitoring system, logging in with one of the default privileged users is advised. Create the first Admin user and then utilize that user to establish additional users while assigning them to specific roles.

It's important to note that permissions applied to each role may vary between the sensor and the on-premises management console.

Reference for Roles and Permissions

In the Defender for IoT system, different user roles offer varying levels of access and permissions. The Admin role grants users comprehensive access to all tools, empowering them to configure systems, create and manage users, and perform various administrative tasks. On the other hand, Security Analysts have more restricted permissions. While they lack admin-level access to configurations, they can still execute actions on devices, acknowledge alerts, and use investigation tools. Security Analysts can access specific options on the sensor through the Discover and Analyze menus and on the on-premises management console via the NAVIGATION and ANALYSIS menus.

Meanwhile, read-only users are limited to viewing tasks, such as observing alerts and devices on the device map. They can access specific options on the sensor through the Discover and Analyze menus in read-only mode and on the on-premises management console through the NAVIGATION menu. These distinct roles cater to the Defender for IoT ecosystem's diverse responsibilities and access requirements.

Permission Levels Assigned Based on Roles for the Operational Technology (OT) Network Sensors

Table 3-10 illustrates role-based permissions for OT network sensors.

Table 3-10. *RBAC for On-Premises Operations*

Permission	Read-Only	Security Analyst	Admin
View the dashboard	Yes	Yes	Yes
Control map zoom views	-	-	Yes
View alerts	Yes	Yes	Yes
Manage alerts: acknowledge, learn, and mute	-	Yes	Yes
View events in a timeline	Yes	Yes	Yes
Authorize devices, known scanning devices, programming devices	-	Yes	Yes
Merge and delete devices	-	-	Yes
View investigation data	Yes	Yes	Yes
Manage system settings	-	-	Yes
Manage users	-	-	Yes
Change passwords	-	-	Yes*
DNS servers for reverse lookup	-	-	Yes
Send alert data to partners	-	Yes	Yes
Create alert comments	-	Yes	Yes
View programming change history	Yes	Yes	Yes
Create customized alert rules	-	Yes	Yes
Manage multiple notifications simultaneously	-	Yes	Yes
Manage certificates	-	-	Yes

Permission Levels Assigned Based on Roles for the On-Premises Management Console

Table 3-11 offers a summary of role-based access control (RBAC) for the on-premises management console, outlining a detailed permission structure.

Table 3-11. *RBAC for On-Premises Operations Management Console*

Permission	Read-Only	Security Analyst	Admin
View and filter enterprise map	Yes	Yes	Yes
Build a site	-	-	Yes
Manage a site (add and edit zones)	-	-	Yes
View and filter device inventory	Yes	Yes	Yes
View and manage alerts	Yes	Yes	Yes
Generate reports	-	Yes	Yes
View risk assessment reports	-	Yes	Yes
Set alert exclusions	-	Yes	Yes
View or define access groups	-	-	Yes
Manage system settings	-	-	Yes
Manage users	-	-	Yes
Change passwords	-	-	Yes
Send alert data to partners	-	-	Yes
Manage certificates	-	-	Yes

Plan Microsoft Defender for IoT with Cybersecurity

The emergence of the Internet of Things (IoT) introduces distinctive security,
privacy, and compliance challenges that businesses worldwide must navigate. Unlike
conventional cybersecurity issues centered on software and its implementation, IoT
complexities arise from the convergence of the cyber and physical realms. Safeguarding
IoT solutions necessitates addressing multifaceted concerns, including the secure
provisioning of devices, establishing secure connectivity between devices and the cloud,
and ensuring secure data protection in the cloud during processing and storage.

The proliferation of IoT devices within enterprise networks is experiencing
exponential growth, encompassing devices like printers, Voice over Internet Protocol
(VoIP) devices, smart TVs, and conferencing systems distributed throughout various
office buildings.

Despite increasing numbers, many IoT devices need robust security measures commonly found on managed endpoints such as laptops and mobile phones. This vulnerability makes unmanaged IoT devices susceptible to exploitation by malicious actors, serving as potential entry points for lateral movement or evasion. Unfortunately, such tactics often result in the unauthorized extraction of sensitive information.

To address these security challenges, Microsoft Defender for IoT seamlessly integrates with Microsoft Defender XDR and Microsoft Defender for Endpoint. This integration delivers comprehensive security coverage for IoT devices, offering purpose-built alerts, recommendations, and vulnerability data.

Within the Microsoft Defender XDR environment, enterprise IoT security enhances the overall security posture by providing specific insights related to IoT devices. This includes alerts, risk assessments, exposure levels, identified vulnerabilities, and actionable recommendations.

Protecting IoT solutions becomes a nuanced endeavor due to several factors working against these security measures. Firstly, resource-constrained devices impose limitations on the robustness of security measures that can be implemented. Often characterized by restricted computing power and storage capacity, these devices need help in enforcing comprehensive security protocols.

Additionally, the geographic distribution of IoT deployments introduces a layer of complexity. IoT solutions are frequently dispersed across diverse locations, making maintaining uniform security measures across the entire network challenging. The global nature of IoT deployments amplifies the need for adaptable security strategies that can accommodate varying regulatory environments and threat landscapes.

Moreover, the sheer volume of devices within an IoT solution compounds the challenge. Managing security for a large number of devices demands scalable and efficient solutions to ensure the integrity and confidentiality of data. Implementing consistent security protocols across numerous devices becomes a logistical challenge, requiring strategic planning and coordination.

In the face of these challenges, businesses engaged in IoT initiatives must adopt a holistic approach to security. Secure provisioning processes must be established to ensure that devices are initialized and configured securely. Establishing secure connectivity channels between devices and the cloud is paramount to protecting data in transit. Furthermore, robust measures for data protection within the cloud, encompassing both processing and storage phases, are indispensable to uphold the confidentiality and integrity of sensitive information.

Intricate landscape of IoT security demands careful consideration of the unique challenges posed by the convergence of the physical and cyber worlds. Businesses must navigate the constraints of resource-constrained devices, address the geographical dispersion of deployments, and manage the complexities associated with a multitude of devices within an IoT solution. Organizations can fortify their IoT implementations against the evolving threat landscape and regulatory requirements by adopting comprehensive security measures encompassing device provisioning, connectivity, and data protection.

From a planning perspective, Microsoft provides security guidelines for individuals and companies involved in IoT solutions. Incorporating these recommendations into your planning will contribute to fulfilling security obligations in alignment with Microsoft's shared responsibility model.

In the planning phase, it's crucial to note that Microsoft Defender for Cloud, which encompasses Azure Security Center and Azure Defender, is the primary defense layer for safeguarding Azure resources. This tool periodically assesses the security state of your Azure resources, identifies potential vulnerabilities, and offers recommendations to address them.

General Recommendations

- Stay up to date.

  To ensure optimal security, utilize the latest versions of supported platforms, programming languages, protocols, and frameworks.

- Keep authentication keys safe.

  Safeguard device IDs and their authentication keys post-deployment to prevent unauthorized access and the potential impersonation of registered devices.

- Use device SDKs when possible.

  Implement security features such as encryption and authentication by leveraging device SDKs. Microsoft's ongoing investment in SDKs ensures continuous support for emerging security advancements.

Identity and Access Management Planning

- Define access control for the hub.

  Understand and define access levels for each component in your IoT Hub solution, specifying permissions such as Registry Read, RegistryReadWrite, ServiceConnect, and DeviceConnect.

- Define access control for backend services.

  Establish access permissions for Azure services consuming data from your IoT Hub, including Cosmos DB, Stream Analytics, App Service, Logic Apps, and Blob Storage.

Data Protection Planning

- Secure device authentication.

  Ensure secure device-to-hub communication by using unique identity keys, security tokens, or on-device X.509 certificates for each device, choosing the appropriate method based on the protocol (MQTT, AMQP, or HTTPS).

- Secure device communication.

  Implement TLS 1.2 for secure communication between devices and IoT Hub, ensuring the highest level of security.

- Secure service communication.

  Utilize TLS for IoT Hub endpoints connecting to backend services. Implement additional security and encryption measures for data storage or analysis at the backend.

Networking Planning

- Protect access to your devices.

  Minimize hardware ports in devices to reduce the risk of unwanted access. Incorporate mechanisms to prevent or detect physical tampering of devices.

- Build secure hardware.

  Integrate security features like encrypted storage or Trusted Platform
  Module (TPM) to enhance device and infrastructure security. Keep
  device operating systems and drivers updated for the latest security
  measures.

Zero-Trust Security Planning

The architectural landscape of operational technology (OT) networks frequently
diverges from conventional IT infrastructure. OT systems operate on distinctive
technologies with proprietary protocols, often featuring aging platforms, limited
connectivity, and power constraints. Additionally, OT networks are characterized by
specific safety requirements and susceptibility to unique physical or local attacks, such
as those initiated by external contractors accessing the network.

Due to their role in supporting critical network infrastructures, OT systems are
typically designed to prioritize physical safety or availability over aspects like secure
access and monitoring. For instance, OT networks may operate independently of other
enterprise network traffic to prevent downtime during routine maintenance or to
address specific security concerns.

The migration of OT networks to cloud-based environments introduces challenges
in applying zero-trust principles. Several factors contribute to this complexity:

- Limited User Management and Authentication Processes

  OT systems may not be inherently designed for multiple users or
  comprehensive role-based access policies, often relying on simplistic
  authentication processes.

- Processing Power Constraints

  OT systems may need more processing power to implement secure
  access policies fully. Consequently, there may be a reliance on
  trusting all received traffic as safe.

- Challenges with Aging Technology

  Aging technology challenges retaining organizational knowledge,
  implementing updates, and utilizing standard security analytics tools
  to gain visibility and drive threat detection.

Despite these challenges, the significance of security in mission-critical systems cannot be overstated. A security compromise in OT systems carries real-world consequences beyond traditional IT incidents. Noncompliance with security measures can impact an organization's ability to adhere to government and industry regulations, underscoring the critical need for a nuanced and adaptive security approach in the evolving landscape of OT networks.

The zero-trust security strategy operates on the foundational principle that a breach is to be expected, necessitating continuous verifications and granting the least necessary privileges. In the context of operational technology (OT) networks, the application of zero trust involves several vital practices:

- Identification and Management of Network Connections

  Rigorous measures are implemented to identify and manage all connections between networks and devices within the OT environment. This includes continuous authentication processes and stringent access controls.

- Limiting and Securing Network Jump Hosts

  Zero-trust principles are applied to network jump hosts, ensuring that access points are restricted and security measures are in place to safeguard these critical entry points.

- Network Segmentation for Data Access Limitation

  A pivotal aspect of zero trust in OT networks is network segmentation. This practice limits data access by creating isolated segments, thereby containing potential breaches and minimizing the impact of security incidents. All communication between devices and segments is encrypted and secured to prevent unauthorized access.

- Preventing Lateral Movement Between Systems

  Zero trust prevents lateral movement between systems within the OT network. By enforcing strict controls on lateral movement, the strategy aims to impede the lateral spread of threats and restrict unauthorized access to critical assets.

- Evaluation of Device Signals for Access Control

  Signals such as device location, health, and behavior are meticulously evaluated using health data. This information is leveraged to gate access, allowing or denying entry based on real-time assessments. Any anomalies or deviations trigger alerts for immediate remediation.

- Monitoring Security Metrics for Perimeter Integrity

  Zero trust extends to continuously monitoring security metrics to ensure the integrity of the security perimeter. This involves tracking and analyzing various security parameters to identify any deviations or potential threats that may compromise the network.

In essence, the zero-trust strategy applied in OT networks encompasses a holistic and dynamic approach to security. By assuming a breach as an inherent possibility, organizations implement robust measures to verify identities, restrict privileges, and fortify the network against potential threats. The emphasis on continuous monitoring, strict access controls, and encryption aligns with the overarching goal of zero trust – to establish a resilient security posture in the face of evolving cyber threats.

Defender for IoT facilitates zero-trust access segmentation by utilizing sites and zones. This approach involves grouping data collected from sensors within the same site or zone, enabling vigilant monitoring to detect any unauthorized traffic traversing across segments. Segmentation empowers organizations to establish policies that enforce the principle of least-privileged access within Defender for IoT.

The definitions for sites and zones are outlined as follows:

- Sites: These entities categorize devices based on specific geographical locations, such as an office situated at a particular address. Grouping devices within a site is instrumental in organizing and managing data associated with a particular physical location.

- Zones: Zones delineate a segment within a site, representing a functional area like a specific production line. This finer level of segmentation allows for more granular control and monitoring of devices and data flows within distinct operational segments, enhancing security and policy implementation.

Monitoring Planning

- Monitor unauthorized access to your devices.

  Leverage the logging feature of the device operating system to monitor security breaches or physical tampering of devices and ports.

- Monitor your IoT solution from the cloud.

  Monitor the overall health of your IoT Hub solution using metrics available in Azure Monitor.

- Set up diagnostics.

  Implement logging of events in your solution and send diagnostic logs to Azure Monitor for enhanced visibility into performance. Utilize Azure Monitor to closely observe operations and diagnose potential issues in your IoT Hub.

By incorporating these planning perspectives, organizations can proactively address security considerations and align their IoT solutions with Microsoft's recommended best practices. This comprehensive approach ensures a robust and secure foundation for IoT deployments.

Integration of Microsoft Defender for IoT with SOC Azure Native Services

As various business-critical industries transition their operational technology (OT) systems to digital IT infrastructures, security operations center (SOC) teams and chief information security officers (CISOs) find themselves increasingly tasked with mitigating threats originating from OT networks.

With these new responsibilities come a set of challenges that SOC teams must navigate, including the following:

Lack of OT Expertise

SOC teams may need more expertise and knowledge regarding OT alerts, industrial equipment, protocols, and network behavior. This knowledge gap often leads to a vague or minimized understanding of OT incidents and their potential business impact.

Communication Gaps Between OT and SOC

Inefficient communication and processes between OT and SOC organizations create silos, hindering the effective collaboration needed to address emerging threats.

Limited Technology and Tools

SOC teams face limitations in technology and tools, such as needing more visibility or automated security remediation for OT networks. Evaluating and correlating information across diverse data sources for OT networks can be challenging, and integrating with existing SOC solutions may incur significant costs.

However, the absence of OT data, context, and integration with existing SOC tools and workflows may result in mishandling or even oversight of OT security and operational threats.

Integrate Defender for IoT and Microsoft Sentinel

Microsoft Sentinel, a scalable cloud service for Security Information and Event Management (SIEM) and security orchestration, automation, and response (SOAR), offers a solution to these challenges. Integrating Microsoft Defender for IoT and Microsoft Sentinel enables SOC teams to collect data across networks, detect and investigate threats, and respond to incidents effectively.

The Defender for IoT data connector and solution in Microsoft Sentinel provides out-of-the-box security content to SOC teams. This facilitates the viewing, analysis, and response to OT security alerts, offering a comprehensive understanding of generated incidents within the broader organizational threat landscape.

To streamline this integration, installing the Defender for IoT data connector alone allows the streaming of OT network alerts to Microsoft Sentinel. Additionally, installing the Microsoft Defender for IoT solution provides extra value, offering IoT/OT-specific analytics rules, workbooks, SOAR playbooks, and incident mappings to MITRE ATT&CK for ICS techniques.

Integrating Defender for IoT with Microsoft Sentinel enhances both platforms' capabilities. It facilitates ingesting more data from Microsoft Sentinel's other partner integrations, contributing to a more robust and comprehensive security posture.

For the purpose of unified detection and response, Table 3-12 illustrates the swift threat detection and response capabilities orchestrated jointly by the OT team leveraging Defender for IoT and the SOC team utilizing Microsoft Sentinel, encompassing the entire attack timeline.

Table 3-12. *Detection and Response Integration with Defender for IOT*

Microsoft Sentinel	Process Step	Defender for IoT
High-confidence OT alerts, generated by Defender for IoT's Section 52 security research group, are triggered based on data ingested to Defender for IoT.	OT alert triggered	Analytics rules automatically open incidents only for relevant use cases, avoiding OT alert fatigue.
OT incident created	SOC teams map business impact, including data about the site, line, compromised assets, and OT owners.	SOC teams move the incident to Active and start investigating, using network connections and events, workbooks, and the OT device entity page.
Alerts are moved to Active, and OT teams investigate using PCAP data, detailed reports, and other device details.	OT incident investigation	SOC teams respond with OT playbooks and notebooks.
OT teams either suppress the alert or learn it for next time, as needed.	OT incident response	After the threat is mitigated, SOC teams close the incident.
After the threat is mitigated, OT teams close the alert.	OT incident closure	-

Changes in alert status are synchronized exclusively from Microsoft Sentinel to Defender for IoT, and the synchronization does not occur in the reverse direction from Defender for IoT to Microsoft Sentinel.

For optimal management of alert statuses in an integrated environment with Defender for IoT and Microsoft Sentinel, handling these statuses collectively with the associated incidents in Microsoft Sentinel is advised.

Once the Defender for IoT data connector is configured, streaming IoT/OT alert data to Microsoft Sentinel allows for creating incidents through various methods. Firstly, one can utilize the default data connector rule, creating incidents for all alerts generated in Microsoft Defender for the IoT analytics rule provided with the data connector.

Alternatively, users can enable some or all of the out-of-the-box analytics rules offered by Microsoft Defender for IoT solutions, helping to mitigate alert fatigue by selectively generating incidents in specific scenarios. Custom analytics rules can be created for more tailored needs, either leveraging the out-of-the-box rules as a starting point or establishing new rules from scratch. A filter is recommended to avoid duplicate incidents for the same alert ID. Regardless of the chosen method, only one incident should be generated for each Defender for IoT alert ID.

Microsoft Sentinel workbooks deployed to the workspace as part of the Microsoft Defender for IoT solution prove invaluable for visualization and monitoring of Defender for IoT data. These workbooks facilitate guided investigations for OT entities based on open incidents, alert notifications, and activities concerning OT assets. Additionally, they offer a hunting experience across the MITRE ATT&CK framework for ICS, providing situational awareness for analysts, security engineers, and MSSPs. Workbooks can display alerts categorized by type, severity, OT device type or vendor, and alerts over time. They also present the outcome of mapping alerts to MITRE ATT&CK for ICS tactics, along with the distribution of tactics by count and period.

Playbooks serve as automated remediation actions that can be executed routinely through Microsoft Sentinel. These playbooks play a pivotal role in automating and orchestrating threat responses, offering the flexibility to be run either manually or automatically. The automatic execution can be triggered in response to specific alerts or incidents, activated by analytics or an automation rule.

Summary

This chapter comprehensively overviews the strategic considerations and preparatory steps involved in deploying and managing Microsoft Defender for IoT. The chapter is organized into key sections, each addressing crucial aspects of the planning process.

Plan Microsoft Defender for IoT Deployment

The first section delved into the strategic planning required for a successful deployment, covering considerations such as network architecture, connectivity, and deployment options.

Prepare for Microsoft Defender for IoT Deployment

The second section provided insights into the necessary preparations, including system requirements, compatibility checks, and any prerequisites for a smooth implementation.

Plan Microsoft Defender for IoT Licenses

The third section outlined the licensing options available for Microsoft Defender for IoT, helping readers understand the licensing landscape and choose the most suitable opportunities based on their organizational needs.

Plan Microsoft Defender for IoT Roles and Permissions

The fourth section delved into the crucial aspect of user access and control. It discussed the roles and permissions within the Defender for IoT ecosystem, ensuring organizations can effectively manage and control user access to resources.

Plan Microsoft Defender for IoT with Cybersecurity

The final section emphasized the integration of Defender for IoT into the broader cybersecurity strategy. This included aligning Defender for IoT with cybersecurity best practices, ensuring a cohesive and comprehensive defense against IoT-specific threats.

This chapter serves as a guide for organizations looking to strategically plan and deploy Microsoft Defender for IoT, covering all essential facets to optimize its effectiveness within the broader cybersecurity framework.

In the book's next chapter, you will read about the deployment of Defender for IoT.

## CHAPTER 4

Deploy Microsoft Defender for IoT

In this book, you are at crucial stages, from the foundational steps to the advanced stage of Microsoft Defender for IoT deployment. Each section of this chapter is thoughtfully curated to provide a structured and in-depth understanding of the deployment processes for securing the Internet of Things (IoT) ecosystem.

Embarking on the Microsoft Defender for IoT deployment is the initial step in fortifying your IoT infrastructure. This section guides you through the fundamental prerequisites, helping you set up licenses, configure vital settings, and establish the groundwork for a robust and secure deployment.

Building upon the foundational knowledge acquired in the first section, you will delve into the intricacies of enabling Microsoft Defender for IoT. Uncovering Defender's wealth of features and capabilities empowers you to maximize its potential in fortifying your IoT environment against evolving threats.

Operational technology (OT) is critical in many industrial and enterprise settings. In this section, you will explore the deployment of OT monitoring solutions provided by Microsoft Defender for IoT. Learn how to monitor network traffic, analyze data, and proactively identify potential threats and vulnerabilities specific to OT networks.

Security concerns often dictate the need for air-gapped environments. This segment addresses the specialized requirements of managing OT sensors in isolated or air-gapped scenarios. Discover best practices to ensure the seamless and secure operation of OT sensors within restricted network environments.

The final section of this chapter transcends individual deployments to focus on the enterprise scale. Delve into the complexities of monitoring large-scale IoT deployments with Microsoft Defender for IoT. Understand how Defender scales to meet the demands of extensive IoT ecosystems, providing comprehensive security solutions for enterprises operating across diverse and complex IoT landscapes.

© Puthiyavan Udayakumar and Dr. R. Anandan 2024
P. Udayakumar and Dr. R. Anandan, *Design and Deploy Microsoft Defender for IoT*,
https://doi.org/10.1007/979-8-8688-0239-3_4

By the end of this chapter, you should be able to understand the following:

- Getting started with Microsoft Defender for IoT deployment

- Enable Microsoft Defender for IoT

- Calibrate and fine-tune the monitoring of OT environment

- Air-gapped OT sensor management

Getting Started with Microsoft Defender for IoT Deployment

Embarking on your Microsoft Defender for IoT deployment journey involves several vital steps to ensure a secure and effective setup. Access the Azure portal, your gateway to Microsoft's cloud services. Once logged in, navigate to the "Security" section and select "IoT Security" under "Advanced Threat Protection."

Within the dedicated dashboard for Defender for IoT, delve into the settings and configurations available. Take the time to familiarize yourself with the options provided, as they are crucial in tailoring the security measures to your specific needs.

Ensuring you have the necessary licenses is paramount, and the portal will guide you through obtaining any required licenses for Microsoft Defender for IoT. Configure basic settings such as region and subscription details as part of the initial setup. Additionally, define an IoT Hub within the Azure portal if you haven't already, as Defender for IoT collaborates closely with IoT Hubs to deliver security features.

Enable Microsoft Defender for IoT within the IoT Hub settings. This step typically involves toggling a switch or selecting a specific configuration option to activate the security features for your IoT devices.

Verify that your IoT devices are correctly registered with the IoT Hub, as this information is crucial for Defender for IoT to monitor and secure your devices effectively. Once set up, explore the "Recommendations" or "Best Practices" section within Defender for IoT settings to address any recommended actions and enhance the overall security posture of your IoT deployment.

Finally, leverage the monitoring features provided by Defender for IoT to analyze network traffic, detect anomalies, and identify potential security threats. Regularly check for updates and alerts from Defender for IoT to stay informed about the security status of your IoT environment, ensuring a proactive approach to safeguarding your IoT devices. This comprehensive process sets the foundation for a robust and secure deployment of Microsoft Defender for IoT.

Quick Overview of Azure Portal and Microsoft Defender for IOT

The Microsoft Azure portal serves as a centralized platform for managing and monitoring various cloud services offered by Microsoft Azure. It provides a unified interface that allows users to deploy, manage, and analyze resources across Azure's extensive suite of services. The Azure portal offers a comprehensive solution for organizations seeking a scalable and flexible cloud computing environment, from virtual machines and databases to machine learning and analytics.

Within the Azure portal, organizations can access and configure Microsoft Defender for IoT, a specialized security solution designed to protect operational technology (OT) environments. Microsoft Defender for IoT provides advanced threat detection and management capabilities tailored to the unique challenges of the industrial, energy, and utility sectors. This solution helps organizations defend against cyber threats targeting their OT infrastructure, safeguard critical assets, and ensure the reliability of industrial processes.

Microsoft Defender for IoT in the Azure portal enables security teams to gain insights into the security posture of their OT environment. It facilitates the monitoring of network traffic, detection of anomalies, and identification of potential cyber threats. Leveraging machine learning and behavioral analytics, Defender for IoT helps in distinguishing normal operational behavior from suspicious or malicious activities within the OT network. The Azure portal is a centralized hub for security analysts to review alerts, investigate incidents, and implement remediation actions, ensuring a proactive and efficient response to potential threats.

Moreover, integrating Microsoft Defender for IoT with the Azure portal gives organizations a unified and streamlined security management experience. Security administrators can leverage Azure's robust identity and access management features to control user permissions, ensuring that only authorized personnel can access sensitive security data. This integration exemplifies Microsoft's commitment to providing holistic, intelligent security solutions, bridging the gap between traditional IT and OT environments.

In summary, the Microsoft Azure portal is a powerful tool for managing Azure resources, and its integration with Microsoft Defender for IoT enhances the security posture of OT environments. This combination allows organizations to benefit from a unified interface for cloud services while effectively safeguarding their critical industrial infrastructure against evolving cyber threats.

Let us start with deployment prerequisites, particularly tailored for customers lacking a Microsoft tenant or Azure subscription. By leveraging Defender for IoT, users can effectively monitor network traffic within their OT networks.

Before commencing the deployment process, ensure you have an email address designated as the contact for your upcoming Microsoft tenant. Additionally, be prepared to input your credit card details for the new Azure subscription; however, rest assured, charges will only apply when transitioning from the Free Trial to the Pay-As-You-Go plan.

Embarking on your journey with Azure Cloud begins by creating a Microsoft Azure account through the dedicated portal. After signing up with a valid email address, accessing the Azure portal becomes your gateway to a world of cloud services. Take a moment to navigate the portal, familiarize yourself with the layout, and utilize the resource management dashboard. Azure operates on a subscription-based model, and as a new user, you can start with a free subscription, offering a limited set of services at no cost for the initial 12 months. Delve into the vast array of Azure services, spanning computing, storage, databases, machine learning, and more. Organize your resources logically by creating a resource group, easing the management and monitoring of interconnected assets. Dive into your Azure journey by deploying your first resource, whether a virtual machine or a web app. Optionally, acquaint yourself with Azure CLI or Azure PowerShell for command-line resource management.

Supplement your hands-on experience with Azure documentation and tutorials, exploring the nuances of specific services and scenarios. Stay connected with the Azure community through forums and social media, tapping into collective knowledge and staying abreast of best practices. As you gain proficiency, explore advanced features and services to tailor your cloud environment for optimal security, scalability, and cost efficiency. Azure's flexibility and scalability empower you to craft a cloud strategy that aligns seamlessly with your unique project requirements.

The following is the high-level process of getting Azure activated with your email ID:

Step 1: Log in to your personal or business account into the Azure portal as shown in Figure 4-1 (https://portal.azure.com/).

Figure 4-1. *Microsoft Azure portal login*

Step 2: For a first-time starter, you need to create an Azure account; you have choice to use your email address or phone number instead (as shown in Figure 4-2).

Figure 4-2. *Microsoft Azure portal account creation*

Step 3: Let us choose to get a new email address, and after selecting, enter the preferred email address; as the next step, you are prompted to enter a password; complete the setup (as shown in Figure 4-3).

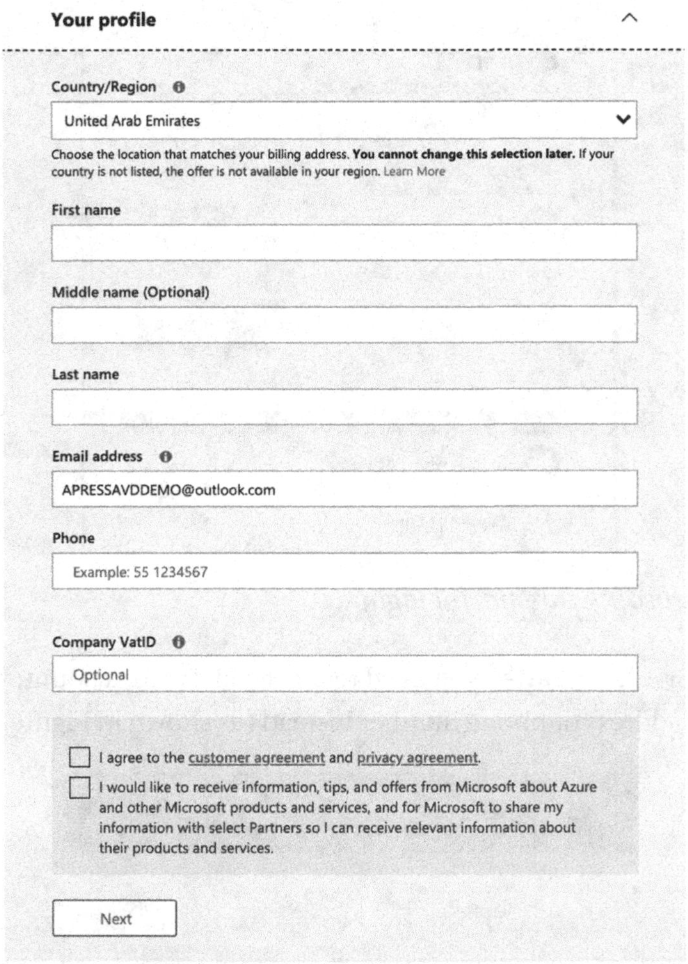

Your profile ∧

- -

Country/Region ❶

| United Arab Emirates | ⌄ |

Choose the location that matches your billing address. **You cannot change this selection later.** If your country is not listed, the offer is not available in your region. Learn More

First name

Middle name (Optional)

Last name

Email address ❶

APRESSAVDDEMO@outlook.com

Phone

Example: 55 1234567

Company VatID ❶

Optional

☐ I agree to the customer agreement and privacy agreement.

☐ I would like to receive information, tips, and offers from Microsoft about Azure and other Microsoft products and services, and for Microsoft to share my information with select Partners so I can receive relevant information about their products and services.

Next

Figure 4-3. *Microsoft Azure portal account creation continued*

Step 4: Complete verification inclusive of credit card setup (as shown in Figure 4-4).

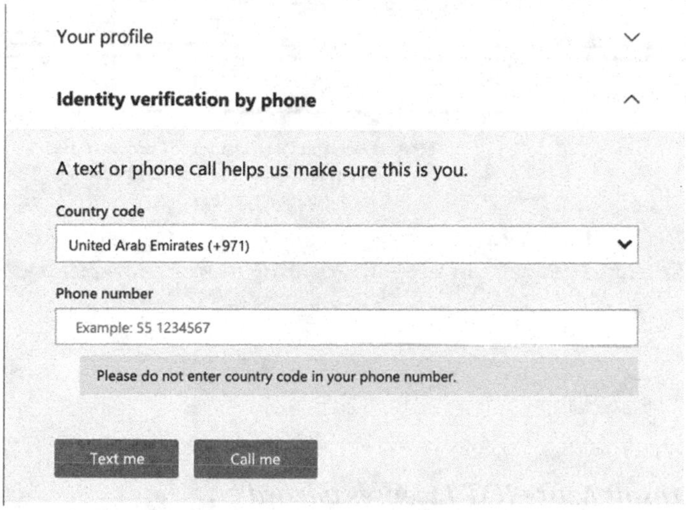

Figure 4-4. *Microsoft Azure portal account validation*

Once you activated your Azure free account, for knowledge, feature evaluation, and proof-of-concept purpose, Microsoft always encourages to make use of trial licenses.

During the trial period, users can take advantage of support for a large site size, accommodating up to 1000 devices, and the trial duration extends for 60 days. To maximize the trial experience, consider deploying virtual sensors or on-premises sensors. These sensors are crucial in monitoring traffic, conducting data analysis, generating alerts, comprehending network risks and vulnerabilities, and much more. The trial period serves as an opportunity to explore and harness the capabilities of Microsoft Defender for IoT in enhancing security and management.

To initiate the process of adding a trial license for Defender for IoT to your Azure subscription, follow these clear steps:

Step 1: Open the Microsoft Defender for IoT – OT Site License (1000 max devices per site) Trial wizard in your preferred browser (as shown in Figure 4-5).

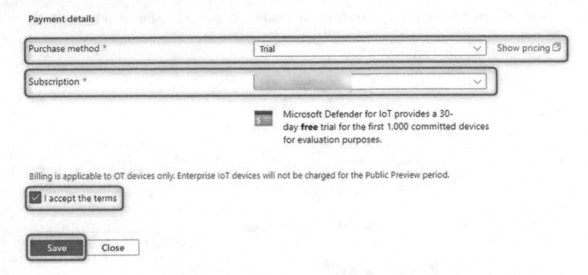

Figure 4-5. *Microsoft Azure IOT Licenses wizard*

Step 2: Enter the email address you wish to associate with the trial license in the Email box and proceed by selecting "Next."

Step 3: Provide your details on the "Tell us about yourself" page and select "Next" to continue.

Step 4: Choose whether you prefer the confirmation message to be sent via SMS to phone. Verify your phone number and select "Send verification code."

Step 5: Upon receiving the verification code, enter it in the designated "Enter your verification code" box.

Step 6: On the "How you'll sign in" page, set up a username and password, and then select "Next."

Note your order number and username on the "Confirmation details" page. Select the "Start using Microsoft Defender for IoT – OT Site License (1000 max devices per site) Trial" button to proceed. It's advisable to copy your full username to the clipboard, as it will be needed to access the Azure portal.

Following these steps, you can seamlessly add a trial license for Defender for IoT to your Azure subscription, ensuring a smooth and well-documented process.

To incorporate an operational technology (OT) plan for Defender for IoT within the Azure portal, leveraging your recently acquired trial license, follow this detailed process:

Step 1: Open the Azure portal and navigate to Defender for IoT. Access the "Plans and Pricing" section, where you'll be prompted to initiate the creation of a new subscription. Refer to Figure 4-6.

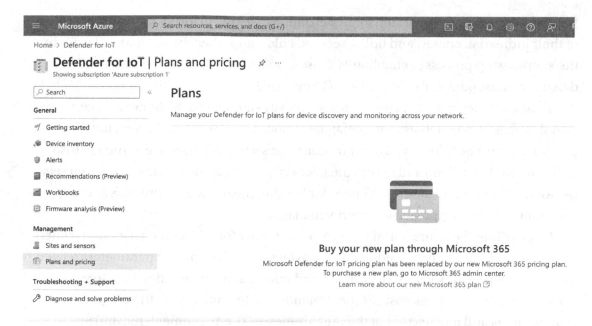

Figure 4-6. *Microsoft Azure – Defender for IOT Plans and pricing page*

Step 2: Click "Go to subscriptions" to proceed to the Azure Subscriptions page, and ensure you opt for the Free Trial option when creating your new subscription.

Step 3: Return to Defender for IoT's "Plans and pricing" page and select "Add plan." In the Plan settings pane, designate your newly created subscription.

The Price plan value is automatically updated to reflect Microsoft 365, aligning with your Microsoft 365 license.

Step 4: Click "Next" to advance and carefully review the particulars of your licensed site. The information on the Review and Purchase pane corresponds to your trial license.

Step 5: Accept the terms and conditions, and then click "Save."

Your freshly added plan will now be visible under the relevant subscription on the "Plans and pricing ➤ Plans" page, indicating successful integration and enabling you to effectively manage and monitor your Defender for IoT deployment.

Enable Microsoft Defender for IoT

Microsoft Defender for IoT is a robust security solution designed to safeguard operational technology (OT) environments from cyber threats, providing advanced threat detection, monitoring, and management capabilities. Enabling Microsoft

Defender for IoT is a crucial step for organizations seeking to fortify the security posture of their industrial, energy, and utility sectors. This comprehensive section will explore the step-by-step process of enabling Microsoft Defender for IoT to ensure a resilient defense against potential cyber risks in OT networks.

To initiate the enabling process, users typically start within the Microsoft Azure portal, a centralized platform for managing various cloud services. Leveraging the Azure portal's user-friendly interface, organizations can seamlessly navigate to the Microsoft Defender for IoT section and access the necessary configurations. This initial step sets the foundation for integrating Defender for IoT into the broader Azure ecosystem, providing a holistic approach to security management.

Once within the Azure portal's Microsoft Defender for IoT section, users are guided through a series of setup procedures. This involves defining specific parameters related to network topology, sensor deployment, and integration with existing infrastructure. Configuring these settings ensures that Defender for IoT aligns with the unique requirements and architecture of the organization's OT environment, maximizing its effectiveness in threat detection and response.

A pivotal aspect of enabling Microsoft Defender for IoT involves deploying dedicated sensors strategically across the OT network. These sensors act as the frontline defense, continuously monitoring network traffic and analyzing data patterns to identify potential anomalies or malicious activities. The deployment process is customizable, allowing organizations to tailor sensor placement based on the criticality of assets and specific network characteristics.

Furthermore, enabling Microsoft Defender for IoT often involves integrating with other security tools and systems, such as Security Information and Event Management (SIEM) solutions. This integration enhances the security ecosystem by streamlining alerting, incident response, and reporting processes. Organizations can seamlessly connect Defender for IoT with their existing security infrastructure, fostering a collaborative and interoperable security environment.

In conclusion, enabling Microsoft Defender for IoT is a strategic imperative for organizations looking to fortify their OT environments against evolving cyber threats. This detailed guide will delve into each step of the enabling process, empowering security professionals to harness the full potential of Defender for IoT within the Azure portal. From initial configurations to sensor deployment and integration with existing security tools, this comprehensive introduction aims to provide actionable insights for a seamless and effective implementation of Microsoft Defender for IoT.

From deployment perspective, Defender for IoT provides agentless, network-layer security that ensures ongoing discovery of IoT/OT assets, effective vulnerability management, and reliable threat detection within operational and enterprise networks. It seamlessly integrates with Microsoft Sentinel and various third-party SOC tools like Splunk, IBM QRadar, ServiceNow, and more without necessitating any modifications to existing environments. Notably, Defender for IoT maintains zero impact on network performance and offers the flexibility to deploy fully on-premises or in Azure-connected environments.

Explore, oversee, and safeguard devices throughout your operational networks, including OT (operational technology), ICS (industrial control systems), IIoT (industrial Internet of Things), and BMS (Building Management Systems). Attain comprehensive insight into unmanaged IoT devices within your corporate network for enterprise IoT.

Defender for IoT empowers you to streamline security management and establish comprehensive threat detection and analysis capabilities across hybrid cloud workloads and your Azure IoT solution. The Azure Defender for IoT suite comprises several integral components:

- IoT Hub Integration

  - Seamless integration with IoT Hub, enabling a centralized point for managing and monitoring security aspects

- Device Agents (Optional)

  - The option to deploy device agents to enhance security measures at the device level

- Send Security Message SDK

  - Facilitates the transmission of security messages for analysis, contributing to the overall threat intelligence

- Analytics Pipeline

  - An analytics pipeline that processes and analyzes security events, ensuring a robust defense mechanism

Now, let's delve into the detailed steps for the outlined tasks:

Task 1: Enable Azure Defender for IoT

Step 1: Log in to the Azure portal using your Azure account credentials, ensuring you are logged in with the account tied to the subscription.

Step 2: On your Azure dashboard, select or search for Defender for IOT.

Step 3: Under "Defender for IoT" in the left-side menu, click "Getting started" (as shown in Figure 4-7). The onboarding process will be initiated upon accessing the security pane for the first time.

Figure 4-7. *Microsoft Azure – Defender for IOT landing page*

Task 2: Configure OT/ICS Security

Utilizing patented agentless technology, sensors rapidly identify and consistently monitor network devices, delivering in-depth visibility into OT/ICS/IoT risks within minutes of connection. These sensors conduct on-site data collection, analysis, and alerting, making them well suited for locations with limited bandwidth or high latency.

Defenders for IoT sensors employ passive, agentless network monitoring to meticulously uncover a comprehensive inventory of your networks' IoT/OT assets. Through this process, the sensors analyze a diverse range of known and proprietary industrial protocols, allowing for a thorough understanding of your IoT/OT network topology and communication paths.

To safeguard your network, the Defender for IoT sensor seamlessly connects to switch SPAN (Mirror) ports and network TAPs, initiating instant collection of network traffic via passive (agentless) monitoring. Deep Packet Inspection (DPI) is then employed to dissect traffic exchanged between serial and Ethernet-based control network equipment. Configuration options enable secure, vendor-approved commands to gather detailed device information as needed, ensuring a robust defense mechanism.

The integration of Microsoft Threat Intelligence updates enhances the protective capabilities of Defender for IoT. Leveraging data collected from tens of thousands of signals daily across Microsoft's ecosystem, including Endpoint, Cloud, Microsoft Entra ID, and Microsoft 365, alongside IoT and OT intelligence from Section 52, the threat intelligence packages provide valuable signatures, malware signatures, CVEs, and indicators of other malicious activities.

Integrating with Microsoft's ecosystem offers substantial benefits to your business. By combining Microsoft Sentinel with Defender for IoT alert detections, you gain a comprehensive view of IT/OT boundaries. Automation of the response process is facilitated by utilizing IoT/OT playbooks. Additionally, integration with Microsoft Defender for Endpoint extends detection and response capabilities, forming an extended detection and response (XDR) framework to prevent attacks proactively.

Setting up OT/ICS Security consists of three stage processes: setting up a sensor, configuring a SPAN port or TAP, and finally registering the sensor with Microsoft Defender for IoT.

Stage 1: Configure Setup a sensor (as shown in Figure 4-8).

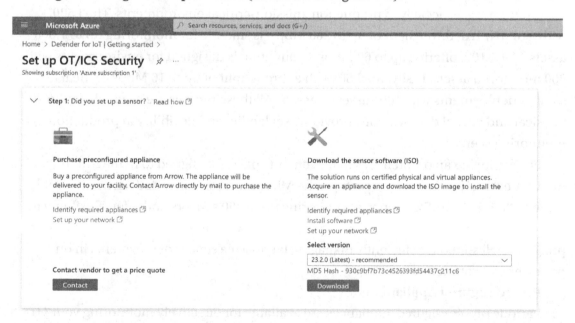

Figure 4-8. *Microsoft Azure – Defender for IOT – Set up OT/ICS Security Stage 1*

Either you can use preconfigured appliance or virtual appliance.

Which Appliances Are Required?

You can choose between physical or virtual appliances to assist you in selecting the optimal appliances for your system and determining the hardware profile that best aligns with your organization's network monitoring requirements. Alternatively, you can refer to the provided specifications to procure hardware that suits your needs independently.

In high-bandwidth corporate IT/OT mixed networks, the Microsoft-recommended hardware profile is the C5600, offering a SPAN/TAP throughput of up to 3 Gbps. This versatile profile can monitor a maximum of 12,000 assets and supports physical and virtual deployments. It is ideal for comprehensive monitoring in mixed IT and OT environments, ensuring efficient network oversight.

Three Microsoft-recommended hardware profiles are recommended for enterprise monitoring at the site level, mainly when collecting multiple traffic feeds. The E1800, E1000, and E500 provide SPAN/TAP throughputs of up to 1 Gbps. Each of these profiles supports monitoring up to 10,000 assets and is adaptable for physical and virtual deployment scenarios. These options cater to the diverse monitoring needs of enterprises operating at the site level, facilitating practical traffic analysis.

Three Microsoft-recommended hardware profiles are suggested in production line monitoring, especially in production/mission-critical environments. The L500, with a SPAN/TAP throughput of up to 200 Mbps, is suitable for monitoring up to 1,000 assets. The L100, offering up to 60 Mbps throughput, is designed for environments with 800 monitored assets. Lastly, the L60, with a throughput of up to 10 Mbps, is ideal for smaller deployments with 100 surveyed assets. All these profiles are available for both physical and virtual deployments, providing scalability and flexibility in production line monitoring scenarios.

For deploying an on-premises management console designed to manage and monitor extensive, multi-sensor setups, the Microsoft-recommended hardware profile is the E1800. This profile supports monitoring up to 300 sensors and offers flexibility in deployment options, allowing for both physical and virtual setups. The E1800 hardware profile is well suited for efficiently managing large-scale sensor deployments in on-premises environments.

Pre-configured Appliances

Various pre-configured appliances are available for effectively monitoring your OT networks, providing options tailored to different network requirements. The C5600, featuring the HPE ProLiant DL360, boasts a maximum bandwidth of up to 3 Gbps, accommodating 12,000 devices. Its physical specifications include a 1U mounting configuration and ports offering flexibility with 15x RJ45 or 8x SFP (OPT). The E1800, utilizing the HPE ProLiant DL20 Gen10 Plus and the Dell PowerEdge R350, supports a maximum bandwidth of up to 1 Gbps and can monitor up to 10,000 devices. This 1U-mounted appliance features ports with 8x RJ45 or 6x SFP (OPT), providing versatility for various network setups. The E500, represented by the Dell Edge 5200 (Rugged MIL-STD-810G), offers a maximum bandwidth of up to 1 Gbps, supporting 10,000 devices.

Designed for rugged environments, this wall-mounted appliance features 8C[8T] CPU/32 GB RAM/512 GB and 3x RJ45 ports. The L500, employing the HPE ProLiant DL20 Gen10 Plus (NHP 2LFF), accommodates a maximum bandwidth of up to 200 Mbps, monitoring up to 1,000 devices. Its 1U mounting configuration and 4x RJ45 ports suit specific deployment scenarios. The L100, utilizing the YS-Techsystems YS-FIT2 (Rugged MIL-STD-810G), supports a maximum bandwidth of up to 10 Mbps, monitoring up to 100 devices. This appliance is ideal for diverse network environments, featuring DIN/VESA mounting and 2x RJ45 ports.

Pre-configured appliances are available for on-premises management consoles in OT settings to streamline the monitoring process. The E1800, incorporating the HPE ProLiant DL20 Gen10 Plus and the Dell PowerEdge R350, supports a maximum of 300 sensors. This 1U-mounted appliance offers ports with 8x RJ45 or 6x SFP (OPT), providing an efficient solution for managing many sensors in an on-premises environment. These pre-configured appliances offer a convenient and reliable option for organizations seeking efficient solutions for network monitoring in both operational technology and on-premises management scenarios.

Virtual Appliances

If you opt to deploy Microsoft Defender for IoT software on your virtual appliances, it's crucial to consider the underlying hypervisor infrastructure. The virtualized hardware responsible for running guest operating systems is provided by hypervisors, also known as virtual machine hosts. Defender for IoT is compatible with several hypervisor software options, including VMware ESXi (version 5.0 and later) and Microsoft Hyper-V (VM configuration version 8.0 and later).

When designing virtual appliances, specific considerations must be considered, especially for both OT sensors and on-premises monitoring consoles.

Microsoft recommends assigning dedicated cores to the CPU with a minimum speed of 2.4 GHz, without dynamic allocation. Given the continuous network traffic recording and analysis, CPU performance is critical to prevent packet drops and degradation.

Static allocation is advised for memory (RAM), considering the high RAM utilization due to constant network traffic recording and analytics.

Regarding network interfaces, Microsoft recommends physical mapping for optimal performance, lowest latency, and efficient CPU usage. Microsoft suggests mapping NICs to virtual machines using SR-IOV or a dedicated NIC. Due to high traffic monitoring levels, expect elevated network utilization. Setting the promiscuous mode on your vSwitch to Accept is also advised to ensure all traffic reaches the virtual machine.

Storage considerations involve allocating sufficient read and write IOPS and throughput to match the performance of the specified appliances. High storage usage is expected due to large volumes of traffic monitoring. Virtual machines' bandwidth results may vary based on protocol distribution and available hardware resources, including CPU model, memory bandwidth, and IOPS.

Specific hardware profiles are outlined with corresponding performance and monitoring specifications for OT network sensor VM requirements. The C5600, E1800, E1000, E500, L500, L100, and L60 profiles are detailed, each with maximum bandwidth, monitored assets capacity, vCPU, memory, and storage specifications.

Additionally, if you intend to deploy an on-premises management console on a virtual appliance for enterprise deployments, the E1800 hardware profile is recommended by Microsoft. This profile features eight vCPUs, 32 GB of memory, and 1.8 TB of storage and supports monitoring up to 300 sensors. These requirements ensure efficient and robust performance for managing a considerable number of sensors in an on-premises environment.

Stage 2: Configure a SPAN port or TAP, as depicted in Figure 4-9.

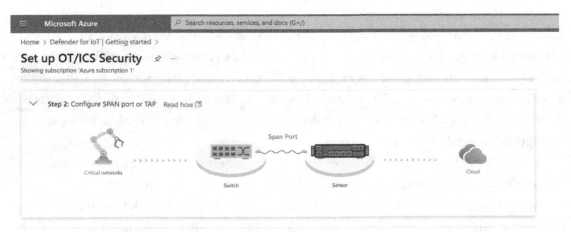

Figure 4-9. *Microsoft Azure – Defender for IOT – Set up OT/ICS Security Stage 2*

Sample CLI SPAN Port Configuration (Cisco 2960)

To configure a SPAN port on a Cisco 2960 via the command-line interface (CLI), follow these sample commands:

```
Cisco2960# configure terminal
Cisco2960(config)# monitor session 1 source interface fastehernet
0/2 - 23 rx
Cisco2960(config)# monitor session 1 destination interface
fastethernet 0/24
Cisco2960(config)# end
Cisco2960# show monitor 1
Cisco2960# running-copy startup-config
```

Sample GUI SPAN Port Configuration (Cisco 2960)

For configuring a SPAN port on a Cisco 2960 using the graphical user interface (GUI), follow these steps:

Step 1: Enter global configuration mode.

Step 2: Configure the first 23 ports as a session source, mirroring only RX packets.

Step 3: Configure port 24 to be a session destination.

Step 4: Return to privileged EXEC mode.

Step 5: Verify the port mirroring configuration.

Step 6: Save the configuration.

Sample CLI SPAN Port Configuration with Multiple VLANs (Cisco 2960)

Defender for IoT can monitor multiple VLANs in your network without additional configuration, provided the network switch is set to send VLAN tags to Defender for IoT. For example, use the following commands on a Cisco switch to support monitoring VLANs:

```
Monitor session:
monitor session 1 source interface Gi1/2
monitor session 1 filter packet type good Rx
monitor session 1 destination interface fastEthernet1/1 encapsulation dot1q

Monitor Trunk Port F.E. Gi1/1:
interface GigabitEthernet1/1
switchport trunk encapsulation dot1q
switchport mode trunk
```

TAP

Whether utilizing active or passive aggregation to mirror traffic, an aggregation Terminal Access Point (TAP) is strategically inserted in line with the network cable. This active or passive TAP duplicates both Receive and Transmit traffic, enabling effective monitoring with Defender for IoT.

A TAP is a hardware device designed to facilitate the seamless flow of network traffic between ports without causing any interruption. Functioning as a conduit, the TAP ensures the continuous creation of an exact copy of both sides of the traffic flow. Importantly, this duplication process occurs consistently, maintaining the integrity of the network without compromise.

Verified TAP Models

Defender for IoT has been tested and found to be compatible with several TAP models. While compatibility with other vendors and models is possible, the following TAP models have undergone testing:

Garland P1GCCAS

When employing a Garland TAP, it is essential to configure your network to support aggregation.

IXIA TPA2-CU3

For users employing an Ixia TAP, ensure that the aggregation mode is activated.

US Robotics USR 4503

When using a US Robotics TAP, activate the aggregation mode by adjusting the selectable switch to AGG.

These TAP models have been specifically tested for compatibility with Defender for IoT, providing users with reliable options for network monitoring. However, it's important to note that compatibility with other TAP models from different vendors may also exist, and users are encouraged to verify compatibility based on specific requirements.

Firewall requirements are listed in Table 4-1.

Table 4-1. *Firewall requirements*

Connection Type	Port Number
Collector and OPM Console Interface: SSL Connection	TCP 443
SSH for Troubleshooting	TCP 22
NTP Server Connection (Collector/OPM to NTP Server)	NTP UDP 123
Mail Server Connection (Collector/OPM to Mail Server)	SMTP 25 (if relevant)
DNS Connection (Collector/OPM to DNS)	53 (if relevant)
Centralized Logging System Connection (Collector/OPM)	Your Defined Port
Active Directory Connection (Collector/OPM to AD)	Your Defined LDAP/S Port (e.g., TCP 389)
SNMP/MIB Keep-Alive Monitoring (Prerequisite: Open port in FW)	UDP 161
Windows Endpoint Monitoring (WMI) (Prerequisite: Firewall rule for outgoing traffic)	UDP 135, TCP >1024

Stage 3: Register this sensor with Microsoft Defender for IOT.

In step 3 of registering your sensor with Microsoft Defender for IoT, you will need to input or select specific values for your sensor:

1. In the "Sensor name" field, provide a meaningful name for your OT sensor. Microsoft recommends including the OT sensor's IP address in the name for easy identification. Keeping track of this registration name in the Azure portal alongside the IP address displayed in the OT sensor console is crucial.

2. In the "Subscription" field, choose your Azure subscription. If you do not have a subscription yet, opt for the "Onboard subscription" to add an OT plan to your Azure subscription.

3. Optionally, enable the "Cloud connected" option to view detected data, manage your sensor from the Azure portal, and connect your data to other Microsoft services like Microsoft Sentinel.

4. Optionally, turn on the "Automatic Threat Intelligence updates" to allow Defender for IoT to push threat intelligence packages to your OT sensor automatically.

5. In the "Site" section, provide the following details:

    a. Resource Name: Select the site to attach your sensors or create a new site by choosing "Create site."

        If creating a new site:

        i. In the "New site" field, enter your site's name and select the check mark button.

        ii. From the "Site size" menu, pick your site's size based on your licenses from the Microsoft 365 admin center. (Note: The "Site size" field isn't included for legacy OT plans.)

    b. Display Name: Enter a meaningful name for your site to be displayed across Defender for IoT.

    c. Tags: Enter tag key and values to aid in identifying and locating your site and sensor in the Azure portal.

    d. Zone: Select the zone for your OT sensor or create a new one by choosing "Create zone."

6. Once all fields are completed, select "Register." A success message will appear, and your activation file will be automatically downloaded.

7. Select "Finish." Your sensor will now be visible under the selected site on the Defender for IoT Sites and Sensors page as depicted in Figure 4-10.

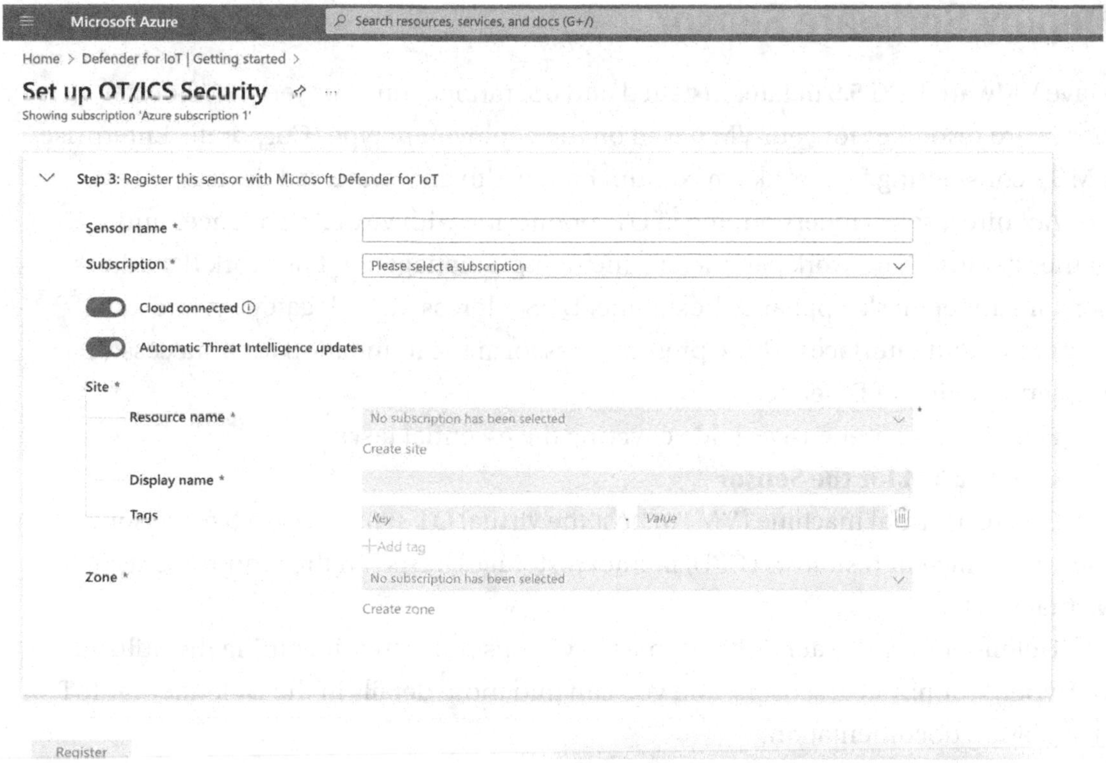

Figure 4-10. *Microsoft Azure – Defender for IOT – Set up OT/ICS Security Stage 3*

Until activation, the sensor's status will be "Pending Activation." Ensure the downloaded activation file is accessible to the sensor console admin for activation. The root of trust signs all files downloaded from the Azure portal to ensure your machines use signed assets exclusively.

Task 3: Configure OT/ICS Security

Onboarding and activating a virtual operational technology (OT) sensor in Microsoft Defender for IoT involves several crucial steps to ensure seamless integration and effective security monitoring.

Before commencing the setup process, ensure that you meet the necessary prerequisites. Firstly, have a completed Quickstart to integrate your Azure subscription with Defender for IoT. Access the Azure portal with roles like Security Admin, Contributor, or Owner, as specified in the Azure user roles documentation for OT and enterprise IoT monitoring. Confirm possession of a network switch supporting traffic monitoring through a SPAN port, and ensure at least one device is connected to the switch's SPAN port for monitoring purposes.

233

Deploy Software Sensor

Have VMware ESXi 5.5 or later installed and operational on your sensor. Allocate hardware resources for your VM based on the deployment type (Corporate, Enterprise, SMB), considering factors like maximum bandwidth and protected devices.

Acquire a solid understanding of OT monitoring with virtual appliances and gather details for network parameters, including a management network IP address, sensor subnet mask, appliance hostname, DNS address, default gateway, and any required input interfaces. These prerequisites form the foundation for a successful implementation of Defender for IoT.

Here is a comprehensive guide covering the essential tasks.

Create a VM for the Sensor

Create a virtual machine (VM) to host the virtual OT sensor. Use a hypervisor and allocate sufficient resources (CPU, memory, storage) based on the requirements of the virtual sensor.

Defender for IoT extends its support to various processes, including the utilization of Hyper-V or physical sensors, and you can find more details in the Defender for IoT installation documentation.

To set up a VM for your sensor:

1. Ensure VMware is operational on your machine.

2. Log in to ESXi, choose the relevant datastore, and access Datastore Browser.

3. Upload the image and close the window.

4. Navigate to Virtual Machines, then choose Create/Register VM.

5. Opt for creating a new virtual machine and proceed to the next step.

6. Assign a sensor name and specify the options as follows: Compatibility – the latest ESXi version, Guest OS family – Linux, Guest OS version – Ubuntu Linux (64-bit).

7. Click Next.

8. Select the relevant data store and proceed to the next step.
    Adjust virtual hardware parameters based on your requirements,
    referencing the specifications in the Prerequisites section. Your
    VM is now set up to install Defender for IoT software.

The subsequent steps involve installing the software, which will be covered later in
this tutorial, following the onboarding of your sensor in the Azure portal, configuring
traffic mirroring, and provisioning the machine for cloud management.

Onboard a Virtual Sensor

Once the VM is set up, initiate the onboarding process for the virtual OT sensor
in Microsoft Defender for IoT. Access the Defender for the IoT console and follow the
onboarding wizard. Provide details such as sensor name, description, and the VM's
network configuration.

To initiate the onboarding process for the virtual sensor, navigate to the Azure portal
and access the Defender for IoT ➤ Getting Started page. At the lower-left corner, choose
Set up OT/ICS Security. Alternatively, from the Defender for IoT Sites and Sensors page,
opt for Onboard OT sensor ➤ OT. By default, on the Set up OT/ICS Security page, the
first two steps of the wizard are as follows:

Step 1: Did you set up a sensor?

Step 2: Configure the SPAN port or TAP, which is collapsed. While software
installation and traffic mirroring configuration occur later in the deployment process,
having your appliances ready and your traffic mirroring method planned is essential.

Step 3: Register this sensor with Microsoft Defender for IoT; provide the following
values: resource name, where you select the site to attach your sensors or create a new
site; display name, for a meaningful site name across Defender for IoT; tags, allowing you
to enter key and values for site and sensor identification in the Azure portal; and zone,
where you select an existing zone or create a new one. Upon completing all fields, select
Register to add your sensor to Defender for IoT. A success message appears, and your
unique activation file is automatically downloaded. This file contains instructions for
your sensor's management mode and is signed by the root of trust for secure use.

Save the downloaded activation file in a location accessible to the user signing
into the console for the first time. This file is crucial for activating the sensor. You can
manually download the file by selecting the relevant link in the Activate your Sensor
box. In the Add outbound allow rules box, choose the Download endpoint details link

to acquire a JSON list of endpoints that must be configured as secure from your sensor. Save the downloaded file locally, and use the listed endpoints in later steps to ensure a successful connection to Azure.

Remember that the list of required endpoints can also be accessed from the Sites and Sensors page. After completing these steps, select Finish at the bottom left of the page. Your new sensor is now visible on the Defender for IoT Sites and Sensors page, with the status "Pending Activation" until the activation process is completed.

Configure a Virtual SPAN Port

Configure a Virtual Switched Port Analyzer (SPAN) port on the virtual switch connected to the VM to capture network traffic for analysis. This enables the virtual sensor to inspect and analyze network packets effectively.

Virtual switches lack inherent mirroring capabilities, but for this tutorial, you can employ promiscuous mode within a virtual switch environment to observe all network traffic passing through the virtual switch.

This process outlines the configuration of a SPAN port using a workaround with VMware ESXi.

Key Note

Promiscuous mode is an operating and security monitoring technique for a VM's interfaces at the same port group level as the virtual switch, allowing visibility into the switch's network traffic. By default, promiscuous mode is disabled but can be defined at either the virtual switch or port group level.

To set up a monitoring interface with promiscuous mode on an ESXi v-Switch:

1. Open the vSwitch properties page and choose Add a standard virtual switch.

2. Label the network as "SPAN Network" and set the MTU field to 4096.

3. Navigate to the Security section, ensuring the Promiscuous Mode policy is configured to Accept mode.

4. Select Add to finalize the vSwitch properties.

5. Highlight the newly created vSwitch and add an uplink.

6. Choose the physical NIC designated for the SPAN traffic, adjust the MTU to 4096, and save your settings.

7. Open the Port Group properties page and opt to Add a Port Group.

8. Name it "SPAN Port Group," set the VLAN ID to 4095, choose "SPAN Network" in the vSwitch drop-down, and add the port group.

9. Access the properties of the OT Sensor VM.

10. For Network Adapter 2, select the recently configured SPAN network.

11. Confirm the settings and connectivity to the sensor, ensuring that mirroring is functioning as expected.

Provision for Cloud Management

For efficient cloud-based management, provision the virtual sensor for cloud integration. Connect the sensor to Microsoft Defender for IoT cloud services, enabling centralized monitoring, reporting, and management.

Set Up Endpoint Details

Access the previously downloaded file to review the list of necessary endpoints. Adjust your firewall rules accordingly to enable your sensor's access to each required endpoint, using port 443.

Download Software for a Virtual Sensor

Access the Microsoft Defender for IoT portal to download the software package for the virtual OT sensor. Ensure compatibility with the VM's operating system and version.

To procure the software for your virtual sensors, initiate the process by navigating to the Defender for IoT ➤ Getting Started page within the Azure portal. Once there, specifically, select the Sensor tab. Within the "Purchase an appliance and install software" box, confirm that the default option corresponds to the latest and recommended software version. Subsequently, click on the "Download" button. Ensure you save the downloaded software in a location accessible from your virtual machine (VM). Notably, all files obtained through the Azure portal undergo signing by the root of trust. This security measure ensures that your machines exclusively utilize authenticated and signed assets, thereby enhancing the integrity and reliability of the acquired software.

Install the Virtual Sensor Software

Transfer the downloaded software package to the VM and install the virtual sensor software. Follow the installation wizard, providing inputs such as sensor ID, registration key, and connection details to link the virtual sensor with the Defender for IoT platform.

To commence the software installation on the virtual sensor, follow these steps. If your virtual machine (VM) is closed, sign in again to ESXi and access your VM settings. Within the settings, navigate to CD/DVD Drive 1, opt for the Datastore ISO file option, and choose the previously downloaded Defender for IoT software. Proceed by selecting "Next" and then "Finish." Power on the VM and open a console.

As the installation initiates, a prompt will appear, starting the installation process. You can manually select the "Install iot-sensor-<version number>" item to proceed or allow it to commence automatically after a 30-second countdown.

Activate the Virtual Sensor

After installation, activate the virtual sensor by verifying its connection to the Defender for IoT platform. Confirm that the sensor is communicating with the cloud services and receiving updates. This step is crucial for enabling real-time threat detection and response.

To initiate the activation process for your sensor, follow these steps. Navigate to the Activation tab and choose the "Upload" option to upload the activation file obtained from the Azure portal. Afterward, select the terms and conditions and proceed to the next step by selecting "Next: Certificates."

In the Certificates tab, deploy an SSL/TLS certificate on your OT sensor. Using a CA-signed certificate for production environments is advisable to configure SSL/TLS certificate settings.

Following these steps, you can successfully onboard and activate a virtual OT sensor in Microsoft Defender for IoT. This integration enhances the security posture of your OT environment by providing comprehensive monitoring and protection against potential threats. Regularly update the sensor software and monitor its performance to ensure the continued security of your IoT infrastructure.

After installing the OT software on your OT sensors, it is crucial to conduct thorough system tests to ensure proper functionality. The validation process outlined here is applicable to all types of appliances.

System Health Validations

Ensuring the validity of IoT (Internet of Things) deployments through system health validations is critical to maintaining a secure, reliable, and efficient connected environment. IoT systems, characterized by the interconnection of various devices and sensors, are integral components of smart homes, industrial processes, healthcare systems, and more. The importance of validating system health lies in its ability to identify and address potential issues that could compromise these interconnected devices' functionality, security, or overall performance.

First and foremost, system health validations play a pivotal role in identifying vulnerabilities and security gaps within an IoT ecosystem. The interconnected nature of IoT devices creates an expanded attack surface, making them susceptible to various cyber threats. By regularly validating the system's health, organizations can proactively detect anomalies or irregularities that may indicate a security breach. This proactive stance is essential in preventing unauthorized access, data breaches, or compromising sensitive information, which could have severe consequences for individuals and businesses alike.

Secondly, validating IoT system health is crucial for ensuring connected devices' reliability and optimal performance. IoT deployments often involve many devices, ranging from sensors and actuators to communication modules and edge devices. Regular health validations enable organizations to monitor these devices' operational status, firmware versions, and connectivity. This information helps identify potential hardware failures, outdated firmware, or communication issues, allowing for timely maintenance or replacements to prevent system downtimes and disruptions.

Moreover, the validation of IoT system health contributes to compliance with industry regulations and standards. Many sectors, such as healthcare, finance, and manufacturing, have specific regulatory requirements governing the security and privacy of connected devices. Conducting systematic health validations ensures that organizations adhere to these regulations, reducing legal risks and potential liabilities. Compliance with standards not only safeguards sensitive data but also fosters trust among users and stakeholders, enhancing the credibility of the IoT ecosystem.

So the importance of validating IoT system health must be addressed in the current landscape of interconnected devices. Organizations can build robust and resilient IoT ecosystems by proactively identifying security vulnerabilities, ensuring reliable device performance, and meeting regulatory compliance. This approach not only safeguards against potential threats but also enhances the overall trustworthiness and effectiveness of IoT deployments, promoting the widespread adoption of these technologies in various domains

These validations are supported through the user interface (UI) or the command-line interface (CLI) and available to the default privileged Admin user.

General Tests

- Sanity Test

  - Verify that the system is running.

- Version

  - Verify that the installed software version is correct.

- ifconfig

  - Confirm that all input interfaces configured during the installation process are running.

- Gateway Checks

  - Utilize the following commands to perform gateway checks:

Use the **route** command to display the gateway's IP address.

```
<root@apress:/# route -n
Kernel IP routing table
Destination     Gateway         Genmask         Flags Metric Ref    Use Iface
0.0.0.0         172.18.0.1      0.0.0.0         UG    0      0        0 eth0
172.18.0.0      0.0.0.0         255.255.0.0     U     0      0        0 eth0
>
```

Use the **arp -a** command to verify the default gateway's MAC address and IP address binding.

```
<root@apress:/# arp -a
cusalvtecca101-gi0-02-2851.network.microsoft.com (172.18.0.1) at
02:42:b0:3a:e8:b5 [ether] on eth0
mariadb_22.2.6.27-r-c64cbca.iot_network_22.2.6.27-r-c64cbca (172.18.0.5) at
02:42:ac:12:00:05 [ether] on eth0
redis_22.2.6.27-r-c64cbca.iot_network_22.2.6.27-r-c64cbca (172.18.0.3) at
02:42:ac:12:00:03 [ether] on eth0
>
```

DNS Checks

Use the cat /etc/resolv.conf command to find the configured IP address for DNS traffic.

```
<root@apress:/# cat /etc/resolv.conf
search reddog.microsoft.com
nameserver 127.0.0.11
options ndots:0
>
```

Use the host command to resolve an FQDN.

```
<root@apress:/# host www.apress.com
www.apress.com is an alias for www.apress.com.edgekey.net.
www.apress.com.edgekey.net is an alias for www.apress.com.edgekey.net.
globalredir.akadns.net.
www.apress.com.edgekey.net.globalredir.akadns.net is an alias for e6858.
dscx.akamaiedge.net.
e6858.dscx.akamaiedge.net has address 72.246.148.202
e6858.dscx.akamaiedge.net has IPv6 address 2a02:26f0:5700:1b4::1aca
e6858.dscx.akamaiedge.net has IPv6 address 2a02:26f0:5700:182::1aca
>
```

Firewall Checks

Use the wget command to verify that port 443 is open for communication.

```
<root@apress:/# wget https://www.apress.com
--2022-11-09 11:21:15--  https://www.apress.com/
Resolving www.apress.com (www.apress.com)... 72.246.148.202,
2a02:26f0:5700:1b4::1aca, 2a02:26f0:5700:182::1aca
Connecting to www.apress.com (www.apress.com)|72.246.148.202|:443...
connected.
HTTP request sent, awaiting response... 200 OK
Length: 99966 (98K) [text/html]
Saving to: 'index.html.1'

index.html.1     100%[====================>]  97.62K  --.-KB/s    in 0.02s

2022-11-09 11:21:15 (5.88 MB/s) - 'index.html.1' saved [99966/99966]
>
```

Ensure that these tests are conducted thoroughly to maintain the optimal performance and health of the system. As the next phase, let's delve into configuring the initial setup settings and initiating the activation process for your OT sensor.

Set Up and Initiate the Activation of Your OT Sensor

Various preliminary setup procedures can be executed through the browser or the command-line interface (CLI).

Opting for the browser approach when connecting physical cables from your switch to the sensor is feasible, allowing for the accurate identification of interfaces. Ensure that you readjust your network adapter to align with the default settings on the sensor.

Alternatively, employ the CLI if you possess networking details without physically connecting cables. Choose the CLI route if your only means of connecting to the sensor is through iLO/iDRAC.

It's important to note that even when configuring your setup via the CLI, the final steps must still be completed using the browser interface.

Configure the Setup Through the Browser

Following these steps helps to configure and activate your OT sensor via the browser.

Sign-In and Password Change

Access the OT sensor console for the first time using a web browser by navigating to the default IP address (e.g., 192.168.0.101) provided during installation.

Enter the default credentials (Username: admin, Password: admin) and change the Admin user password as prompted.

Define Network Details

In the Management interface tab, specify the following network details for your sensor:

- Management Interface: Select the desired interface for management purposes.

- IP Address: Enter the IP address for sensor access.

- Subnet Mask: Specify the sensor's subnet mask.

- Default Gateway: Set the default gateway address.

- DNS: Enter the DNS server IP address.

- Hostname: Assign a hostname to the sensor.

- Enable proxy for cloud connectivity (optional): Define a proxy server if needed

Define Monitored Interfaces

In the Interface configurations tab, configure settings for monitored interfaces:

- Enable/Disable Toggle: Select interfaces to be monitored.

- Advanced Settings: Optionally modify each interface's mode, description, and auto-negotiation settings.

- Save changes.

Reboot the Sensor

Proceed to the next step by selecting "Next: Reboot" and initiate a reboot. After rebooting, you'll be redirected to the specified sensor IP address.

Activate the Sensor

- In the Activation tab, upload the sensor's activation file downloaded from the Azure portal.

- Select terms and conditions, then proceed to the "Next: Certificates" step.

SSL/TLS Certificate Settings

In the Certificates tab, deploy an SSL/TLS certificate on your OT sensor:

Import trusted CA certificate (recommended): Deploy a CA-signed certificate.

Enter certificate details and upload private key, certificate, and optional certificate chain files.

Complete Setup

Select "Finish" to finalize the setup and access your sensor console.

Note: If initial settings were configured via CLI, this browser-based configuration resumes after the sensor reboots, directing you to the Defender for IoT ➤ Overview page and the Activation tab.

Configure the Initial Setup Settings via CLI

Following these steps helps to configure and activate your OT sensor via CLI.

On the installation screen, press Enter after the default networking details are displayed.

1. At the D4Iot login prompt, sign in using the default credentials:

    i. Username: admin

    ii. Password: admin (entered characters are not displayed)

2. When prompted, please enter a new password for the Admin user, ensuring it meets specified requirements.

3. The Package configuration Linux configuration wizard opens. Navigate using arrows, select options with the SPACE bar, and press Enter to proceed.

4. Choose the interfaces you want to monitor in the wizard's "Select monitor interfaces" screen. Ensure selected interfaces are connected to avoid health notifications.

5. In the "Select management interface" screen, select the Azure portal or on-premises management console connectivity interface.

6. Enter the desired IP address, subnet mask, default gateway, DNS server IP address, and hostname for the sensor.

7. Optionally, configure the sensor as a proxy server by selecting "Yes" in the "Run this sensor as a proxy server (Preview)" screen and providing proxy credentials if prompted.

8. The configuration process initiates, the sensor reboots, and a final sign-in prompt appears.

9. Open a browser to the defined sensor IP address to continue the setup.

Configuring Proxy Settings on the OT Sensor for Azure Connection
Defining Proxy Settings on the OT Sensor

a. **Access System Settings**
   Sign in to the OT sensor and navigate to System Settings ➤ Sensor Network Settings.

b. **Enable Proxy and Provide Details**
   Activate the Proxy option and input the necessary details for your proxy server:

   1. Proxy host

   2. Proxy port

   3. Proxy username (optional)

   4. Proxy password (optional)

c. Certificate Option

   Select "Client certificate" to upload an authentication certificate for SSL/TLS proxy server access if required.

d.   Save Configuration

Save the configured proxy settings.

If a proxy is already configured, then proceed to define proxy settings on the sensor console.

Setting Up a New Azure Proxy

You may opt for an Azure proxy to establish a connection between your sensor and Defender for IoT in the following scenarios:

- When you need private connectivity between your sensor and Azure

- When your site is linked to Azure through ExpressRoute

- When your site is connected to Azure over a VPN

Prerequisites

Ensure you have

- A Log Analytics workspace for monitoring logs.

- Remote site connectivity to the Azure VNET.

- Outbound HTTPS traffic on port 443 is allowed from your sensor to the required Defender for IoT endpoints.

Configuring Sensor Proxy Settings

Let's explore the process of setting up proxy configurations on your OT sensor for connecting to Azure. It is a seven-stage process.

Stage 1: Defining a Storage Account for NSG Logs

Azure Storage is a cloud-based storage service provided by Microsoft Azure, offering a comprehensive suite of scalable and highly available storage solutions for various data types and scenarios. It is a foundational component for storing and managing data in the Azure cloud environment. Azure Storage provides a versatile range of storage services designed to cater to specific storage needs.

Here are key components and services within Azure Storage:

- Blob Storage: Azure Blob Storage is designed for storing massive amounts of unstructured data, such as documents, images, videos, and log files. It is highly scalable and supports different access tiers based on data access frequency.

- File Storage: Azure File Storage offers fully managed file shares in the cloud, allowing organizations to create a distributed file system accessible through the Server Message Block (SMB) protocol. It is suitable for applications that require shared file access.

- Table Storage: Azure Table Storage is a NoSQL data store suitable for semi-structured data. It provides a key/attribute store with a schema-less design, making it a flexible option for applications that require scalable and low-latency storage.

- Queue Storage: Azure Queue Storage enables the building of scalable and decoupled applications by providing a messaging queue for asynchronous communication between components. It helps create loosely coupled systems that can handle bursts of incoming requests.

- Disk Storage: Azure Disk Storage provides scalable and high-performance block storage for Azure Virtual Machines. It offers managed disks that simplify the management of storage associated with virtual machines, ensuring durability and availability.

Key features and characteristics of Azure Storage include the following:

- Scalability: Azure Storage is designed to scale dynamically based on demand, allowing organizations to store and manage vast amounts of data efficiently.

- Durability and Redundancy: Data in Azure Storage is replicated to ensure durability and high availability. Redundancy options include locally redundant storage (LRS), geo-redundant storage (GRS), and zone-redundant storage (ZRS).

- Security: Azure Storage provides robust security features, including encryption at rest, role-based access control (RBAC), and shared access signatures (SAS) for fine-grained access control.

- Integration with Azure Services: Azure Storage integrates with various Azure services, allowing organizations to leverage data for analytics, machine learning, and other scenarios.

- Global Reach: Azure Storage has a global presence with data centers worldwide, enabling organizations to deploy applications and store data close to their end users for reduced latency.

Overall, Azure Storage is a flexible and reliable solution for organizations looking to store, manage, and access data in the cloud, supporting various use cases across different industries and application scenarios.

Azure Storage is a cloud-based storage service provided by Microsoft Azure, offering scalable, secure, and highly available storage solutions for various data types, including blobs, files, tables, and queues. To ensure the security of data stored in Azure Storage, Network Security Groups (NSGs) play a crucial role in implementing network security controls.

Network Security Groups in Azure act as virtual firewalls, allowing or denying inbound and outbound traffic to resources within an Azure virtual network. When protecting Azure Storage using NSGs, the focus is primarily on securing access to storage accounts and associated services.

One fundamental approach is to control network traffic to and from Azure Storage accounts. NSGs enable rules that regulate incoming and outgoing traffic based on source and destination IP addresses, port ranges, and protocols. Administrators can implement fine-grained controls over network communication by associating NSGs with subnets or individual resources.

For Azure Storage, the following key considerations can be addressed using NSGs:

- Restricting Access to Storage Accounts: NSGs can be configured to allow only specific IP ranges or applications to access Azure Storage accounts. This restriction is crucial in preventing unauthorized access and potential data breaches.

- Securing Communication Protocols: NSGs help in specifying rules for allowed communication protocols. For instance, administrators can limit access to secure communication protocols such as HTTPS, ensuring encrypted data in transit.

- Isolating Storage Resources: NSGs allow for separating storage resources within a virtual network. By associating NSGs with the relevant subnets or resources, organizations can segment their network to enhance security and compliance.

- Whitelisting Trusted Sources: By defining rules that allow trusted IP addresses or ranges, organizations can ensure that only authorized entities can access or modify data within Azure Storage.

- Logging and Monitoring: NSGs provide logging capabilities, allowing administrators to monitor and audit network traffic to and from Azure Storage. This facilitates the detection of suspicious activities and helps maintain a secure storage environment.

Implementing NSGs for Azure Storage involves creating and configuring the NSG rules based on the organization's specific security requirements. Regularly reviewing and updating NSG configurations is essential to adapt to evolving security needs and maintain a robust defense against potential threats to Azure Storage resources.

Create a new storage account in the Azure portal with specified settings.

In the Azure portal, initiate the creation of a new storage account with the following specifications:

Basics

- Performance: Standard

- Account Kind: Blob Storage

- Replication: LRS

Network:

- Connectivity Method: Public endpoint (selected network)

- In Virtual Networks: None

- Routing Preference: Microsoft network routing

Data Protection

- Keep all options cleared.

Advanced

- Keep all default values.

Stage 2: Defining Virtual Networks and Subnets

Create the following Virtual Network (VNet) and its corresponding subnets:

- Name: MD4IoT-VNET

- Recommended Size: /26 or /25 with Bastion

- Subnets

  - GatewaySubnet: /27

  - ProxyserverSubnet: /27

  - AzureBastionSubnet (optional): /26

Stage 3: Defining a Virtual or Local Network Gateway

A Virtual Network Gateway (often referred to as a Network Gateway) in Azure is a networking component that provides a way to connect your on-premises network to an Azure virtual network. It acts as a bridge between the on-premises infrastructure and Azure, facilitating secure and encrypted communication over the Internet.

Key features and aspects of Virtual Network Gateway include the following:

- VPN Gateway: One of the primary functions of the Virtual Network Gateway is to enable the establishment of Virtual Private Network (VPN) connections. It supports both Site-to-Site VPNs and Point-to-Site VPNs.

- Site-to-Site VPN: Connects on-premises networks to Azure virtual networks, extending your corporate network to the cloud. This is typically done using an Internet connection.

- Point-to-Site VPN: Allows individual computers to connect to an Azure virtual network over the Internet. This is useful for remote users or devices.

- ExpressRoute Gateway: Besides VPN connectivity, Virtual Network Gateway supports connections via Azure ExpressRoute. ExpressRoute provides a dedicated, private connection from on-premises to Azure, offering higher bandwidth and lower latencies than typical Internet-based connections.

- Local Network Gateway: The Local Network Gateway is a related concept that represents the on-premises VPN device or the public IP address of the on-premises VPN gateway. It defines the necessary information for the Azure VPN Gateway to connect to the on-premises network.

  - IP Address: Specifies the public IP address of the on-premises VPN device

- Address Space: Defines the on-premises address space (local
  network ranges)

- BGP (Border Gateway Protocol) Settings: Optional BGP settings
  for dynamic routing if BGP is used

By configuring a Virtual Network Gateway and associating it with a Virtual Network and a Local Network Gateway, you can establish secure and reliable connections between your on-premises infrastructure and Azure. This connectivity is crucial for scenarios where you must extend your data center to the cloud or enable secure communication between on-premises and cloud-based resources.

Establish a VPN or ExpressRoute Gateway for virtual gateways, or configure a local gateway based on how your on-premises network connects to Azure. Attach the gateway to the previously created GatewaySubnet subnet.

Stage 4: Defining Network Security Groups (NSG)

Azure Network Security Groups (NSG) are a fundamental element of Azure's network security features. NSGs act as virtual firewalls, enabling you to control inbound and outbound traffic to and from Azure resources. They provide a way to implement network security policies based on rules that allow or deny traffic based on various attributes such as source and destination IP addresses, port numbers, and protocols.

Key features and aspects of Azure Network Security Groups include the following:

- Rule-Based Access Control: NSGs operate on a rule basis, where
  each rule defines a set of conditions for allowing or denying traffic.
  Rules are defined based on source and destination IP addresses, port
  ranges, and protocols.

- Inbound and Outbound Rules: NSGs allow you to define both
  inbound and outbound rules. Inbound rules control traffic coming
  into Azure resources, while outbound rules control traffic leaving
  Azure resources.

- Priority and Order: Rules are assigned a priority, and the order of
  rules matters. Traffic is evaluated against the rules in order, and the
  first rule that matches the traffic is applied. Lower numeric values
  indicate higher priority.

- Default Rules: NSGs have default rules that allow all outbound traffic but deny all inbound traffic unless explicitly allowed by a rule. These default rules help to secure resources by default and require explicit configuration for inbound access.

- Association with Subnets or Network Interfaces: NSGs can be associated with subnets, individual network interfaces, or both. When associated with a subnet, the NSG rules apply to all resources within that subnet.

- Stateful Filtering: NSGs are stateful, meaning that if you allow inbound traffic for a specific connection, the corresponding outbound traffic for that connection is automatically allowed. This simplifies rule configuration.

- Logging: NSGs support logging, allowing you to capture information about allowed and denied traffic. These logs can be helpful for monitoring and troubleshooting network security issues.

By using Azure Network Security Groups, you can implement a layered security approach to protect your Azure resources and control communication between different components of your applications deployed in the Azure cloud.

Create an NSG and define the following inbound rules:

- Create rule 100 to allow traffic from sensors (sources) to the private IP address of the load balancer (destination) using port tcp3128.

- Duplicate rule 4095 from the 65001 system rule, as rule 65001 will be overwritten by rule 4096.

- Establish rule 4096 to deny all traffic for micro-segmentation.

- Optionally, for Bastion users, create rule 4094 to permit Bastion SSH to servers, with the Bastion subnet as the source.

Assign the NSG to the ProxyserverSubnet created earlier.
Configure NSG logging:

a. Select the new NSG.

b. Choose Diagnostic setting ➤ Add diagnostic setting.

   c. Provide a name for the diagnostic setting; select the category as allLogs.

   d. Opt for Sent to Log Analytics workspace; then choose your Log Analytics workspace.

   e. Choose to send NSG flow logs and define the required values.

Basics tab:

- Enter a meaningful name.

- Select the previously created storage account.

- Define the required retention days.

Configuration tab:

- Select Version 2.

- Enable Traffic Analytics.

- Select your Log Analytics workspace.

Stage 5: Defining an Azure Virtual Machine Scale Set

Azure Virtual Machine Scale Sets (VMSS) are a service in Microsoft Azure that enables you to deploy and manage a group of identical, load-balanced virtual machines. They are designed to provide high availability to your applications and allow for automatic scaling based on demand.

Key features of Azure Virtual Machine Scale Sets include the following:

- Scalability: VMSS allows you to quickly scale the number of virtual machines in the set based on changing demand. You can manually adjust the number of VM instances or set up auto-scaling rules to dynamically adjust the capacity based on metrics like CPU usage or network traffic.

- Load Balancing: VMSS includes built-in load balancing to distribute incoming network traffic across all instances in the set. This ensures that each virtual machine receives a balanced share of the workload.

- High Availability: VMSS is designed for high availability by distributing virtual machines across multiple fault domains and update domains. This minimizes the risk of application downtime during planned or unplanned maintenance events.

- Automatic OS Image Updates: VMSS can automatically update the operating system images for all instances in the set. This feature simplifies keeping virtual machines up to date with the latest security patches and updates.

- Custom VM Images: You can use custom VM images to create a VMSS. This allows you to configure a virtual machine with your desired software and configurations, capture it as a custom image, and then use that image to deploy multiple identical instances.

- Integrated with Azure Services: VMSS integrates with other Azure services, such as Azure Virtual Network, Azure Load Balancer, and Azure Auto Scaling. This integration helps you build comprehensive and scalable solutions.

- Flexible Update Policies: VMSS provides flexibility in updating virtual machines. You can define update policies to control how many virtual machines are updated at a time, set maintenance windows, and specify parameters for automatic updates.

- Monitoring and Diagnostics: Azure Monitor and Azure Diagnostics can be used to monitor the performance of virtual machines in the scale set. You can collect and analyze metrics, logs, and traces to gain insights into the behavior of your application.

Azure Virtual Machine Scale Sets are particularly useful for applications that require rapid scaling to handle varying workloads, such as web applications, API services, and microservices architectures. They simplify the deployment and management of many identical virtual machines, providing a cost-effective and efficient solution for scalable and resilient applications.

Define an Azure Virtual Machine Scale Set to manage a group of load-balanced virtual machines. Adjust the number of virtual machines based on your needs.

- To create a scale set for your sensor connection:

  - Create a scale set with the following parameter definitions:

  - Orchestration Mode: Uniform

  - Security Type: Standard

  - Image: Ubuntu server 18.04 LTS – Gen1

- Size: Standard_DS1_V2

- Authentication: Based on your corporate standard

- Keep the default value for Disks settings.

- Generate a network interface in the ProxyserverSubnet without defining a load balancer.

- Specify scaling settings as follows:

  - Define the initial instance count as 1.

  - Set the scaling policy to Manual.

  - Configure management settings, such as the upgrade mode, boot diagnostics, identity, overprovisioning, and automatic OS upgrades.

- Define health settings:

  - Enable application health monitoring.

  - Specify the TCP protocol and port 3128.

  - Under advanced settings, define the spreading algorithm as Max Spreading.

- For the custom data script, create a configuration script depending on the port and services in use.

```
# Recommended minimum configuration:
# Squid listening port
http_port 3128
# Do not allow caching
cache deny all
# Allowlist sites allowed
acl allowed_http_sites dstdomain .azure-devices.net
acl allowed_http_sites dstdomain .blob.core.windows.net
acl allowed_http_sites dstdomain .servicebus.windows.net
acl allowed_http_sites dstdomain .download.microsoft.com
http_access allow allowed_http_sites
# Allowlisting
```

```
acl SSL_ports port 443
acl CONNECT method CONNECT
# Deny CONNECT to other unsecured ports
http_access deny CONNECT !SSL_ports
# Default network rules
http_access allow localhost
http_access deny all
```

- Encode the contents of your script file in base-64.

  - Copy the encoded file contents and create the configuration script.

    ```
    #cloud-config
    # Updates packages
    apt_upgrade: true
    # Install squid packages
    packages:
     - squid
    run cmd:
     - systemctl stop squid
     - mv /etc/squid/squid.conf /etc/squid/squid.conf.factory
    write_files:
    - encoding: b64
      content: <replace with base64 encoded text>
      path: /etc/squid/squid.conf
      permissions: '0644'
    run cmd:
     - systemctl start squid
     - apt-get -y upgrade; [ -e /var/run/reboot-required ]
    && reboot
    ```

Stage 6: Creating an Azure Load Balancer

Azure Load Balancer is a Layer 4 (TCP, UDP) load balancer that distributes incoming network traffic across multiple servers to ensure no single server is overwhelmed with too much traffic. It plays a crucial role in optimizing the availability and reliability of applications by distributing incoming requests or network traffic among multiple servers. This distribution ensures that no single server bears the entire load, thereby improving applications' fault tolerance and performance.

Key features of Azure Load Balancer include the following:

- Load Balancing Algorithms: Azure Load Balancer uses a hash-based distribution algorithm to distribute incoming traffic across backend servers. It supports a variety of algorithms, such as round-robin and hash-based distribution, to ensure efficient load balancing.

- Health Probes: Azure Load Balancer regularly checks the health of backend servers by sending health probes. If a server is deemed unhealthy, the load balancer stops sending traffic to that server until it recovers.

- Public and Private Load Balancing: A load balancer can be configured to distribute traffic for both public and private IP addresses. It allows for scenarios where public-facing applications and internal applications have different load-balancing requirements.

- Backend Pool Configuration: Backend pools consist of the virtual machines or instances that will receive the traffic. Azure Load Balancer allows the configuration of backend pools to include multiple VMs for redundancy and scalability.

- Session Persistence: While Azure Load Balancer is primarily a Layer 4 load balancer, it can be used with application gateways for Layer 7 load balancing and session persistence.

- Availability Sets and Virtual Machine Scale Sets Integration: Azure Load Balancer integrates seamlessly with Azure Virtual Machine Scale Sets and Availability Sets to ensure high availability and fault tolerance.

- Outbound Connection Management: It helps manage outbound connections by providing a stable public IP address for outbound connections initiated by resources in the backend pool.

- Azure Load Balancer is a fundamental component in building scalable and reliable applications in Azure. It is suitable for various scenarios, including web applications, API services, and other workloads that benefit from distributing traffic across multiple servers.

Create a load balancer with standard SKU, defining front-end IP, backend pool, load-balancing rules, and health probe.

To create an Azure load balancer for your sensor connection:

a. Generate a load balancer with a standard SKU and an Internal type to ensure it remains closed to the Internet.

b. Define a dynamic front-end IP address in the proxysrv subnet created earlier, setting the availability to zone-redundant.

c. For the backend, select the virtual machine scale set created earlier.

d. On the port defined in the sensor, create a TCP load-balancing rule connecting the front-end IP address with the backend pool (default port is 3128).

e. Create a new health probe and define a TCP health probe on port 3128.

f. Define load balancer logging.

g. In the Azure portal, navigate to the created load balancer.

Stage 7: Configuring a NAT Gateway

To set up a NAT gateway for your sensor connection, follow these steps:

a. Begin by creating a new NAT Gateway.

b. In the Outbound IP tab, choose to create a new public IP address.

c. Navigate to the Subnet tab, and opt for the ProxyserverSubnet subnet that you previously established.

Your proxy is now configured. Proceed by defining proxy settings on your OT sensor.

Setting Up Connectivity for Multi-cloud Environments

This section explains how to connect your sensor to Defender for IoT in Azure from sensors deployed in public clouds such as AWS or Google Cloud. Choose the appropriate multi-cloud connectivity method based on the provided flow chart and configure your sensor accordingly.

After deploying sensors in public clouds, configure the proxy settings on your OT sensor to complete the setup.

Calibrate and Fine-Tune the Monitoring of OT Environment

Calibrating and fine-tuning the monitoring of operational technology (OT) environments is paramount in maintaining critical industrial processes' security, efficiency, and reliability. OT systems, encompassing industrial control systems and Supervisory Control and Data Acquisition (SCADA) systems, play a fundamental role in managing essential infrastructure such as power grids, manufacturing plants, and transportation systems. Given the increasing sophistication of cyber threats targeting these systems, the need for a proactive and adaptive monitoring approach cannot be overstated.

One primary reason for calibrating OT monitoring is to establish a baseline of normal behavior within the industrial network. This baseline serves as a reference point, enabling the detection of deviations or anomalies that may indicate potential security incidents. As OT environments are dynamic and subject to frequent changes, calibration ensures that the monitoring system remains aligned with the evolving nature of industrial processes. With a well-defined baseline, it becomes easier to differentiate between regular operational activities and suspicious behavior, leading to false positives or, conversely, overlooking genuine threats.

Moreover, the calibration process allows organizations to customize monitoring parameters based on the unique characteristics of their OT infrastructure. Fine-tuning involves optimizing the sensitivity of sensors, defining specific protocols, and tailoring detection mechanisms to focus on the most relevant indicators of compromise. This level of customization is crucial in mitigating the risk of false alarms, which, if not properly managed, can lead to alert fatigue among security personnel. By minimizing false positives, security teams can direct their attention more effectively toward genuine threats, ensuring a more efficient and responsive security posture.

In the context of OT environments, where the consequences of security breaches can be severe, the continuous calibration of monitoring systems contributes to the overall resilience of industrial processes. It allows organizations to adapt to evolving cyber threats, emerging attack vectors, and changes in the operational landscape. Additionally, fine-tuning the monitoring system facilitates the identification of vulnerabilities and weaknesses, enabling organizations to implement timely remediation measures and enhance their overall cybersecurity posture.

Furthermore, calibration is essential for optimizing the allocation of resources within the OT network. Organizations can avoid unnecessary strain on network resources by configuring monitoring sensors to focus on specific activities or critical areas. This targeted approach not only improves the efficiency of the monitoring system but also ensures that critical OT processes operate without disruption. In environments where real-time responsiveness is crucial, resource optimization through fine-tuning becomes a key factor in maintaining operational continuity.

So calibrating and fine-tuning the monitoring of OT environments is a multifaceted practice that addresses the unique challenges posed by industrial control systems. It establishes a baseline for normal behavior, customizes monitoring parameters, mitigates false positives, enhances resilience against cyber threats, and optimizes the allocation of resources. As industrial processes become increasingly interconnected and reliant on digital technologies, the importance of proactive and adaptive monitoring strategies cannot be overstated in safeguarding critical infrastructure's integrity, availability, and security.

Microsoft Defender for IoT/OT network sensors performs deep packet detection for IT and OT traffic, capturing network device data like device attributes and behavior. After installing, activating, and configuring your OT network sensor, you can use the tools outlined in this section to analyze automatically detected traffic, add extra subnets as necessary, and manage the information included in Defender for IoT alerts.

Prerequisites

Before following the procedures in this section, ensure you have

- Installed, configured, and activated an OT network sensor

- Access your OT network sensor and on-premises management console as an Admin user

Analyze Your Deployment

After onboarding a new OT network sensor to Microsoft Defender for IoT, validate the correct deployment by analyzing the monitored traffic.

To explore your network, sign in to your OT sensor as an Admin user, navigate to System settings ➤ Basic ➤ Deployment, and select "Analyze." Check each interface tab to understand the monitoring state and make necessary adjustments.

Every interface tab displays the following information:

- The tab displays the connection status, identifiable by a green or red connection icon in the tab name. For instance, the eth1 interface exhibits a green icon in the provided image, signifying a connected status.

- At the top of the tab, the cumulative count of identified subnets and VLANs is presented.

- Details on the protocols identified within each subnet are outlined.

- For each subnet, the count of detected unicast addresses is specified.

- The presence or absence of broadcast traffic in each subnet is indicated, serving as an indicator of a local network.

If the displayed traffic on the Deployment page doesn't align with your expectations, consider refining your deployment. This may involve adjusting the sensor's network placement or ensuring the correct connectivity of your monitoring interfaces. If modifications are made, and you wish to assess whether the traffic has improved, choose the "Analyze" option again to review the updated monitoring status.

Fine-Tune Your Subnet List

After analyzing the monitored traffic and refining your sensor deployment, there may be a need for further adjustments to your subnet list. Follow this procedure to ensure accurate configuration.

While the OT sensor automatically learns your network subnets during the initial deployment, it is advisable to analyze the detected traffic and make updates as necessary for optimizing map views and device inventory.

Utilize this procedure to define subnet settings, specifying how devices are presented in the sensor's device map and the Azure device inventory.

In the device map, IT devices are automatically grouped by subnet. You can expand and collapse each subnet view as needed for detailed exploration.

After configuring the subnets in the Azure device inventory, employ the Network location (Public preview) filter to distinguish between local and routed devices based on your subnet list. Devices associated with listed subnets appear local, while those linked to detected ones not included in the list are displayed as routed.

While the OT network sensor autonomously learns network subnets, verifying the learned settings and making updates as required for optimizing map views and device inventory are recommended. Any subnets not listed are treated as external networks.

To fine-tune your subnet list to optimize map views and device inventory, in the OT sensor settings, under System settings ➤ Basic ➤ Subnets, update the listed subnets using options like importing/exporting, clearing all defined subnets, or manually defining settings such as IP address, mask, and name. Save your updates.

Manually Define a Subnet as ICS

If an OT subnet isn't automatically marked as an ICS subnet, edit the device type for devices in the relevant subnet within the OT sensor's device inventory. This manual change designates the subnet as an ICS subnet.

To manually update the device type and change the subnet:

1. Log in to your OT sensor console and navigate to Device inventory.

2. Choose a device from the pertinent subnet within the device inventory grid, and then click "Edit" in the toolbar at the top of the page.

3. In the "Type" field, pick a device type from the drop-down list categorized under ICS or IoT.

Customize Port and VLAN Names

Enrich device data by customizing port and VLAN names on your OT network sensors. In the OT sensor settings, under System settings ➤ Network monitoring, customize port names and VLAN names to highlight specific activities or identify VLANs more efficiently.

To set up VLAN names on an OT network sensor:

1. Log in to your OT sensor as an Admin user.

2. Go to System Settings, and then, under Network monitoring, click VLAN Naming.

3. In the VLAN naming pane that appears, input a VLAN ID and
    a unique VLAN name. VLAN names can have up to 50 ASCII
    characters.

4. Click "+ Add VLAN" to customize another VLAN, and save your
    changes after completing the customization.

For Cisco switches: Add the monitor session 1 destination interface XX/XX
encapsulation dot1q command to the SPAN port configuration, where XX/XX represents
the name and number of the port.

To personalize a port name:

1. Log in to your OT sensor as an Admin user.

2. Navigate to System settings, and under Network monitoring,
    choose Port Naming.

3. In the Port Naming pane that appears, input the desired port
    number, the port's protocol, and a descriptive name. Supported
    protocol values include TCP, UDP, and BOTH.

4. Click "+ Add port" to customize another port, and save your
    changes when you're finished.

Configure DHCP Address Ranges

Define DHCP address ranges on each OT network sensor to handle IP address
changes in dynamic networks. In the OT sensor settings, under System settings ➤
Network monitoring ➤ DHCP Ranges, add single or multiple ranges, import/export
ranges, or clear existing configurations. Save your changes.

To establish DHCP address ranges:

1. Sign in to your OT sensor and navigate to System settings ➤
    Network monitoring ➤ DHCP Ranges.

2. Choose one of the following options.

3. To add a single range, click "+ Add range" and input the IP address
    range along with an optional name.

4. Create a .CSV file for multiple ranges with columns for the From,
    To, and Name data for each range. Utilize the Import function to
    import the file to your OT sensor. Imported range values from a
    .CSV file will overwrite any existing range data on your sensor.

5. To export currently configured ranges to a .CSV file, select Export.

6. To clear all presently configured ranges, choose Clear All. Range names can be up to 256 characters.

7. Click Save to apply and save your changes.

Configure Traffic Filters (Advanced)

To optimize network monitoring, configure capture filters via the OT sensor CLI to block high-bandwidth traffic at the hardware layer, reducing alert fatigue and enhancing appliance performance and resource usage.

Confirm and Revise the Inventory of Detected Devices

Let's explore the process of examining your device inventory and improving security monitoring by refining device details.

Prerequisites

Before proceeding with the steps outlined in this section, ensure the following:

- An OT sensor is installed, configured, and activated with detected device data.

- Access to your OT sensor is available as a Security Analyst or Admin user.

View Your Device Inventory on the Azure Portal

1. Log in to your OT sensor and navigate to the Device inventory page.

2. Click Edit Columns to display additional information in the grid, allowing a thorough review of the detected data for each device.

   Microsoft recommends examining data in columns such as Name, Class, Type, Subtype, Authorization, Scanner device, and Programming device.

3. Understand the devices detected by the OT sensor and identify sensors where device properties need clarification.

Edit Device Properties per Device

For each device requiring property adjustments:

1. Select the device in the grid and click Edit to access the editing pane.

2. Edit any of the following device properties as necessary:

- Authorized Device: Select if the device is a known entity on your network to avoid triggering alerts for learned traffic on approved devices.

- Name: Update the default IP address to a meaningful name for the device.

- Description: Provide a meaningful description for the device if left blank by default.

- OS Platform: If the operating system value is blocked for detection, select the device's operating system from the drop-down list.

- Type: If the device's type is blocked for detection or needs modification, choose a device type from the drop-down list.

- Purdue Level: If the device's Purdue level is detected as Undefined or Automatic, select an appropriate level to fine-tune your data.

- Scanner: Indicate if the device is a scanning device to avoid triggering alerts for scanning activities.

- Programming Device: Mark if the device is a programming device to avoid triggering alerts for programming activities.

3. Click Save to apply the changes.

Merge Duplicate Devices

As you review the detected devices, check for multiple entries for the same device on your network.

For instance, this may occur when a device has multiple network cards or interfaces.

Devices with identical IP and MAC addresses are automatically merged. Merge any duplicate devices to ensure each entry represents a unique device in your network.

Key Note

Device merges are irreversible, so ensure correct merging to avoid complications.

Select two or more authorized devices in the inventory to merge multiple devices and then click Merge.

Enhance Device Data (Optional)

To enhance device visibility and gather additional details beyond default data:

- For increased visibility to Windows-based devices, utilize the Defender for IoT Windows Management Instrumentation (WMI) tool.

- If network policies prevent specific data ingestion, consider importing extra data in bulk.

Establish a Baseline for Learning OT Alerts

Let's explore the process of establishing a baseline for learned traffic on your OT sensor.

Understand Learning Mode

An OT network sensor initiates automatic monitoring upon connection to the network and your sign-in. Devices start populating the device inventory, and alerts are triggered for security or operational incidents in your network.

Initially, this occurs in learning mode, directing the OT sensor to understand typical network activity, encompassing devices, protocols, and regular file transfers between specific devices. Consistently detected activity forms the baseline traffic for your network.

Key Note

Utilize the learning mode period to assess alerts and designate those representing authorized and expected activity as learned. Learned traffic doesn't generate new alerts upon subsequent detections.

Once the learning mode is disabled, any activity diverging from the established baseline triggers an alert.

Learn Mode Timeline

Creating your baseline of OT alerts may span a few days to several weeks, contingent on network size and complexity. Learning mode automatically concludes when a reduction in newly detected traffic is observed, typically two to six weeks after deployment.

Manually turn off learning mode earlier if you believe current alerts accurately portray your network activity.

Prerequisites

The procedures in this section can be performed from the Azure portal, an OT sensor, or an on-premises management console.

Before starting, ensure you have

- Installed, configured, and activated an OT sensor with alerts triggered by detected traffic

- Access to your OT sensor as a Security Analyst or Admin user.

Triage Alerts

Toward the end of deployment, triage alerts to establish an initial baseline for network activity.

1. Log in to your OT sensor and go to the Alerts page.

2. Utilize sorting and grouping options to prioritize critical alerts. Review each alert to update statuses and learn alerts for OT-authorized traffic.

Next Steps

Once learning mode is disabled, transition from learning to operational mode and integrate Defender for IoT data with Microsoft Sentinel to unify your SOC team's security monitoring.

Before initiation, ensure that your workspace satisfies the following prerequisites:

1. Possess Read and Write permissions for your Microsoft Sentinel workspace. For detailed information, refer to Permissions in Microsoft Sentinel.

2. Hold Contributor or Owner permissions on the subscription you intend to link with Microsoft Sentinel.

3. Have an active Defender for IoT plan on your Azure subscription, configured to stream data into Defender for IoT.

Begin by activating the Defender for IoT data connector to seamlessly transmit all Defender for IoT events into Microsoft Sentinel.

To enable the Defender for IoT data connector:

1. In Microsoft Sentinel, navigate to Configuration, choose Data connectors, and locate the Microsoft Defender for IoT data connector.

2. At the bottom right, click Open connector page.

3. On the Instructions tab, within the Configuration section, click Connect for each subscription from which you wish to stream alerts and device information into Microsoft Sentinel.

Note   If you've made any connection modifications, it may take ten seconds or more for the Subscription list to update.

Air-Gapped OT Sensor Management

Let us get started with what air-gapped OT sensor management is all about.

Getting Started

Air-gapped OT sensor management refers to the administration and control of operational technology (OT) sensors in an environment deliberately isolated from external networks, including the Internet. This isolated setup, often termed an "air-gapped network," is a security measure employed to enhance the protection of critical infrastructure, sensitive data, and industrial control systems. Air-gapping aims to minimize the risk of unauthorized access, cyberattacks, and data breaches.

Key Components

- Operational Technology (OT) Sensors

  OT sensors are specialized devices designed to monitor and analyze network traffic within industrial environments. These sensors play a crucial role in identifying anomalies and potential threats and ensuring the security of critical infrastructure components.

- Air-Gapped Network

  An air-gapped network is physically and logically isolated from external networks, such as the Internet and enterprise networks. This isolation is achieved by disconnecting the network from external communication channels, preventing unauthorized access, and reducing the attack surface.

- Management Console

  The management console is the central hub for configuring, monitoring, and controlling OT sensors. In an air-gapped environment, the management console is typically deployed within the isolated network to facilitate local management of sensors.

- Command-Line Interface (CLI) and API

  Administrators may use the command-line interface (CLI) and application programming interface (API) to interact with and manage OT sensors. These interfaces enable direct sensor communication, allowing configuration changes, data retrieval, and overall management.

Air-Gapped OT Sensor Management Process

Air-gapped OT sensor management is a meticulous process designed to ensure the security and reliability of operational technology (OT) sensors within an isolated network environment. The air-gapped setup is deliberately disconnected from external networks, creating a closed ecosystem to minimize the risk of cyber threats and unauthorized access. The management process involves several key steps to deploy, configure, monitor, and maintain OT sensors within this secure enclave.

Deployment

OT sensors are strategically deployed within the air-gapped network to monitor industrial processes, control systems, and network traffic.

The management console, CLI, and API are also deployed within the air-gapped network to facilitate local management.

Configuration

Initial configurations of OT sensors, including network settings, monitoring parameters, and alert thresholds, are performed through the management console, CLI, or API.

Monitoring

OT sensors monitor network traffic, detect anomalies, and generate alerts for potential security incidents.

Administrators can access real-time monitoring data and alerts through the management console or retrieve information using CLI/API.

Incident Response

In the event of a security incident or anomaly detection, administrators can initiate incident response actions through the management console or by using CLI/API.

Periodic Maintenance

Routine maintenance tasks, software updates, and sensor configuration adjustments can be carried out using the management console, CLI, or API.

Backup and Recovery

Regular backup of sensor configurations and data is essential for data integrity and recovery in case of system failures. Administrators can manage backup processes using the designated tools.

Transition Planning

In scenarios where air-gapped networks need to transition to different architectures, administrators plan and execute the transition, ensuring a seamless shift in management practices.

Challenges and Considerations

Managing operational technology (OT) sensors in air-gapped environments presents unique challenges and considerations that demand specialized attention. In air-gapped setups, OT sensors operate within isolated networks, disconnected from external communication channels to enhance security. While this approach significantly mitigates certain cybersecurity risks, it introduces a set of complexities in terms of deployment, monitoring, and maintenance.

Let us delve into the challenges associated with air-gapped OT sensor management, addressing key considerations to ensure the robustness and effectiveness of security measures within these closed environments. From deployment strategies to ongoing maintenance practices, understanding the intricacies of isolating sensors is paramount for organizations seeking to safeguard critical infrastructure and industrial processes.

Limited Connectivity

Air-gapped environments restrict external connectivity, limiting remote management and update options.

Physical Access Requirements

Since air-gapped networks are physically isolated, any management or maintenance tasks may require direct physical access to the network components.

Security Concerns

While air-gapped networks enhance security, they are not immune to all threats. Administrators must remain vigilant and implement additional security measures to address potential risks.

Air-gapped OT sensor management is a critical aspect of securing industrial environments where the isolation of networks is essential for safeguarding critical infrastructure. This approach ensures that industrial processes remain secure, resilient, and operational in the face of evolving cyber threats. Administrators play a pivotal role in managing and maintaining OT sensors within these isolated environments, employing a combination of tools and protocols to uphold the security and reliability of industrial control systems.

Microsoft Defender for IoT for Air-Gapped OT Sensor Network

Microsoft Defender for IoT is a robust solution tailored to assist organizations in achieving and sustaining compliance within their operational technology (OT) environments. It offers a comprehensive threat detection and management suite, ensuring coverage across parallel networks. The versatility of Defender for IoT extends its support to various sectors, such as industrial, energy, and utility domains, including compliance like NERC CIP or IEC 62443.

Unique Challenges in Air-Gapped Networks

Certain industries, like governmental organizations, financial services, nuclear power operators, and industrial manufacturing, often operate air-gapped networks. These networks are physically isolated from unsecured environments such as enterprise networks, guest networks, or the Internet. Defender for IoT plays a pivotal role in helping these organizations comply with global standards for threat detection, network segmentation, and more.

Balancing Security and Digital Transformation

While digital transformation has streamlined operations for many businesses, it poses challenges in air-gapped networks. The inherent security provided by isolation complicates the integration of modern architectural designs, such as zero trust. These challenges highlight the necessity to monitor air-gapped networks actively to detect and respond to potential threats.

Architectural Guidance for Hybrid and Air-Gapped Networks

To address these challenges, the section recommends integrating Defender for IoT sensors into existing IT infrastructure, both on-site and remotely, rather than maintaining a closed architecture. This integration facilitates smoother security operations, efficient management, and easy maintenance.

270

Microsoft Architecture Recommendations

The suggested architecture involves connecting OT sensors to multiple security management systems in both cloud and on-premises environments. The architecture includes routers in different logical zones, firewalls, and integration with local IT infrastructure. Communication lines for alerts, syslog messages, and APIs are clearly defined, ensuring a robust and efficient deployment.

In Figure 4-11, three sensors connect with four routers strategically placed in distinct logical zones throughout the organization. Positioned behind a firewall, these sensors seamlessly integrate with the local on-premises IT infrastructure. This infrastructure includes local backup servers, remote access connections through Secure Access Service Edge (SASE), and the transmission of alerts to an on-premises Security Information and Event Management (SIEM) system.

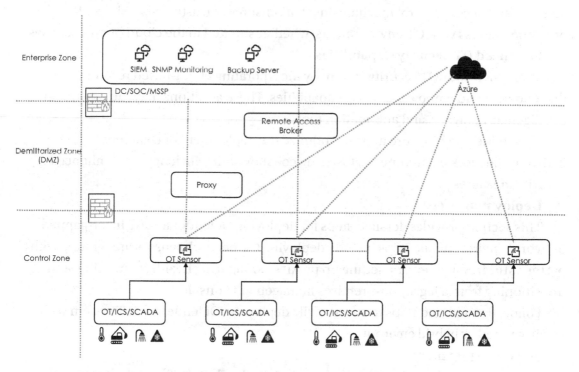

Figure 4-11. *Hybrid or air-gapped OT sensor management*

The architecture diagram visually represents communication pathways for alerts, syslog messages, and APIs. A solid black line signifies communication for alerts, while on-premises management communication is depicted with a solid purple line. Cloud/ hybrid management communication is presented with a dotted black line.

The provided guidance for Defender for IoT architecture in hybrid and air-gapped networks offers several benefits.

Utilize Existing Organizational Infrastructure

Leverage your organizational infrastructure to monitor and manage your operational technology (OT) sensors efficiently. This approach minimizes the necessity for additional hardware or software investments.

Seamless Organizational Security Stack Integrations

Seamlessly integrate with organizational security stack components that are progressively reliable and robust, regardless of whether your operations are on the cloud or on-premises.

Global Security Team Collaboration

Facilitate collaboration with your global security teams by implementing robust auditing and access control mechanisms. This ensures consistent visibility and protection across your OT environments, whether situated in the cloud or on-premises.

Enhanced OT Security Capabilities

Strengthen your OT security system by incorporating cloud-based resources that enhance and empower existing capabilities. These additions may include threat intelligence, analytics, and automation tools.

This refined architecture aims to optimize the deployment of Defender for IoT in diverse network environments, fostering collaboration, efficiency, and enhanced security measures.

Deployment Steps

This section provides detailed steps for deploying Defender for IoT in air-gapped or hybrid environments. Steps include deploying OT network sensors, integrating with partner SIEM/syslog servers, setting up proxies, configuring health monitoring, and transitioning from a legacy on-premises management console.

Follow the outlined steps to successfully deploy the Defender for IoT system within an air-gapped or hybrid environment.

Sensor Deployment

Execute the deployment of each operational technology (OT) network sensor according to your predefined plan.

Sensor Integration

For each sensor, perform the following integration steps.

Integrate with partner Security Information and Event Management (SIEM) or syslog servers. Configure email notifications.

For instance:

- Establish the connection between Microsoft Defender for IoT and Microsoft Sentinel.

- Conduct investigations and detect threats related to Internet of Things (IoT) devices.

- Forward OT alert information to on-premises environments.

Utilize the Defender for IoT API to create management dashboards. Refer to the Defender for IoT API reference for detailed information.

Proxy Setup

Implement a proxy or a series of chained proxies to facilitate communication with the management environment.

Health Monitoring

Establish health monitoring using either an SNMP (Simple Network Management Protocol) Management Information Base (MIB) server or a command-line interface (CLI).

Server Management Interface Configuration

Configure access to the server management interface, including interfaces like iDRAC (Integrated Dell Remote Access Controller) or iLO (Integrated Lights-Out).

Backup Server Configuration

Set up a backup server, ensuring configurations are in place to save backups to an external server.

By meticulously following these steps, you can effectively deploy the Defender for IoT system in environments characterized by air-gapped or hybrid configurations, ensuring robust security and operational efficiency.

Transitioning from Legacy Management Console

The legacy on-premises management console will be supported on January 1, 2025. The following emphasizes transitioning to the new architecture using on-premises and cloud APIs. It outlines a step-by-step process for this transition, ensuring a more efficient, secure, and reliable deployment.

As you transition your OT sensors to a new architecture, follow these steps to ensure a seamless and secure deployment.

Step 1: Legacy Integration and Permissions Assessment

Examine your OT sensors to identify legacy integrations and existing permissions configured for on-premises security teams. Consider aspects such as backup systems and user groups with access to sensor data.

Step 2: Sensor Connection to On-Premises and Cloud Resources

Establish connections for your sensors to on-premises, Azure, and other necessary cloud resources based on specific site requirements. This may involve linking to on-premises Security Information and Event Management (SIEM) systems, proxy servers, backup storage, and partner systems. Adopt a hybrid approach, ensuring certain sites remain air-gapped or isolated using data diodes.

Step 3: Access Permissions and Procedures Update

Set up permissions and update procedures to align with the new deployment architecture. This involves ensuring sensor access is configured appropriately based on the revised setup.

Step 4: Security Use Case Review and Validation

Review and validate all security use cases and procedures to confirm a smooth transition to the new architecture. This step is crucial to ensuring security measures remain effective and aligned with the updated deployment.

Step 5: On-Premises Management Console Decommissioning

After completing the transition, decommission the on-premises management console. This marks the shift toward the new architecture and streamlines your sensor management for enhanced efficiency and security.

By following these steps diligently, you can successfully transition to a new architecture for your OT sensors, fostering improved security practices and operational effectiveness.

Retirement Timeline for On-Premises Management Console

The retirement plan for the on-premises management console entails the following specifics:

Post-January 1, 2025

Sensor versions released after January 1, 2025, will no longer be compatible with the on-premises management console. Users are advised to transition to alternative management methods for optimal sensor control.

Between January 1, 2024, and January 1, 2025

Sensor software versions launched from January 1, 2024, to January 1, 2025, will continue to support the on-premises management console release. Users with these versions can maintain their current management setup.

Management of Air-Gapped Sensors

Direct management alternatives are available for air-gapped sensors incapable of connecting to the cloud. Users can leverage the sensor console, command-line interface (CLI), or application programming interface (API) for seamless management and control. This ensures continued functionality even in environments with restricted cloud connectivity.

Summary

This chapter provided comprehensive information for organizations looking to implement and optimize their security posture in operational technology (OT) environments. The deployment process was broken down into critical sections, providing a step-by-step approach for users.

Getting Started with Microsoft Defender for IoT Deployment

The initial section laid the foundation for deploying Microsoft Defender for IoT. It covered the prerequisites, outlining the essential requirements for the deployment process. This ensures that organizations have the necessary components before proceeding with the deployment.

Enable Microsoft Defender for IoT

This section delved into the specifics of enabling Microsoft Defender for IoT, detailing the configuration steps and best practices. Following these guidelines, users can activate the robust security features Defender provides for IoT, enhancing threat detection and management capabilities within their OT environments.

Calibrate and Fine-Tune the Monitoring of OT Environment

Recognizing the dynamic nature of OT environments, this section emphasized the importance of calibration and fine-tuning. It explored the need for adjustments in monitoring settings to align with the unique characteristics of the organization's OT landscape. This step ensures the precision and efficiency of the monitoring system.

Air-Gapped OT Sensor Management

In addressing the challenges posed by air-gapped networks, this section provided insights into managing OT sensors in isolated environments. It explored strategies for effectively monitoring and securing air-gapped systems, emphasizing the significance of maintaining security operations in environments physically separated from external networks.

In summary, the chapter guides you through the deployment journey of Microsoft Defender for IoT, starting with the foundational steps, progressing to enabling the platform, and culminating in the nuanced processes of calibration and air-gapped sensor management. This structured approach equips organizations with the knowledge and tools to fortify their OT security infrastructure against evolving threats.

In the book's next chapter, you will read about the management of Microsoft Defender for IoT.

CHAPTER 5

Manage Microsoft Defender for IoT

In this book, you are at final stages, from the foundational steps to the final stage of Microsoft Defender for IoT management and security. This chapter serves as a comprehensive reference point for organizations seeking to optimize their security operations within operational technology (OT) environments.

First Section: Getting Started with Microsoft Defender for IoT Management

The initial segment of this comprehensive guide lays the groundwork for users embarking on the journey of managing and monitoring Microsoft Defender for IoT. Covering essential prerequisites and foundational steps, this section ensures a solid understanding of the preliminary requirements, setting the stage for a seamless transition into subsequent sections.

Second Section: Manage Your Defender for IoT System

The following portion of the chapter is dedicated to the active management of the Microsoft Defender for IoT system. Offering practical guidance on day-to-day management tasks, system optimization, and maintenance, this section empowers users to tailor the Defender for IoT system to their organization's unique requirements. This segment ensures ongoing operational efficiency and adaptability from user access controls to system configurations.

Final Section: Security Baseline Microsoft Defender for IoT

Recognizing that security is paramount in IoT, the final leg of our journey unfolds with an exploration of the "Security Baseline for Microsoft Defender for IoT." Here, we unravel the importance of establishing a robust security baseline and guide you through defining, configuring, and enforcing security measures tailored to your organization's unique needs. By the conclusion of this section, you will possess the knowledge and tools necessary to fortify your IoT ecosystem against potential threats.

© Puthiyavan Udayakumar and Dr. R. Anandan 2024
P. Udayakumar and Dr. R. Anandan, *Design and Deploy Microsoft Defender for IoT*,
https://doi.org/10.1007/979-8-8688-0239-3_5

This final chapter stands as a testament to our commitment to equipping you with the insights needed to harness the full potential of Microsoft Defender for IoT. Whether you are taking your first steps or seeking advanced strategies for enhancement, the collective knowledge within these sections is designed to empower you in creating a resilient and secure IoT infrastructure.

By the end of this chapter, you should be able to understand the following:

- Getting started with Microsoft Defender for IoT management

- Manage your Defender for IoT system

- Security baseline Microsoft Defender for IoT

Getting Started with Microsoft Defender for IoT Management

In the rapidly evolving landscape of the Internet of Things (IoT), managing security has become a mission-critical endeavor for organizations across industries. Microsoft Defender for IoT emerges as a comprehensive and sophisticated platform designed to address the multifaceted challenges of securing IoT ecosystems. Delving deeper into the essential aspects of managing IoT security through Defender for IoT reveals a wealth of features contributing to the platform's efficacy.

Device management is not merely about tracking the presence of devices but involves orchestrating their entire life cycle. Defender for IoT empowers organizations to establish stringent policies for device onboarding, ensuring that only authorized entities can access the network. The platform's intuitive interface allows for seamless identification of new devices, troubleshooting potential issues, and implementing targeted security measures.

Sensors, the frontline components in the defense against IoT threats, require meticulous management to optimize their effectiveness. Defender for IoT provides organizations with granular control over sensor deployment, allowing for strategic placement to maximize coverage. Regular calibration and fine-tuning of sensor settings are facilitated, ensuring that these guardians of the IoT realm operate with peak efficiency.

The management of alerts is a pivotal function in any robust security framework. Defender for IoT categorizes alerts based on severity, enabling security teams to prioritize responses according to the potential impact on the organization. The adaptive alerting system evolves with the organization's security posture, offering tailored configurations that align with specific operational needs.

User management is a linchpin in the overall security strategy. Defender for IoT offers sophisticated user controls, allowing organizations to define roles and permissions precisely. This ensures that access to sensitive security data is restricted to authorized personnel, fortifying the collaborative efforts of security teams in incident response and resolution.

Billing plan management is an ancillary concern, but it becomes a strategic element in the context of IoT. Defender for IoT allows organizations to choose billing plans that align with their budget constraints and scale seamlessly with the evolving security requirements. This adaptive approach ensures cost-effectiveness without compromising on security measures.

The distinctive capability of managing both OT and IoT on-premises resources sets Defender for IoT apart. Recognizing the unique challenges these environments pose, the platform extends its reach to integrate on-premises resources seamlessly into the broader security strategy. This holistic approach ensures that organizations can secure their IoT landscape comprehensively, regardless of deployment locations.

Microsoft Defender for IoT emerges as a dynamic and responsive solution, offering nuanced management capabilities across diverse facets of IoT security. From the meticulous oversight of devices and sensors to the strategic handling of alerts, users, billing plans, and the intricacies of on-premises resource management, the platform stands as a beacon in navigating the complexities of the IoT security landscape. As organizations continue to embrace the potential of IoT, the role of Defender for IoT in fortifying these digital frontiers becomes increasingly indispensable.

Manage Your Defender for IoT System

In the dynamic landscape of IoT cybersecurity, managing devices, users, alerts, and billing is paramount to ensuring the robust security posture of an organization. Microsoft Defender for IoT emerges as a comprehensive solution, offering a multifaceted approach to safeguarding industrial environments and critical infrastructure. Four elements are covered in this section: device management, user management, alert management, and billing management.

Device Management

Effectively managing devices within Defender for IoT involves orchestrating their connectivity, configurations, and security protocols. This includes onboarding, monitoring, and maintaining devices to ensure optimal functionality and resilience against potential threats. The centralized device management capabilities empower organizations to enforce security policies, implement updates, and streamline operations across diverse IoT ecosystems.

User Management

User access and privileges play a pivotal role in the security architecture. Defender for IoT enables organizations to intricately manage user roles, ensuring that each individual has the appropriate permissions for their responsibilities. Whether it's configuring access levels for administrators, security analysts, or read-only users, the system provides a granular approach to user management, enhancing accountability and control.

Alert Management

In the face of evolving cyber threats, timely and accurate alerts are critical for swift response and mitigation. Defender for IoT excels in alert management by providing comprehensive insights into detected anomalies, potential security breaches, and other noteworthy events. Users can navigate through the alert system, categorize severity levels, and implement proactive measures to address security incidents promptly.

Billing Management

Understanding the financial aspects of utilizing Defender for IoT is essential for optimizing resources and ensuring cost-effectiveness. The billing management features empower organizations to track usage, assess resource consumption, and manage subscription plans efficiently. This transparency aids in budgeting, resource allocation, and aligning the cybersecurity strategy with the organization's financial objectives.

In this holistic approach to managing devices, users, alerts, and billing, Microsoft Defender for IoT emerges as a robust solution designed to fortify the cybersecurity posture of industrial environments. By integrating these management components seamlessly, organizations can proactively protect their assets, respond effectively to emerging threats, and maintain operational integrity in an increasingly interconnected world.

Let us get started with managing devices from Microsoft Defender for IoT.

Manage Devices

Defender for IoT's device inventory proves invaluable in acquiring comprehensive insights into specific devices, encompassing critical details such as manufacturer, type, serial number, firmware, and more. This meticulous device profiling equips your teams to proactively investigate vulnerabilities, fortifying your defenses against potential threats to your most crucial assets.

Key Functions of Device Management

- Holistic Device Management

   Efficiently manage all your IoT/OT devices by establishing an up-to-date inventory encompassing managed and unmanaged devices. This comprehensive approach ensures a centralized view of your device landscape, fostering effective control and oversight.

- Risk-Based Protection

   Employ a risk-based approach to device protection, identifying potential risks like missing patches and vulnerabilities. Prioritize fixes based on a meticulous risk-scoring system and leverage automated threat modeling to enhance the security posture of your devices.

- Dynamic Inventory Maintenance

   Keep your inventory current by systematically removing irrelevant devices and supplementing it with organization-specific information. This dynamic maintenance approach allows you to emphasize your organization's preferences, ensuring that your inventory aligns with the evolving needs of your cybersecurity strategy.

Incorporating Defender for IoT's device inventory into your cybersecurity framework empowers your organization to understand your device landscape's intricacies and proactively address vulnerabilities. This proactive stance is instrumental in preserving the integrity of your critical assets and maintaining a robust defense against emerging cybersecurity challenges.

Defender for IoT's device inventory encompasses various device classes, each serving specific functions within various sectors. These include manufacturing devices like industrial robots and packaging systems, building devices such as HVAC systems and smart lighting, healthcare devices like glucose meters and monitors, transportation/utilities devices including turnstiles and fire safety systems, and energy and resources devices like DCS controllers and PLCs. Additionally, the inventory covers endpoint devices such as workstations and servers, enterprise devices like smart devices and communication tools, retail devices including barcode scanners and humidity sensors, and a category for transient devices detected briefly, requiring thorough investigation for network impact understanding. Moreover, unclassified devices, lacking a predefined category, are also accounted for within the Defender for IoT device inventory.

Table 5-1 enumerates the columns accessible in the Azure portal's Defender for IoT device inventory.

Table 5-1. *IoT Device Inventory Fields Table via the Azure Portal*

Field	Description
Authorization	Editable field indicating whether the device is marked as authorized, subject to changes based on device security
Business function	Editable field describing the device's business function
Class	Editable field specifying the device's class (default: IoT)
Data source	Source of data, such as micro agent, OT sensor, or Microsoft Defender for Endpoint (default: MicroAgent)
Description	Editable field containing the device's description
Device ID	Azure-assigned ID number for the device
Firmware model	The device's firmware model
Firmware vendor	Editable field indicating the vendor of the device's firmware
Firmware version	Editable field specifying the device's firmware version
First seen	Date and time when the device was initially detected (format: MM/DD/YYYY HH:MM:SS AM/PM)
Importance	Editable field indicating the device's importance level: Low, Medium, or High
IPv4 address	IPv4 address of the device
IPv6 address	IPv6 address of the device
Last activity	Date and time of the device's last event transmission (format: MM/DD/YYYY HH:MM:SS AM/PM)

(continued)

Table 5-1. (*continued*)

Field	Description
Location	Editable field for specifying the physical location of the device
MAC address	The device's MAC address
Model	Editable field indicating the device's hardware model
Name	Mandatory and editable field specifying the device's name as discovered or entered by the user
Network location (Public preview)	Indicates whether the device is defined as local or routed based on configured subnets
OS architecture	Editable field indicating the device's operating system architecture
OS distribution	Editable field specifying the device's operating system distribution (e.g., Android, Linux, Haiku)
OS platform	Editable field indicating the device's detected operating system
OS version	Editable field specifying the device's operating system version (e.g., Windows 10, Ubuntu 20.04.1)
PLC mode	Specifies the PLC operating mode, including Key state (physical/logical) and Run state (logical)
Programming device	Editable field indicating whether the device functions as a programming device for PLCs, RTUs, and controllers
Protocols	Specifies the protocols used by the device
Purdue level	Editable field specifying the Purdue level in which the device exists
Scanner device	Editable field indicating whether the device performs scanning-like activities in the network
Sensor	Specifies the sensor to which the device is connected
Serial number	The device's serial number
Site	Specifies the device's site (enterprise IoT sensors are automatically added to the enterprise network site)
Slots	Indicates the number of slots the device has
Subtype	Editable field indicating the device's subtype (default: Managed Device)

(*continued*)

Table 5-1. (*continued*)

Field	Description
Tags	Editable field for specifying the device's tags
Type	Editable field specifying the device type (default: Miscellaneous)
Vendor	The name of the device's vendor, as defined in the MAC address
VLAN	Specifies the device's VLAN
Zone	Specifies the device's zone

Options for Managing Devices

The Defender for IoT device inventory is accessible through various interfaces, each offering distinct capabilities.

Azure Portal

- OT devices detected by all cloud-connected OT sensors are accessible.

- Linked incidents in Microsoft Sentinel.

- Utilize Defender for IoT workbooks for comprehensive visibility into cloud-connected device inventory, including related alerts and vulnerabilities.

- Devices detected by Microsoft Defender for Endpoint agents are also included for Azure subscriptions with legacy enterprise IoT plans.

Microsoft Defender XDR

- Enterprise IoT devices identified by Microsoft Defender for Endpoint agents.

- Correlate devices across Microsoft Defender XDR, consolidating purpose-built alerts, vulnerabilities, and recommendations.

OT Network Sensor Consoles

- Description: Devices detected by the specific OT sensor in use.

- Visualize all detected devices through a network device map.

- Explore related events on the Event timeline.

On-Premises Management Console

- Devices detected across all connected OT sensors.

- Augment device data by manual import or script-based methods.

These diverse entry points provide flexibility in managing Defender for IoT device inventory, allowing users to choose the interface that best aligns with their specific requirements and operational context.

Effectively manage your network devices detected by cloud-connected sensors, encompassing operational technology (OT), Internet of Things (IoT), and information technology (IT), using the Device Inventory page in Defender for IoT on the Azure portal. This centralized platform allows you to identify new devices efficiently, troubleshoot potential issues, and gain comprehensive insights into your network ecosystem.

Administer Your Device Inventory Through the Azure Portal

Accessing the Device Inventory page is straightforward. Navigate to Defender for IoT ➤ Device inventory on the Azure portal. The user-friendly interface provides multiple options to modify or filter the displayed devices, enhancing your ability to tailor the view according to your needs. You can sort devices by selecting column headers, filtering them based on specific criteria using the search box, adding custom filters, and modifying the columns shown for a personalized experience. Table 5-2 illustrates the view device inventory properties via the Azure portal.

Table 5-2. *View IoT Device Inventory via the Azure Portal*

Option	Steps
Sort devices	1. Click on a column heading to arrange devices by that category.
	2. Click the same column heading again to change the sorting order.
Filter devices shown	1. Use the search box to find specific device details.
	2. Click Add filter to choose which devices to display. In the filter box: Pick a category, an operator, and a value. Click Apply to use your filter. Apply several filters at once.
	Note: Search results and filters aren't saved after refreshing the Device Inventory page. The default Last Active Time and Network Location (Preview) filters are already active.

(continued)

Table 5-2. (*continued*)

Option	Steps
Modify columns shown	1. Click Edit columns. 2. In the Edit columns section: Click + Add Column to insert new columns. Drag and drop fields to change their order. To remove a column, click the Delete icon. Click Reset to revert to default settings. 3. Click Save to keep any changes.
Group devices	1. Above the grid, choose a category (like Class, Data source, Location, Purdue level, Site, Type, Vendor, or Zone) to group devices. 2. Inside each group, devices keep the same order. 3. To undo grouping, click No grouping.

To see complete information about a particular device, click on the row corresponding to that device. Initial details will appear in a side pane on the right. You can also choose "View full details" to access the device details page and delve deeper into the information. Table 5-3 showcases extensive information about the device, presenting various tabs.

Table 5-3. *Complete Information About the IoT Device via the Azure Portal*

Section	Description
Attributes	Provides comprehensive device information, showcasing details such as class, data source, firmware specifications, activity, type, protocols, Purdue level, sensor, site, zone, and more.
Backplane	Reveals the configuration of the backplane hardware, offering insights into slots and racks. Selecting a slot in the backplane view allows users to delve into the specifics of the underlying devices.
Vulnerabilities	Highlights current vulnerabilities specific to the device, leveraging Defender for IoT's coverage for supported OT vendors. The platform detects firmware models and versions to provide vulnerability data.

(*continued*)

Table 5-3. (*continued*)

Section	Description
	The information is sourced from the repository of standards-based vulnerability data documented in the US government National Vulnerability Database (NVD). Users can click on the CVE name for detailed information.
	A useful tip is to utilize the Defender for IoT Vulnerability workbook to view vulnerability data across the network.
Alerts	Showcases current open alerts associated with the device. Users can select any alert for additional details and access the full alert information by choosing "View full details."
Recommendations	Displays current recommendations tailored to the device, such as "Review PLC operating mode" and "Review unauthorized devices." More information on recommendations can be found in the documentation on enhancing security posture with security recommendations.

Identifying Devices with Connectivity Issues

If you have concern that specific devices may not be actively communicating with Azure, we suggest checking whether these devices have had any recent communication with Azure at all.

The following is the procedure to do so:

1. On the Device Inventory page, ensure the Last Activity column is visible.

2. Select Edit columns ➤ Add column ➤ Last Activity ➤ Save.

3. Click on the Last Activity column to sort the devices based on their last activity.

4. Filter the grid to display active devices within a specific
time range:

   a. Click Add filter.

   b. In the Column field, select Last Activity.

   c. Choose a predefined time range or define a custom range.

   d. Click Apply.

5. Review the filtered list to confirm the connectivity status of the
devices.

Editing Device Details

While overseeing your network devices, it might be necessary to revise their details.
This could involve adjusting security settings due to changes in assets, customizing the
inventory for improved device identification, or correcting misclassifications of devices.
The following is the procedure to do so:

1. Select one or more devices from the grid and click Edit.

2. If multiple devices are selected, use Add field type to add fields for
all selected devices.

3. Modify the device fields as needed.

Click Save to apply changes, which will be saved for all selected devices. The
following is the reference of Editable Fields:

General Information

- Name: Mandatory; supported for editing when dealing with a
single device.

- Authorized Device: Toggle security status on or off.

- Description: Provide a meaningful description.

- Location: Specify a meaningful location.

- Category: Use Class, Type, and Subtype options for categorization.

- Business Function: Describe the device's business function.

- Hardware Model: Select from the drop-down menu.

- Hardware Vendor: Select from the drop-down menu.

- Firmware: Provide firmware name and version.

- Purdue Level: Indicate the Purdue level.

- Tags: Enter meaningful tags.

Settings

- Importance: Modify the device's importance (Low, Normal, High).

- Programming Device: Toggle on or off.

Exporting Device Inventory to CSV

Export your device inventory to a CSV file for data management or sharing purposes beyond the Azure portal. The export allows a maximum of 30,000 devices at a time. The following is the procedure to do so:

1. On the Device Inventory page, click Export.

2. The export includes devices with applied filters; save the file locally.

Deleting a Device

If devices are no longer in use, remove them from the device inventory to disconnect them from Defender for IoT. Inactivity in devices may result from misconfigured SPAN ports, changes in network coverage, or the device being unplugged. Deleting inactive devices helps maintain an accurate representation of current network activity, provides a clearer understanding of the monitored device count in managing Defender for IoT licenses and plans, and reduces screen clutter. The following is the procedure to do so:

1. In the Device Inventory page, select the device to delete.

2. Click Delete in the toolbar at the top.

3. Confirm deletion by selecting Yes.

Merging Duplicate Devices

You might find it necessary to combine duplicate devices when the sensor identifies distinct network entities linked to a single, unique device. The following is the procedure to do so:

1. On the Device Inventory page, select two or more devices
    to merge.

2. Click Merge in the toolbar (up to ten devices at a time, if in the
    same zone or site).

3. In the Merge pane, choose

    - Merge: To merge and return to the Device Inventory page

    - Merge & View: To merge and open merged device details

A success message confirms the merge into a single, unique device. The merged
device retains details of the most recent activity or update.

**Overseeing OT and IT Devices Using the Device Inventory in the Sensor Console
(Microsoft Defender for IoT)**

The Device Inventory page in the sensor console of Microsoft Defender for IoT
provides a comprehensive platform for overseeing and handling operational technology
(OT) and information technology (IT) devices. Here's a step-by-step process to
effectively utilize the Device Inventory page.

To access identified devices on the Device Inventory page within the Azure portal,
navigate to Defender for IoT ➤ Device Inventory. Table 5-4 shows the devices inventory
viewed via the sensor console.

Table 5-4. *IoT Devices Inventory Viewed via the Sensor Console*

Option	Steps
Sort devices	1. Click on a column header to organize devices by that column. 2. Click the same column header again to change the sorting direction.
Filter devices shown	1. Use the search box to find specific device details. 2. Alternatively, select Add filter to filter the displayed devices. In the Add filter box: Specify the filter by column name, operator, and value. Click Apply to apply the filter. Multiple filters can be applied simultaneously. Note: Search results and filters are not saved upon refreshing the Device Inventory page. The default Last Active Time and Network Location (Preview) filters are active.
Modify columns shown	1. Click Edit columns. 2. In the Edit columns pane: Click + Add Column to insert new columns. Rearrange columns by dragging and dropping fields. To remove a column, click the Delete icon. To reset columns to default settings, click Reset. 3. Click Save to retain changes.
Group devices	1. Above the grid, choose a category (e.g., Class, Data source, Location, Purdue level, Site, Type, Vendor, or Zone) to group devices. 2. Within each group, devices maintain the same column sorting. 3. To eliminate grouping, select No grouping.

Table 5-5. *The Complete Information About the IoT Device via the Sensor Console*

Section	Description
Attributes	Provides a comprehensive overview of the device, showcasing details like class, data source, firmware specifics, activity, type, supported protocols, Purdue level, associated sensor, site, zone, and more.
Backplane	Offers insights into the backplane hardware configuration, revealing slot and rack information. By selecting a specific slot in the backplane view, you can access detailed information about the underlying devices. Typically, visible for Purdue level 1 devices with occupied slots, such as PLCs, RTUs, and DCS devices.

(continued)

Table 5-5. (*continued*)

Section	Description
Vulnerabilities	Presents current vulnerabilities specific to the device. Defender for IoT delivers vulnerability coverage for supported OT vendors, detecting firmware models and versions. Vulnerability data is sourced from the US government National Vulnerability Database (NVD). Clicking on the CVE name provides additional details and descriptions.
Alerts	Displays ongoing alerts associated with the device. You can select any alert to access more details and choose View Full Details to open the alert page, providing comprehensive information on the alert and enabling you to take necessary actions.
Recommendations	Highlights current recommendations tailored for the device, such as Review PLC operating mode and Review unauthorized devices.

Access the Complete Details of the Device

To access the complete details of the device, click on the respective device row to access comprehensive information about a particular device. Preliminary details will be displayed in a side pane on the right, where you can also choose to view full details, allowing you to delve deeper into the device's specifics on the dedicated details page.

Detect Devices Experiencing Connectivity Issues

If you suspect that specific devices are not actively communicating with Azure, it is advisable to confirm whether these devices have recently been shared with Azure. Follow these steps:

1. On the Device Inventory page, ensure the Last Activity column is visible.

2. Select Edit Columns ➤ Add Column ➤ Last Activity ➤ Save.

3. Click on the Last Activity column to arrange the grid based on that column.

4. Filter the grid to display active devices within a specific time frame:

   a. Choose Add Filter.

   b. In the Column field, opt for Last Activity.

   c. Select a predefined time range or define a custom range for filtering.

   d. Click Apply.

5. Search for the devices you are verifying within the filtered list of devices.

Update Device Information

As you oversee your network devices, revising their details might be necessary. This could involve adjusting security values due to asset changes, personalizing the inventory for improved device identification, or correcting misclassifications.

To modify device details:

1. Choose one or more devices in the grid, then click Edit.

2. If multiple devices are selected, click Add Field Type to include the fields you wish to edit for all chosen devices.

3. Adjust the device fields as necessary, and click Save upon completion.

All changes made are saved for the selected devices.

Table 5-6 shows the Device Inventory page supporting the editing of the device fields.

Table 5-6. *Modification of the IoT device details*

Name	Description
General Information	
Name	Mandatory. Editable only when modifying a single device.
Authorized device	Toggle on or off based on changing device security needs.
Description	Input a meaningful description for the device.
Location	Input a meaningful location for the device.
Category	Utilize the Class, Type, and Subtype options to categorize the device.
Business function	Input a meaningful description of the device's business function.
Hardware model	Select the device's hardware model from the drop-down menu.
Hardware vendor	Select the device's hardware vendor from the drop-down menu.
Firmware	Define the device's firmware name and version. Choose to delete or add firmware.
Purdue level	Specify the Purdue level in which the device exists.
Tags	Enter meaningful tags for the device. Choose to delete or add tags.
Settings	
Importance	Modify the device's importance level by selecting Low, Normal, or High.
Programming device	Toggle the Programming Device option on or off based on your device's needs.

Export the Device Inventory to CSV

Export your device inventory to a CSV file to manage or share data efficiently outside the Azure portal. This process allows you to export up to 30,000 devices at once.

Steps for Exporting Device Inventory

1. Visit the Device Inventory page.

2. Click on the "Export" option.

The device inventory will be exported with the currently applied filters, and you can save the file locally.

Delete a Device

If you have devices that are no longer in use, removing them from the device inventory ensures they are no longer connected to Defender for IoT.

Devices may become inactive due to misconfigured SPAN ports, changes in network coverage, or being unplugged from the network. Deleting inactive devices is essential to accurately represent current network activity, understand the monitored device count, and reduce on-screen clutter.

Steps to Delete a Device

1. On the Device Inventory page, select the device you want to delete.

2. Click "Delete" in the toolbar at the top of the page.

3. Confirm the deletion by selecting "Yes" when prompted.

Combine Duplicate Devices

It might be necessary to merge duplicate devices if the sensor identifies distinct network entities linked to a single, unique device.

Instances of this situation could involve a laptop with Wi-Fi and a physical network card, a switch with multiple interfaces, an HMI with four network cards, or a single workstation with multiple network cards.

Manually Consolidate Devices

Navigate to the Device Inventory page. Choose two or more devices you wish to merge, then click on the "Merge" option in the toolbar at the top. You can merge up to ten devices simultaneously, provided all selected devices belong to the same zone or site.

It's important to note that OT devices can only be merged with other OT devices. On the other hand, enterprise IoT devices and those detected by Microsoft Defender for Endpoint agents can be merged with other enterprise IoT or Defender for Endpoint devices.

In the Merge pane, opt for one of the following:

1. Select "Merge" to combine the chosen devices and return to the inventory page.

2. Choose "Merge & View" to consolidate the devices and access the details of the merged device.

A confirmation message will appear at the top right, indicating the successful merging of devices into a single, unique entity.

The merged device, now visible in the grid, preserves the device's details with the latest activity or the most recent update to its identifying information.

Examine Devices Displayed on a Device Map

OT device maps visually depict the network devices identified by the OT network sensor and illustrate their connections.

Utilize a device map to access, analyze, and oversee device information comprehensively or segment it based on network criteria, such as specific interest groups or Purdue layers. In air-gapped environments with an on-premises management console, employ a zone map to observe devices across all connected OT sensors in a designated zone.

Manage Users

Microsoft Defender for IoT offers tools for user access management in the Azure portal and on-premises.

Organize Users via Microsoft Azure Portal

Within the Azure portal, user management operates at the subscription level, utilizing Microsoft Entra ID and Azure role-based access control (RBAC). By assigning Microsoft Entra users specific Azure roles at the subscription level, they can add or update Defender for IoT pricing plans, access device data, manage sensors, and oversee device data throughout the Defender for IoT environment.

For enhanced user management in the context of OT network monitoring, Defender for IoT introduces the site level. This feature allows you to add granularity to user management, enabling assigning roles at the site level. This way, you can apply distinct permissions for the same users across different sites, providing a more tailored approach to access control.

Establish Azure user definitions for Defender for IoT on a per-subscription basis. Administer user access through Azure role-based access control (RBAC), assigning roles to users or user groups according to their specific functional needs.

Facilitate user access to Azure resources through the following methods:

1. Azure Portal: Grant individual users access to Azure resources directly through the Azure portal.

2. Azure PowerShell: Extend access to Azure resources by granting groups access via Azure PowerShell.

Utilize Azure user roles tailored for operational technology (OT) and enterprise Internet of Things (IoT) monitoring.

For an added layer of precision in Azure access policies, manage access control on a site-based level (currently in Public preview). This approach involves defining specific permissions for each Defender for the IoT site, contributing to a zero-trust security strategy. Defender for IoT sites typically represent collections of devices in a specific geographical location, such as those within an office building at a particular address.

Site-based access control activities empower you to

- Verify your access to the site or inspect access for other users, groups, service principals, or managed identities

- Review existing role assignments on the site, including those that explicitly deny specific actions

- Access a comprehensive list of available roles specific to the site

To oversee site-based access control:

1. Navigate to the Defender for IoT ➤ Sites and Sensors page within the Azure portal. Choose the OT site where you intend to allocate permissions.

2. In the Edit site pane that appears on the right, opt for "Manage site access control (Preview)."

3. A snapshot of the site-based access option will be visible on the Sites and Sensors page.

4. Access the Access control page within Defender for IoT for your selected site. This page mirrors the interface found directly in the Access control tab on any Azure resource.

Develop and Organize Users on an OT Network Sensor

Microsoft Defender for IoT offers tools to administer user access within on-premises environments, specifically in the OT network sensor and the legacy on-premises management console. On the other hand, Azure users are overseen at the Azure subscription level through Azure role-based access control (RBAC).

The upcoming section will delve into directly managing on-premises users on an OT network sensor.

Default Privileged Users

The default privileged users in the OT network sensor include the Admin user, who is automatically installed during the sensor setup. This Admin user is granted access to advanced tools for troubleshooting and system configuration. During the initial configuration of a sensor, Microsoft recommends signing in with the Admin user, creating an initial user with administrative privileges, and then establishing additional users tailored for security analysts and read-only access.

Notably, sensor versions are 23.1 at the earliest. x comes pre-equipped with cyberx and cyberx_host privileged users. In version 23.1.x and above, these users are installed by default but are not activated initially. Users need to reset their passwords to enable the cyberx and cyberx_host users, especially for use with the Defender for IoT CLI.

Integrate Active Directory

As Microsoft recommends, set up an Active Directory connection on your OT sensor. This configuration allows on-premises users to be integrated with Active Directory, enabling them to sign in to the sensor and utilize Active Directory groups. By employing Active Directory groups, permissions can be collectively assigned to all users within a specific group. This approach is particularly advantageous when dealing with many users for whom you wish to allocate read-only access. Using Active Directory in such cases facilitates permissions management at the group level, streamlining the administration process.

To create an Active Directory connection:

1. Access OT sensor system settings:

   - Sign in to your OT sensor.

   - Navigate to System Settings ➤ Integrations ➤ Active Directory.

2. Enable Active Directory integration:

   - Toggle on the "Active Directory Integration Enabled" option.

3. Enter Active Directory server details:

    -   Provide the following values for your Active Directory server:

    -   Domain Controller FQDN: Enter the fully qualified domain name (FQDN) precisely as it appears on your LDAP server (e.g., host1. subdomain.contoso.com).

    -   Domain Controller Port: Specify the port configured for your LDAP (e.g., use port 636 for LDAPS/SSL connections).

    -   Primary Domain: Enter the domain name (e.g., subdomain. contoso.com) and choose the connection type (LDAPS/NTLMv3 recommended, LDAP/NTLMv3, or LDAP/SASL-MD5).

4. Add Active Directory groups:

    -   Select "+ Add" to include Active Directory groups for each required permission level.

    -   Ensure the group name matches the definition in your Active Directory configuration on the LDAP server.

    -   Use these group names when adding new sensor users with Active Directory.

    -   Supported permission levels include Read-only, Security Analyst, Admin, and Trusted Domains.

Key notes for LDAP parameters:

-   Define values exactly as they appear in Active Directory, except for case sensitivity.

-   Use lowercase characters only, even if the Active Directory configuration uses uppercase.

-   LDAP and LDAPS cannot be configured for the same domain; however, you can configure each in different domains and use them simultaneously.

5. Add additional Active Directory servers (optional):

- Select "+ Add Server" at the top of the page to integrate with multiple Active Directory servers.

- Provide the required values for each additional server.

6. Save configuration:

- Once all Active Directory servers are added, select "Save" to complete the integration process.

Add New OT Sensor Users

In this section, let us explore the method to create a new user for a specific OT network sensor.

Prerequisites

This procedure is accessible for admin, cyberx, and cyberx_host users and any user with the Admin role.

Steps

1. Sign in and access users.

2. Sign in to the sensor console.

3. Navigate to Users ➤ + Add user.

- On the "Create a user ➤ Users" page, provide the following details:

- Username: Enter a meaningful username for the user.

- Email: Input the user's email address.

- First Name: Enter the user's first name.

- Last Name: Input the user's last name.

- Role: Choose one of the user roles – Admin, Security Analyst, or Read Only.

- Password: Select the user type (Local or Active Directory User).

- For local users, set a password adhering to the following requirements:

- At least eight characters

- Both lowercase and uppercase alphabetic characters

- At least one number

- At least one symbol

- Local user passwords can only be modified by Admin users.

4. Save changes:

- Click "Save" once all necessary details are entered.

Your newly created user is now added and will be visible on the sensor Users page.

Additional Actions

- Select the Edit icon for the desired user to edit a user and make the necessary changes.

- To delete a user, click the Delete button corresponding to the user you want to remove.

Key Note for Active Directory Integration

If you wish to associate groups of users with specific permission levels using Active Directory, configure an Active Directory connection first and then proceed with this procedure.

Change a Sensor User's Password

In this section, let us explore the steps for Admin users to modify local user passwords on a sensor. Admin users have the authority to change passwords for themselves and for Security Analyst or Read-Only users. Additionally, privileged users can alter their passwords and other Admin users' passwords.

Note   If you need to recover access to a privileged user account, refer to the documentation on recovering privileged access to a sensor.

Prerequisites

This procedure is applicable only to cyberx, admin, or cyberx_host users or users with the Admin role.

To change a sensor user's password:

   a. Sign in:

      i. Log in to the sensor.

     ii. Access the Users section.

    iii. Locate the user:

   b. On the Users page, identify the user for whom the password needs modification.

   c. Edit the user:

      i. On the user row, select the options (...) menu.

     ii. Choose "Edit" to open the user pane.

   d. Change the password:

      i. In the user pane, within the "Change password" section:

- Enter and confirm the new password.
- If changing your own password, provide your current password.

   e. Password requirements:

      i. Ensure the new password meets the following criteria:

- Minimum of eight characters
- Combination of both lowercase and uppercase alphabetic characters
- At least one number
- At least one symbol

  5. Save changes:

      i. Select "Save" to apply the password changes.

Recovering Privileged Access to an OT Sensor

In this section, let us explore recovering privileged access to a sensor, specifically for the cyberx, admin, or cyberx_host users.

Prerequisites

This procedure applies only to the cyberx, admin, or cyberx_host users.

Steps

1. Initiate password reset:

   a. Begin the sign-in process to the OT network sensor.

   b. On the sign-in screen, click on the Reset password link.

2. Choose user and copy identifier:

   a. In the Reset password dialog, choose the user whose password needs recovery (cyberx, admin, or cyberx_host).

   b. Copy the unique identifier code displayed in the Reset password identifier.

3. Navigate to the Azure portal:

   a. Open the Defender for IoT Sites and Sensors page in the Azure portal. You may open the Azure portal in a new browser tab or window while keeping the sensor tab open.

4. Ensure correct subscription:

   a. In your Azure portal settings ➤ Directories + subscriptions, confirm that the subscription linked to your sensor's Defender for IoT onboarding is selected.

5. Recover password in the Azure portal:

   a. Find the relevant sensor on the Sites and Sensors page, and select the options menu (...) on the right ➤ Recover my password.

6. Enter the unique identifier in Azure:

   a. In the Recover dialog, enter the unique identifier copied from your sensor and click Recover. This action triggers the automatic download of a password_recovery.zip file.

7. Upload the password recovery file:

   a. Return to the sensor tab, navigate to the Password recovery screen, and choose Select file.

   b. Upload the password_recovery.zip file downloaded earlier from the Azure portal.

Key Note: If an error indicates an invalid file, ensure the correct subscription is selected in Azure portal settings.

8. Generate and retrieve a new password:

    a. Click Next. A system-generated password for your sensor will be displayed. Make a note of this password as it won't be shown again.

    b. Click Next again to sign in to your sensor using the new password.

This process ensures the recovery of privileged access to the OT sensor for the specified user.

Tracking and Auditing User Activity in Microsoft Defender for IoT

Once you've established user access on the Azure portal, OT network sensors, and on-premises management consoles, monitoring and auditing user activity across the entire Microsoft Defender for IoT ecosystem is crucial.

Audit Azure User Activity

Utilize Microsoft Entra user auditing resources to audit Azure user activity within Defender for IoT.

Audit User Activity on OT Network Sensors

Audit and track user activity on the sensor's Event timeline. This timeline details events on the sensor, affected devices, and timestamps of each event. Follow these steps:

1. Sign in to the sensor console as the default privileged Admin user or any user with an Admin role.

2. Select Event Timeline from the left-hand menu, ensuring the filter is set to show User Operations.

3. Utilize additional filters or search using CTRL+F to locate specific information.

Audit User Activity on On-Premises Management Console

Defender for IoT recommends transitioning to Microsoft cloud services or existing IT infrastructure for central monitoring, and the on-premises management console will be retired on January 1, 2025.

To audit and track user activity on the on-premises management console:

1. Sign in to the on-premises management console and go to System Settings ➤ System Statistics ➤ Audit log.

2. The dialog displays data from the currently active audit log. New logs are generated every 10 MB, with one previous log stored in addition to the active log file.

3. Audit logs include alert ID, user changes, exclusion rules, console upgrades, and more.

Manage Alerts

Managing alerts in the realm of Microsoft Defender for IoT involves a comprehensive strategy combining the Azure portal's capabilities and the OT sensor console. Collectively, these two interfaces give users a centralized and detailed overview of network security events. The Azure portal is a robust platform for users to access and analyze alerts, offering a customizable display of key information such as alert severity, name, detection engine, and status. This centralized hub enables users to efficiently manage and organize alerts, applying filters and grouping options to streamline their focus.

On the OT sensor side, a dedicated console allows users to access alerts tailored to the specifics of the operational technology (OT) environment. The roles of Admin, Security Analyst, or Viewer determine the level of access and visibility into the alerts on the sensor. Like the Azure portal, the OT sensor console provides a detailed view of alert information, facilitating effective monitoring and management.

A synchronized approach between the Azure portal and the OT sensor ensures a seamless workflow for users engaged in alert management. This includes modifying alert statuses or severities, learning or muting alerts, accessing packet capture (PCAP) data, and appending predefined comments. By adopting this dual-interface strategy, organizations can enhance their network security operations, responding promptly to potential threats and maintaining a vigilant stance in the evolving cybersecurity landscape.

View and Manage Alerts via the Azure Portal

Microsoft Defender for IoT alerts plays a crucial role in enhancing your network's security and operational aspects by providing real-time information about logged events. This guide outlines managing these alerts within the Azure portal, covering alerts triggered by both OT and enterprise IoT network sensors.

Real-time details about events logged in your network make Microsoft Defender for IoT alerts essential to network security and operations. OT networks are equipped with sensors that detect changes or suspicious activity in network traffic and send alerts.

Defender for IoT alerts can be accessed through various platforms, providing users with flexibility and convenience. These alert notifications are accessible via the Azure portal, OT network sensor consoles, and the on-premises management console. Additionally, enterprise IoT security offers alerts for devices detected by Defender for Endpoint within Microsoft 365 Defender.

While users can view detailed information about alerts, investigate their context, and manage alert statuses from any of these locations, each platform also provides unique functionalities for extra alert actions. The following outlines the specific alerts supported for each location and the additional actions exclusive to that particular platform:

Azure Portal

- Description: Alerts from all cloud-connected OT sensors

- Extra alert actions:

  - View related MITRE ATT&CK tactics and techniques.

  - Utilize out-of-the-box workbooks for visibility into high-priority alerts.

  - Access alerts from Microsoft Sentinel and conduct deeper investigations with Microsoft Sentinel playbooks and workbooks.

OT Network Sensor Consoles

- Description: Alerts generated by the respective OT sensor

- Extra alert actions:

  - View the alert's source and destination in the device map.

  - Examine related events on the Event timeline.

- Forward alerts directly to partner vendors.

- Create alert comments.

- Establish custom alert rules.

- Unlearn alerts.

On-Premises Management Console

- Description: Alerts generated by connected OT sensors

- Extra alert actions:

  - Forward alerts directly to partner vendors.

  - Create alert exclusion rules.

Microsoft 365 Defender

- Description: Alerts generated for enterprise IoT devices detected by Microsoft Defender for Endpoint

- Extra alert actions:

  - Manage alert data alongside other Microsoft 365 Defender data, including advanced hunting.

In summary, the diverse range of platforms for accessing Defender for IoT alerts ensures users can choose the most suitable interface for their needs while offering specific additional actions tailored to each platform's capabilities.

So you can access OT alerts directly on each OT network sensor console or connected to the on-premises management console.

To streamline alert management, integrate Microsoft Sentinel, allowing you to view Defender for IoT alerts within Microsoft Sentinel and handle them alongside security incidents.

It's important to note that if enterprise IoT security is enabled in Microsoft Defender XDR, alerts related to enterprise IoT devices detected by Microsoft Defender for Endpoint are exclusively accessible within Defender for Endpoint.

Requirements

To receive alerts in Defender for IoT, it's essential to have an OT onboarded and ensure that network data is streaming into Defender for IoT.

The necessary permissions for accessing alerts on the Azure portal include being a Security Reader, Security Admin, Contributor, or Owner.

Permissions as a Security Admin, Contributor, or Owner are required to manage alerts on the Azure portal actively. Alert management tasks include modifying statuses or severities, learning an alert, or accessing PCAP data.

Viewing Alerts in the Azure Portal

1. Navigate to the Alerts page in Defender for IoT on the Azure portal. By default, the grid displays the following details:

   - Severity: Predefined alert severity modifiable as needed.

   - Name: The alert title.

   - Site: The associated site is listed on the Sites and Sensors page.

   - Engine: Defender for IoT detection engine triggering the alert (Micro-agent indicates the Defender for IoT Device Builder platform).

   - Last Detection: Time of the latest alert detection.

     If an alert is New and the same traffic reoccurs, the Last Detection time is updated for the existing alert. If the alert is Closed and traffic reoccurs, a new alert is triggered, and the Last Detection time remains unchanged.

   - Status: Alert status (New, Active, Closed). Refer to Alert statuses and triaging options for more details.

   - Source Device: IP address, MAC address, or the device name originating the triggering traffic.

   - Tactics: The MITRE ATT&CK stage.

2. To access more details, click the Edit Columns button on the right. In the Edit columns pane, choose Add Column and include the following extra columns:

   - Source Device Address: IP address of the source device

   - Destination Device Address: IP address of the destination device

   - Destination Device: Destination IP or MAC address or device name

- First Detection: Initial alert detection time

- ID: Unique alert ID

- Last Activity: Last alert modification time, including manual
  updates or automated changes

- Protocol: Protocol detected in the network traffic

- Sensor: Sensor detecting the alert

- Zone: Zone assigned to the detecting sensor

- Category: Alert category (e.g., operational issues, custom alerts,
  or illegal commands)

- Type: Internal alert name

Filter and Group Alerts

Utilize the search box and time range and Add filter options to filter alerts based on
specific parameters or locate a particular alert.

For instance, filter alerts by category using the provided options, as depicted in
Figure 5-1.

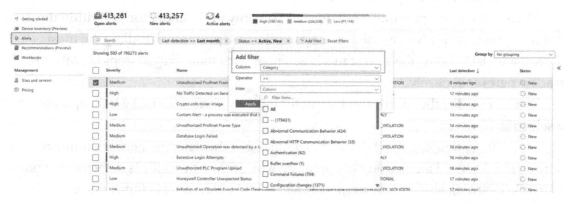

Figure 5-1. *Alerts view from Microsoft Defender for IoT*

Group alerts by specific parameters using the Group by menu at the top right,
allowing you to collapse the grid into subsections. Supported grouping options include
Engine, Name, Sensor, Severity, and Site.

Review and Address a Specific Alert

Navigate to the Alerts page and choose an alert in the grid to unveil additional details in the right-side pane. Within this alert detail pane, you'll find information such as the awake description, traffic source and destination, and more.

Alerts view is depicted in Figure 5-2.

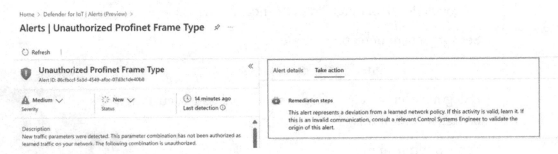

Figure 5-2. *Alerts remediation steps from Microsoft Defender for IoT*

Opt to View Full Details for a more in-depth exploration. This will lead you to the alert details page, offering comprehensive insights into the alert and a series of remediation steps available on the Take Action tab.

Manage Alert Severity and Status

Microsoft advises promptly updating alert severity in Defender for IoT within the Azure portal once you've assessed an alert to prioritize promptly handling the most critical alerts. Updating the alert status is essential once remediation steps are taken to track progress effectively.

You can modify the severity and status for individual alerts or make bulk updates for a selection of alerts.

Learn an golden signal to Microsoft Defender that the detected network traffic is authorized. Learned alerts won't trigger again when the same traffic is detected on your network. Learning applies only to specific alerts, and unlearning is supported exclusively from the OT network sensor.

To handle a single alert:

- In Defender for IoT in the Azure portal, navigate to the Alerts page on the left and select an alert in the grid.

- In the details pane on the right or the alert details page itself, determine the new status and severity.

To manage multiple alerts in bulk:

- In Defender for IoT in the Azure portal, go to the Alerts page on the left and choose the alerts in the grid that require modification.

- The toolbar utilizes the "Change status" and "Change severity" options to update the status and/or severity for all selected alerts.

To learn or unlearn alerts:

In Defender for IoT in the Azure portal, access the Alerts page on the left and perform one of the following:

- Select one or more learnable alerts in the grid and choose "Learn" in the toolbar.

- On an alert details page for a learnable alert, within the Take Action tab, select "Learn."

Accessing Alert PCAP Data

To expedite your investigation, you may need to access raw traffic files, commonly called packet capture or PCAP files. If you're an SOC or OT security engineer, you can directly access PCAP files from the Azure portal to enhance the efficiency of your investigation.

To access raw traffic files associated with a specific alert, select "Download PCAP" in the top-left corner of your alert details page.

The portal initiates a request for the file from the sensor that identified the alert and then transfers it to your Azure storage.

The duration for downloading the PCAP file may vary and could take several minutes, influenced by the strength of your sensor connectivity.

Export Alerts

Exporting alerts to a CSV file lets you share and generate reports offline. Follow these steps in Defender for IoT on the Azure portal:

1. Navigate to the Alerts page on the left.

2. Utilize the search box and filters to display the specific alerts for Export.

3. On the toolbar above the grid, click Export and then Confirm.

The system generates the file, and you will receive a prompt to save it locally.

View and Manage Alerts on the OT Sensor

Monitor and manage alerts on your OT sensor using Microsoft Defender for IoT to enhance network security. Real-time details about events in your network are provided through these alerts, triggered by changes or suspicious activity detected by OT network sensors. Here are the steps and details for viewing and managing alerts on an OT sensor.

Prerequisites

- Ensure your OT sensor has a configured SPAN port and Defender for IoT monitoring software installed.

- View alerts on an OT sensor. Sign in to your OT sensor console as an Admin, Security Analyst, or Viewer user.

- To oversee alerts on an OT sensor, log in to your sensor with credentials as either an Admin or a Security Analyst user. Engage in various alert management tasks, such as adjusting statuses or severities, learning or muting alerts, accessing PCAP data, or appending predefined comments to an alert.

Navigate to the Alerts Page on the Left

Log in to your OT sensor console and navigate to the Alerts page on the left.

Default Grid Details

The default grid displays the following details:

- Severity: Predefined alert severity (Critical, Major, Minor, Warning).

- Name: Alert title.

- Engine: The Defender for IoT detection engine triggers the alert.

- Last Detection: The last time the alert was detected.

  If the status is New, and the same traffic is seen again, the Last Detection time updates.

  A new alert is triggered if the status is Closed and traffic is seen again.

- Status: Alert status (New, Active, Closed).

- Source Device: Source device IP address, MAC, or device name.

Additional Columns

To view more details, select the "Edit Columns" button and add extra columns like Destination Device, First Detection, Alert ID, Last Activity, etc.

Manage Alerts on the OT Sensor

To manage alerts, sign in as an Admin or Security Analyst. Activities include modifying statuses or severities, learning/muting alerts, accessing PCAP data, or adding predefined comments.

Filter Alerts

Use the search box and time range and Add filter options to filter alerts based on specific parameters or to locate a particular alert. Group alerts can use custom groups created in Device Inventory or Device Map.

Group Alerts Displayed

Collapse the grid into subsections using the Group by menu based on Severity, Name, Engine, or Status. This provides more specific information about alert count breakdowns, such as the number of alerts with a particular severity or status.

Examine and Address a Particular Alert

To access and address specific alerts, log in to the OT sensor and navigate to the Alerts section in the left-hand menu. Upon selecting a particular alert from the grid, a detailed view is presented on the right-side pane, showcasing vital information such as the alert description, traffic source, and destination. For a deeper dive, click "View full details," which redirects to the alert details page, providing a comprehensive breakdown of the alert and offering remediation steps under the "Take Action" tab. Figure 5-3 depicts the full details of Alert view.

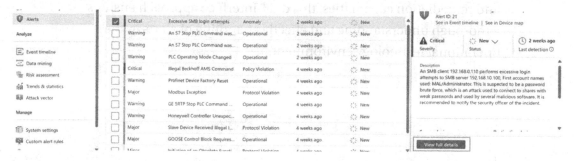

Figure 5-3. *Alerts view full details from Microsoft Defender for IoT*

To gain additional contextual insights, explore various tabs:

- Map View: This tab provides a graphical representation of the source and destination devices in a map view, offering a visual understanding of their interconnectedness with other devices linked to your sensor. Figure 5-4 depicts Map view of Alerts.

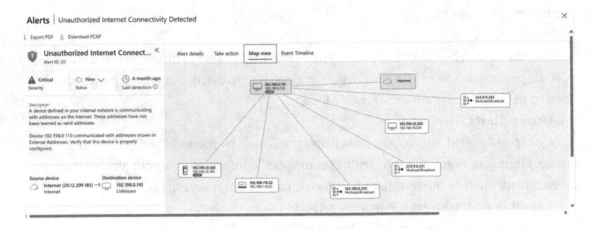

Figure 5-4. *Alerts Map view from Microsoft Defender for IoT*

- Event Timeline: This tab allows users to review the specific event and recent activities on the associated devices. It offers filter options to tailor the displayed data, providing a more customized and focused perspective. Combining the OT sensor's detailed view and remediation capabilities, this dual-interface approach ensures a thorough understanding and effective handling of alerts in the operational technology environment.

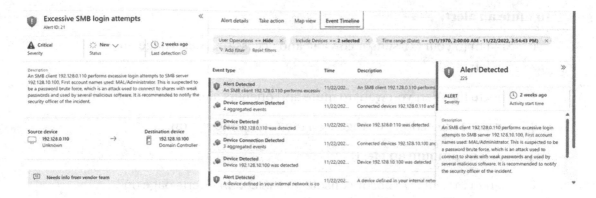

Figure 5-5. Alerts timeline from Microsoft Defender for IoT

Manage Alert Status and Triage Alerts

Ensure you update the alert status after taking remediation steps to record the progress. Whether for a single alert or a selection of alerts in bulk, you can easily update their status.

Learning an alert informs Defender for IoT that the detected network traffic is authorized. Learned alerts will not trigger again when the same traffic is detected on your network. Alternatively, you can mute an alert when learning is not applicable and you wish to disregard a specific scenario on your network.

To manage alert status:

1. Sign in to your OT sensor console and navigate to the Alerts page on the left.

2. Choose one or more alerts in the grid for which you want to update the status.

3. Utilize the toolbar's Change Status button or the Status option in the details pane on the right to modify the alert status.

4. The Status option is also accessible on the alert details page.

To learn one or more alerts:

1. Sign in to your OT sensor console and go to the Alerts page on the left, then perform either of the following:

2. Choose one or more learnable alerts in the grid and select Learn in the toolbar.

3. On an alert details page, select Learn within the Take Action tab.

To mute an alert:

1. Sign in to your OT sensor console and access the Alerts page on the left.

2. Locate the Alert you want to mute and open its alert details page.

3. On the Take Action tab, toggle on the Alert mute option.

To unlearn or unmute an alert:

1. Sign in to your OT sensor console and select the Alerts page on the left.

2. Find the Alert you've learned or muted and open its alert details page.

3. Toggle off the Alert Learn or Alert Mute option on the Take Action tab.

After unlearning or unmuting an alert, alerts will be re-triggered whenever the sensor detects the selected traffic combination.

Access Alert PCAP Data and Export Alerts to CSV or PDF

If you need to access raw traffic files, commonly referred to as packet capture files or PCAP files, for investigative purposes, follow these steps.

To access raw traffic files for a specific alert, choose Download PCAP from the top-left corner of the alert details page. Your browser will prompt you to either open or save the PCAP file locally.

For exporting alerts to a CSV or PDF file for offline sharing and reporting:

Exporting to CSV

1. Sign in to your OT sensor console and navigate to the Alerts page on the left.

2. Use the search box and filter options to display only the alerts you intend to export.

3. In the toolbar above the grid, select Export to CSV.

The file is generated, and you will be prompted to open or save it locally.

Exporting to PDF

1. Sign in to your OT sensor console and access the Alerts page on the left.

2. Choose one of the following methods:

   - On the Alerts page, select an alert, then choose Export to PDF from the toolbar above the grid.

   - On an alert details page, select Export to PDF.

The PDF file is generated, and you will be prompted to save it locally.

These actions enable you to efficiently manage and utilize PCAP data and export alert information for comprehensive offline analysis and reporting purposes.

Speed Up Workflows for On-Premises Operational Technology (OT) Alerts

Microsoft Defender for IoT alerts is crucial in fortifying your network security and streamlining operational efficiency by providing real-time insights into events recorded within your network. Designed explicitly for operational technology (OT), these alerts are activated by OT network sensors when they identify alterations or suspicious activities in network traffic warranting immediate attention.

This section outlines various strategies to mitigate OT network alert fatigue within your team.

- Facilitate communication and documentation across your alerts by generating alert comments for your teams to append to individual alerts.

- Craft custom alert rules to pinpoint specific network traffic within your system.

- Implement alert exclusion rules to curtail the number of alerts your sensors trigger.

Key Prerequisites

- To create alert comments or custom alert rules on an operational technology (OT) network sensor, you need to have an OT network sensor installed and access it as an Admin user.

317

- For establishing a DNS allowlist on an OT sensor, having an OT network sensor installed and access as a Support user is essential.

- To create alert exclusion rules on an on-premises management console, you should have an on-premises management console installed and access it as an Admin user.

Generate alert comments for an operational technology (OT) sensor.

1. Log in to your OT sensor account and navigate to System Settings ➤ Network Monitoring ➤ Alert Comments.

2. Within the Alert Comments pane, input the new comment in the Description field and click "Add." The newly added comment will be displayed in the Description list below the field.

3. Click "Submit" to incorporate your comment into the roster of available comments for each alert on your sensor.

Team members can utilize these custom comments in each alert on your sensor.

Generate personalized alert regulations on an operational technology (OT) sensor.

Establish custom alert rules on an operational technology (OT) sensor to activate alerts for specific activities on your network that are not covered by default functionalities.

For instance, in a Modbus environment, you may introduce a rule to identify any written commands to a memory register on a designated IP address and Ethernet destination.

To create a custom alert rule:

1. Log in to your OT sensor account and navigate to Custom Alert Rules ➤ + Create Rule.

2. In the Create Custom Alert Rule pane, specify the following fields:

   - Alert Name: Provide a meaningful name for the alert.

   - Alert Protocol: Choose the protocol you wish to detect. In certain scenarios, opt for protocols like TNS or TDS for database events; HTTP, DELTAV, SMB, or FTP for file events; and HTTP for package download events. For open ports (dropped) events, select TCP or UDP, depending on the port type. If tracking changes in OT protocols like S7 or CIP, utilize relevant parameters such as tag or subfunction.

- Message: Formulate a message to be displayed when the alert is triggered. These messages support alphanumeric characters and any traffic variables detected. Include details like source and destination addresses using curly brackets ({}) for variables.

- Direction: Specify source and destination IP addresses for detecting traffic.

- Conditions: Define one or more conditions that must be met to trigger the alert. Using the AND operator, utilize the + sign to create a condition set with multiple conditions. If using MAC or IP addresses as variables, convert the values from dotted-decimal to decimal format. At least one condition is required to create a custom alert rule.

- Detected: Establish a date and time range for the traffic to be detected, aligning with maintenance or working hours.

- Action: Specify an action for Defender for IoT to take when the alert is triggered automatically. Choose to have Defender for IoT create an alert or event with the specified severity.

- PCAP Included: If opting to create an event, adjust the PCAP included option as needed. For alerts, the PCAP is always included and cannot be removed.

3. Select "Save" when the rule configuration is complete.

Revise a personalized alert rule by choosing the rule and then accessing the options (...) menu ➤ Edit. Adjust the alert rule as required and save the modifications.

Alterations made to customized alert rules, including adjustments to severity levels or protocols, are documented in the Event timeline page on the OT sensor.

To prevent the execution of custom alert rules without removing them entirely, disable the rules. On the Custom Alert Rules page, pick one or more rules, and then choose Disable, Enable, or Delete from the toolbar as necessary.

Permit Internet connectivity within an operational technology (OT) network.

Enable Internet connections on an operational technology (OT) network by minimizing unauthorized Internet alerts by creating a domain allowlist on your OT sensor. Configuring a DNS allowlist entails the sensor cross-referencing each unauthorized Internet connection attempt with the specified list before triggering an alert. If a domain's fully qualified domain name (FQDN) is part of the allowlist, the sensor refrains from triggering an alert and seamlessly permits the associated traffic.

All OT sensor users can access a comprehensive list of currently configured domains through a data mining report. This report encompasses FQDNs, resolved IP addresses, and the timestamp of the last resolution.

To establish a DNS allowlist:

1. Log in to your OT sensor as the Admin user and navigate to the Support page.

2. In the search box, enter "DNS" and identify the engine associated with the Internet Domain Allowlist description.

3. Select "Edit" for the Internet Domain Allowlist row, adjusting configurations as necessary.

4. In the Edit Configuration pane, input one or more domain names in the FQDN allowlist field, separating multiple entries with commas. The sensor will refrain from generating alerts for unauthorized Internet connectivity attempts on the specified domains.

5. Click "Submit" to save your changes.

To inspect the current, allow list in a data mining report.

While selecting a category in your custom data mining report, choose "Internet Domain Allowlist" under the DNS category.

The generated data mining report showcases the permitted domains and the corresponding IP addresses being resolved for those domains. Additionally, the report includes the Time-to-Live (TTL) duration, measured in seconds, during which the resolved IP addresses will not trigger an Internet connectivity alert.

Establish exclusion rules for alerts on the on-premises management console to guide your sensors in disregarding specific network traffic that typically triggers an alert.

For instance, if you know that all the operational technology (OT) devices monitored by a specific sensor will undergo maintenance procedures for two days, create an exclusion rule instructing Defender for IoT to suppress alerts detected by this sensor during the predefined period.

To create an alert exclusion rule:

1. Log in to your on-premises management console and access Alert Exclusion in the left-hand menu.

2. On the Alert Exclusion page, click the + button at the top-right to introduce a new rule.

3. In the Create Exclusion Rule dialog, input the following details:

    *   Name: Provide a meaningful name for your rule (without quotes).

    *   By Period: Choose a time zone and the specific period for the exclusion rule to be active, then click ADD. This option allows the creation of separate rules for different time zones. For instance, if you need to apply an exclusion rule between 8:00 AM and 10:00 AM in three different time zones, create three separate exclusion rules using the same period and relevant time zone.

    *   By Device Address: Select and input the following values, then click ADD:

        *   Determine whether the designated device is a source, destination, or both.

        *   Specify whether the address is an IP address, MAC address, or subnet.

        *   Enter the value of the IP address, MAC address, or subnet.

    *   By Alert Title: Choose one or more alerts to add to the exclusion rule, then click ADD. To find alert titles, enter all or part of an alert title and select the desired one from the drop-down list.

    *   By Sensor Name: Select one or more sensors to add to the exclusion rule, then click ADD. To find sensor names, enter all or part of the sensor name and select the desired one from the drop-down list.

- Important Note: Alert exclusion rules follow AND logic, meaning alerts are excluded only when all rule conditions are met. If a condition is not defined, all options are included. For example, if the name of a sensor is not specified in the rule, the rule applies to all sensors.

  A summary of the rule parameters is displayed at the bottom of the dialog.

4. Verify the rule summary at the bottom of the Create Exclusion Rule dialog and click SAVE.

Create Alert Exclusion Rules via API

Utilize the Defender for IoT API to generate alert exclusion rules from an external ticketing system or another system managing network maintenance processes.

Employ the maintenance Window (Create alert exclusions) API to define the sensors, analytics engines, start time, and end time for applying the rule. Exclusion rules created via API are displayed in the on-premises management console as read-only.

Share On-Premises Operational Technology (OT) Alert Data Proactively

Microsoft Defender for IoT alerts elevates your network security and operational capabilities by providing real-time insights into events recorded within your network. Operational technology (OT) alerts are activated when OT network sensors identify alterations or suspicious activities in network traffic, demanding your prompt attention.

This section outlines the steps to configure your OT sensor or on-premises management console for forwarding alerts to partner services, syslog servers, email addresses, and more. The forwarded alert information encompasses crucial details, including

- Date and time of the alert

- Engine responsible for detecting the event

- Alert title and descriptive message

- Alert severity

- Source and destination names and IP addresses

- Identification of suspicious traffic

- Notifications regarding disconnected sensors

- Reports on remote backup failures

Requirements

To establish forwarding alert rules in your desired location, ensure the presence of either an OT network sensor or an on-premises management console with administrative user access. Configure SMTP settings on the OT sensor or the on-premises management console.

Setting Up Forwarding Rules on an OT Sensor

1. Log in to the OT sensor and navigate the Forwarding section on the left-hand menu. Click on + Create a new rule.

2. In the Add forwarding rule pane, provide a meaningful rule name and configure rule conditions and actions as outlined here:

    i. Minimal Alert Level: Choose the minimum severity level for forwarding alerts. For instance, selecting "Minor" will forward minor alerts and any above this severity level.

    ii. Any Protocol Detected: Toggle on to forward alerts from all protocol traffic or toggle off and specify the desired protocols.

    iii. Traffic Detected by Any Engine: Toggle on to forward alerts from all analytics engines or toggle off and select specific engines.

    iv. Actions: Choose the server type for forwarding alerts and provide any necessary details. To add multiple servers to the same rule, select + Add server and input additional details.

3. Once you've configured the rule, click Save. The rule will be displayed on the Forwarding page.

4. Test the created rule:

    i. Click the options menu (...) for your rule and choose Send Test Message.

    ii. Verify the received information at the target service.

Editing or Deleting Forwarding Rules on an OT Sensor

1. Log in to the OT sensor and go to the Forwarding section on the left-hand menu.

2. Click the options menu (...) for the desired rule, and choose one of the following:

   i. Edit: Update the fields as necessary, then click Save.

   ii. Delete: Confirm the deletion by selecting Yes.

Creating Forwarding Rules on an On-Premises Management Console

1. Log in to the on-premises management console and navigate to the Forwarding section in the left-hand menu.

2. Click the + button at the top-right to create a new rule.

3. In the Create Forwarding Rule window, provide a meaningful name for the rule and set rule conditions and actions as follows:

   i. Minimal Alert Level: Use the drop-down list at the top-right to choose the minimum alert severity level for forwarding. For instance, selecting "Minor" forwards minor alerts and any alerts above this severity level.

   ii. Protocols: Select All to forward alerts from all protocol traffic or choose Specific to include specific protocols only.

   iii. Engines: Choose All to forward alerts triggered by all sensor analytics engines or select Specific to include specific engines only.

   iv. System Notifications: Choose the Report System Notifications option to be notified about disconnected sensors or remote backup failures.

   v. Alert Notifications: Select the Report Alert Notifications option to be notified about an alert's date and time, title, severity, source and destination names and IP addresses, suspicious traffic, and the detecting engine.

   vi. Actions: Click Add to add an action, specify any necessary parameter values, and repeat as required for multiple actions.

4. Once the rule configuration is complete, click SAVE. The rule will be listed on the Forwarding page.

5. Test the created rule:

   i. Click the "Test This Forwarding Rule" button on the row for your rule. A
       success notification will be displayed if the message is sent successfully.

   ii. Verify in your partner system that the information sent by the sensor has
       been received.

Editing or Deleting Forwarding Rules on an On-Premises Management Console

1. Sign in to your on-premises management console and go to the
    Forwarding section in the left-hand menu.

2. Locate the row for your rule, then choose the Edit or
    Delete button.

   a. If editing, update the fields as needed and click SAVE.

   b. If deleting, click CONFIRM to confirm the deletion.

Set Up Alert Forwarding Rule Actions

In the upcoming section, let's delve into configuring settings for supported
forwarding rule actions, whether on an OT sensor or the on-premises management
console. Table 5-7 provides the action type and configuration details.

Table 5-7. *Action Type and Configuration Details*

Action Type	Configuration Details
	Configure an Email action to forward alert data to the specified email address.
	In the Actions section, provide the following details:
Email Address Action	– Name: Email
	– Email: Enter the destination email address for forwarding alerts.
	– Timezone: Select the desired time zone for alert detection in the target system.

(continued)

Table 5-7. (*continued*)

Action Type	Configuration Details

Configure a syslog server action to forward alert data to the chosen syslog server format.
In the Actions area, enter the following details:

Syslog Server Actions	— Name: Syslog Server
	— Server: Select one of the Syslog formats: SYSLOG Server (CEF format), SYSLOG Server (LEEF format), SYSLOG Server (Object), or SYSLOG Server (Text Message).
	— Host/Port: Enter the host name and port of the syslog server.
	— Timezone: Select the time zone for alert detection in the target system.
	— Protocol: For text messages, choose between TCP and UDP.
	— Enable Encryption: For CEF format, toggle on to configure TLS encryption with a certificate file, key file, and passphrase.

Supported from the on-premises management console only

Configure a Webhook action to integrate with Defender for IoT alert events, sending data to an external system.

In the Actions section, provide the following details:

Webhook Server Action	— Name: Webhook
	— URL: Enter the webhook server URL.
	— Key/Value: Customize HTTP headers with key/value pairs, adhering to specified character limitations.

Supported from the on-premises management console only

Configure a Webhook extended action to send additional data to the webhook server.
In the Actions area, provide the following details:

(*continued*)

Table 5-7. (*continued*)

Action Type	Configuration Details
Webhook Extended Action	— Name: Webhook Extended
	— URL: Enter the endpoint data URL.
	— Key/Value: Customize HTTP headers with key/value pairs, adhering to specified character limitations.
Configure a NetWitness action to transmit alert information to a NetWitness server. In the Actions section, provide the following details:	
NetWitness Action	— Name: NetWitness
	— Server: Select NetWitness.
	— Hostname/Port: Enter the NetWitness server's hostname and port.
	— Timezone: Specify the time zone for the timestamp in alert detection at the SIEM.

Configure Alert Groups in Partner Services

Set up forwarding rules for partner integrations when integrating Defender for IoT with a partner service. This facilitates the transmission of alert or device inventory information to another security or device management system and communication with partner-side firewalls.

Partner integrations play a crucial role in breaking down silos among security solutions, improving device visibility, and expediting system-wide responses for swift risk mitigation.

In these scenarios, leverage supported actions to input credentials and information to enable seamless communication with integrated partner services.

Establish alert groups within partner services by configuring forwarding rules for sending alert data to syslog servers, QRadar, and ArcSight. These alert groups are automatically applied and accessible within these partner servers.

Alert groups serve as a valuable organizational tool for security operations center (SOC) teams using these partner solutions, allowing them to manage alerts according to enterprise security policies and business priorities. For instance, alerts related to new detections are categorized into a discovery group, encompassing alerts about new devices, VLANs, user accounts, MAC addresses, and more.

In partner services, alert groups appear with specific prefixes:

- Prefix "cat" for QRadar, ArcSight, Syslog CEF, and Syslog LEEF

- Prefix "Alert Group" for Syslog text messages

- Prefix "alert_group" for Syslog objects

To leverage alert groups effectively in your integration, ensure that your partner services are configured to display the alert group names.

By default, alerts are grouped into various categories, including but not limited to

- Abnormal communication behavior

- Custom alerts

- Remote access

- Abnormal HTTP communication behavior

- Discovery

- Restart and stop commands

- Authentication

- Firmware change

- Scan

- Unauthorized communication behavior

- Illegal commands

- Sensor traffic

- Bandwidth anomalies

- Internet access

- Suspicion of malware

- Buffer overflow

- Operation failures

- Suspicion of malicious activity

- Command failures

- Operational issues

- Configuration changes

- Programming

Manage Billing Plans

The deployment of Microsoft Defender for IoT for OT monitoring is overseen using a site-based license acquired through the Microsoft 365 admin center. Apply it to your OT plan within the Azure portal following the license acquisition.

Before performing the upcoming procedure, make sure that you have the following:

- A Microsoft 365 tenant with access to the Microsoft 365 admin center as Global or Billing admin.

- An Azure subscription. If you need to, sign up for a free account.

- A Security Admin, Contributor, or Owner user role for the Azure subscription that you're using for the integration.

- An understanding of your site size.

Acquiring a Defender for IoT license involves the following steps outlined in this procedure for purchasing licenses in the Microsoft 365 admin center.

To purchase Defender for IoT licenses:

1. Navigate to the Microsoft 365 admin center and access Billing
   ➤ Purchase services. If this option is unavailable, opt for
   Marketplace instead.

2. Search for Microsoft Defender for IoT, and then identify the
   appropriate license based on your site size.

3. Follow the provided options to acquire the license and integrate it
   into your Microsoft 365 products.

Ensure you specify the required licenses corresponding to the sites you intend to monitor at the selected size. Incorporating an OT plan for Defender for IoT in the Azure portal is outlined in this procedure, based on the licenses acquired through the Microsoft 365 admin center.

To add an OT plan in Defender for IoT:

1. Within Defender for IoT, navigate to Plans and Pricing ➤ Add plan.

2. In the Plan settings pane, designate the Azure subscription where the plan will be added. Only one subscription can be added, and you must possess a Security admin, Contributor, or Owner role for the chosen subscription.

   Key Note: If your subscription is not listed, verify your account details and ensure your permission with the owner. Additionally, confirm that you have the correct subscriptions selected in your Azure settings ➤ Directories + subscriptions page. The Price plan is automatically updated to reflect your Microsoft 365 licenses.

3. Select Next and review the details for any licensed sites. The information on the Review and purchase pane mirrors the licenses procured through the Microsoft 365 admin center.

   a. Choose to accept the terms and conditions.

   b. If using an on-premises management console, opt to Download the OT activation file (optional).

Upon completion, click Save. The file is saved locally if you downloaded the on-premises management console activation file. This file will be used later when activating your on-premises management console.

Canceling an OT Plan in Defender for IoT

Follow these steps to terminate a Defender for IoT plan associated with OT networks in your Azure subscription. This might be necessary if you are transitioning to a different subscription or the service is no longer required.

Prerequisites

Before canceling, delete any sensors linked to the subscription.

To cancel an OT network plan:

1. Navigate to Defender for IoT ➤ Plans and pricing in the Azure portal.

2. On the subscription row, click the options menu (...) on the right and select Cancel plan.

3. In the cancellation dialog, confirm your decision by selecting "I agree to cancel the Defender for IoT plan from the subscription."

The changes will be effective one hour after confirmation.

Please note that canceling an OT plan in the Azure portal does not automatically cancel your Defender for IoT license. If you need to modify your billed licenses, cancel your Defender for IoT license separately from the Microsoft 365 admin center.

Supervise Support for Enterprise IoT Monitoring Using Microsoft Defender for IoT

Security monitoring for enterprise IoT with Defender for IoT is compatible with a Microsoft 365 E5 (ME5) or E5 Security license. Alternatively, additional stand-alone per-device licenses can be acquired as add-ons to Microsoft Defender for Endpoint.

Requirements

Before proceeding with the steps outlined in this document, ensure that you possess
1. Either of the following license combinations:

- A Microsoft 365 E5 (ME5) or E5 Security license and a Microsoft Defender for Endpoint P2 license

- Sole possession of a Microsoft Defender for Endpoint P2 license

2. Access to the Microsoft Defender Portal with Global administrator privileges

Obtain a Stand-Alone Enterprise IoT Trial License

Acquire a trial license for stand-alone enterprise IoT monitoring with Microsoft Defender for IoT, designed explicitly for customers possessing only a Microsoft Defender for Endpoint P2 license. For ME5/E5 Security plan subscribers, enterprise IoT monitoring is automatically available, and a trial is unnecessary. Initiate the trial through the Microsoft Defender for IoT - IoT Device License - add-on wizard in the Microsoft 365 admin center.

To initiate an enterprise IoT trial:

1. Navigate to the Microsoft 365 admin center ➤ Marketplace.

2. Search for "Microsoft Defender for IoT - IoT Device License - add-on" and filter the results by "Other services."

3. Under the add-on details, select "Start free trial." On the Checkout page, choose "Try now."

Calculate the number of monitored devices for enterprise IoT monitoring using the following procedure:

1. Access Assets ➤ Devices to open the Device inventory page in Microsoft Defender XDR.

2. Sum the total devices listed on both the Network and IoT devices tabs.

3. Round up the total to a multiple of 100 and compare it with the available licenses.

For example, if you have 473 network devices and 1206 IoT devices, totaling 1679 devices, and you possess 320 ME5 licenses covering 1600 devices, you need 79 stand-alone licenses to cover the remaining devices.

Purchase stand-alone licenses if additional licenses are required.

Obtain stand-alone, per-device licenses under specific circumstances: for ME5/ E5 Security customers who surpass the allocation of five devices per license or for Defender for Endpoint customers seeking to integrate enterprise IoT security into their organizational framework. These licenses offer flexibility and scalability to accommodate additional devices beyond the standard allocation, ensuring comprehensive coverage for enhanced security monitoring.

Purchase stand-alone licenses; follow this procedure:

1. Go to the Microsoft 365 admin center Billing ➤ Purchase services (or Marketplace).

2. Search for "Microsoft Defender for IoT - IoT Device License - add-on" and filter the results by "Other services."

3. Enter the desired license quantity on the add-on page, choose a billing frequency, and select "Buy."

Turning Off Enterprise IoT Security

Disable enterprise IoT monitoring within Microsoft Defender XDR; this feature is applicable exclusively to customers without any stand-alone, per-device licenses integrated into Microsoft Defender XDR. If you have discontinued the service, you can turn off the Enterprise IoT security option, ensuring that resources are not allocated to this feature.

Disable enterprise IoT security; follow this procedure:

1. Go to Settings ➤ Device discovery ➤ Enterprise IoT in Microsoft Defender XDR.

2. Toggle the option to "Off."

For canceling a legacy enterprise IoT plan:

1. Access Settings ➤ Device discovery ➤ Enterprise IoT in the Microsoft Defender XDR portal.

2. Select "Cancel plan."

Key Note: Cancellation of a legacy enterprise IoT plan is available only for specific customers not utilizing ME5/E5 Security, and it takes effect one hour after confirmation. Charges are applied based on the plan's effective duration.

Security Baseline for Microsoft Defender for IoT

Ensuring robust security is a pivotal element in deploying any solution, and when it comes to IoT, unique considerations emerge, primarily due to the integration of remote physical devices.

Imagine being part of a team implementing an Azure IoT solution for your company. The organization relies on your team to guarantee that the solution aligns with its stringent security requirements. In light of the distinctive challenges posed by the threat landscape in an IoT environment, it becomes imperative for the team to comprehend these intricacies and adopt effective mitigation strategies. Thus, a comprehensive examination of IoT security recommendations and threat mitigation techniques becomes a strategic step in crafting a well-informed approach to security for the IoT implementation.

Microsoft provides the following security recommendations for individuals and companies engaged in IoT solutions, which, when implemented, contribute to fulfilling security obligations within Microsoft's shared responsibility model.

Several of these recommendations can be automatically overseen by Microsoft Defender for Cloud, now referred to as Microsoft Defender for Cloud (formerly Azure Security Center and Azure Defender). As the initial line of defense for safeguarding Azure resources, it regularly evaluates the security status of your Azure resources, identifying potential vulnerabilities and offering recommendations for mitigation.

General Recommendations

Stay up to date: Employ the latest versions of supported platforms, programming languages, protocols, and frameworks.

Keeping IoT devices up to date is crucial for maintaining a secure and resilient environment, and Microsoft Defender for IoT provides valuable features to help achieve this. Regularly updating IoT devices ensures they receive the latest security patches, bug fixes, and feature enhancements, reducing the risk of exploited vulnerabilities. Leveraging Microsoft Defender for IoT, administrators can stay informed about the current state of their IoT device fleet. The platform enables monitoring device health, detecting anomalies, and providing real-time alerts for potential security threats. By staying up to date with the latest security insights and leveraging the capabilities of Microsoft Defender for IoT, organizations can enhance the overall security posture of their IoT ecosystem, protecting against evolving cyber threats and ensuring the continued reliability of their connected devices.

Keep authentication keys safe: Safeguard device IDs and authentication keys post-deployment to prevent unauthorized devices from posing as registered devices.

Securing authentication keys is paramount for maintaining the integrity and confidentiality of IoT devices, and Microsoft Defender for IoT plays a crucial role in fortifying this aspect. To keep authentication keys safe, organizations can utilize the robust features offered by Microsoft Defender for IoT, which includes monitoring and safeguarding these sensitive credentials. The platform enables continuous surveillance of device authentication mechanisms, ensuring that unauthorized access attempts are promptly detected and thwarted. By leveraging Microsoft Defender for IoT's security measures, such as encryption and secure communication protocols, administrators can establish a fortified defense against potential threats seeking to compromise authentication keys. This proactive approach helps maintain the trustworthiness of IoT devices, ensuring they operate securely within the network and mitigating the risk of unauthorized access or malicious activities.

Use device SDKs when possible: Leverage device SDKs to benefit from security features, including encryption and authentication, ensuring the development of a robust and secure device application.

Privileged Access Management (PAM): Deploying Privileged Access Management (PAM) in Microsoft Defender for IoT involves accessing the Defender for IoT portal, ensuring adequate permissions, and navigating to the Privileged Access Management section. Within this section, configure role-based access control (RBAC) by defining roles and assigning appropriate permissions to users or groups. Establishing role-based controls follows the principle of least privilege. Additionally, set up Privileged Access Policies, specifying rules and conditions for privileged access, including factors such as time-based restrictions, approval workflows, and multifactor authentication requirements. This comprehensive approach aims to manage, monitor, and control access within the IoT environment, minimizing the risk of unauthorized activities and potential security threats.

Deploying Backup and Recovery in Microsoft Defender for IoT involves implementing a robust strategy to safeguard critical data and configurations, ensuring business continuity in the face of potential disruptions or data loss incidents. Begin by accessing the Defender for IoT portal and navigating to the Backup and Recovery section. Configure backup settings, specifying the frequency and retention policies for data backups. Utilize cloud storage solutions, such as Azure Storage, for storing backup data securely. Implement a routine backup schedule to capture changes and updates regularly. In case of data loss or system failure, the recovery process involves accessing the backup data and restoring it to the desired state, ensuring minimal downtime and maintaining the integrity of the IoT environment. This proactive approach enhances the overall resilience and reliability of the IoT deployment.

Identity and Access Management Recommendations

In the realm of Microsoft Defender for IoT, robust identity and access management practices play a pivotal role in fortifying the security of your IoT infrastructure. The following strategies, aligned with Microsoft's recommended best practices, contribute to a comprehensive approach to identity and access management.

Centralized Identity and Authentication System

Implementation: Integrate a centralized identity and authentication system, such as Azure Active Directory (AAD), to manage user identities and control access to IoT resources.

Benefits: Centralization streamlines user management, enabling consistent authentication processes and access control policies across the IoT ecosystem.

Local Authentication Methods for Data Plane Access

Implementation: Leverage local authentication methods for enhanced security at the data plane level. This involves implementing strong authentication mechanisms directly on IoT devices to ensure secure communication and data exchange.

Benefits: By enforcing local authentication methods, you add layer of protection to prevent unauthorized access to critical data and resources.

Restrict Resource Access Based on Conditions

Implementation: Implement conditional access policies that dynamically adjust access controls based on specific conditions, such as device health, location, or user roles.

Benefits: Dynamic access restrictions provide adaptive security, allowing fine-grained control over resource access. For instance, access may be granted only to devices with updated security patches or users with specific permissions.

Restrict the Exposure of Credentials and Secrets

Implementation: Employ secure practices for managing credentials and secrets, such as using Azure Key Vault. Minimize exposure by avoiding hard-coding credentials within device configurations.

By safeguarding credentials and secrets, you reduce the risk of unauthorized access and potential exploitation. Centralized management in Azure Key Vault adds an extra layer of security and simplifies key life cycle management.

These identity and access management measures align with Microsoft Defender for IoT's overarching goal of providing a robust security foundation for IoT environments. By incorporating these strategies, organizations can mitigate potential vulnerabilities, enforce access controls, and elevate the overall security posture of their IoT deployments. Regularly reviewing and adapting these practices ensures ongoing resilience against emerging security threats in the evolving landscape of IoT cybersecurity.

Define access control for the hub: Clearly outline the access permissions for each component in your IoT Hub solution, considering functionalities and utilizing default shared access policies.

Define access control for backend services: Understand and grant appropriate access permissions for Azure services consuming data from your IoT Hub solution, such as Cosmos DB, Stream Analytics, App Service, Logic Apps, and Blob Storage.

Data Protection Recommendations

In the Microsoft Defender for IoT context, robust data protection measures are paramount to safeguard sensitive information within your IoT ecosystem. The following practices align with Microsoft's recommendations for ensuring data protection.

Discover, Classify, and Label Sensitive Data

Implementation: Employ tools and processes to discover, classify, and label sensitive data within your IoT environment. Leverage solutions like Azure Information Protection to automatically classify and label data based on sensitivity.

Monitor Anomalies and Threats Targeting Sensitive Data

Implementation: Utilize Microsoft Defender for IoT to continuously monitor and analyze anomalies and threats, specifically targeting sensitive data. Leverage advanced threat detection mechanisms to identify and respond to potential security incidents promptly.

Encrypt Sensitive Data in Transit

Implementation: Ensure that all sensitive data transmitted between IoT devices and hubs is encrypted using secure communication protocols. Microsoft Defender for IoT supports encryption standards, such as TLS (Transport Layer Security), for securing data in transit.

Enable Data at Rest Encryption by Default

Implementation: Activate data at rest encryption by default for stored data within your IoT environment. This ensures that the data remains encrypted and unreadable even if unauthorized access occurs.

Use Customer-Managed Key Option in Data at Rest Encryption When Required

Implementation: Employ the customer-managed key (CMK) option within Azure Key Vault to exert control over the encryption keys used for data at rest. This option allows organizations to manage and audit their encryption keys independently.

Use a Secure Key Management Process

Implementation: Establish and adhere to a secure key management process to handle encryption keys effectively. Regularly rotate keys, restrict access to authorized personnel, and implement secure key storage practices.

Use a Secure Certificate Management Process

Implementation: Implement a robust certificate management process to secure digital certificates within your IoT infrastructure. This includes obtaining certificates from trusted sources, monitoring certificate validity, and promptly updating or renewing certificates as needed.

Secure device authentication: Guarantee secure communication between devices and IoT Hub by utilizing unique identity keys, security tokens, or on-device X.509 certificates for each device.

Secure device communication: Ensure secure device-to-IoT Hub connections using the TLS standard, with IoT Hub supporting versions 1.2 and 1.0 for maximum security.

Secure service communication: Safeguard the connection to backend services, protecting sensitive information once data reaches Azure Storage or Event Hubs.

These data protection practices align with Microsoft Defender for IoT's commitment to fortifying the security posture of IoT environments. By adopting these measures, organizations can enhance their resilience against potential data breaches, comply with regulatory requirements, and maintain the confidentiality and integrity of sensitive information within their IoT deployments. Regular assessments and adjustments to these practices ensure ongoing efficacy in the face of evolving cybersecurity challenges.

Networking Recommendations

Establishing network segmentation boundaries in alignment with Microsoft Defender for IoT is crucial for enhancing the overall security posture of your IoT infrastructure. Network segmentation involves dividing a network into multiple segments or zones, each with its own security measures and access controls. This practice helps contain potential security breaches and limits the lateral movement of threats within the network.

When implementing network segmentation for IoT environments, it is essential to consider the following key aspects:

- Device Classification: Categorize your IoT devices based on their functions, sensitivity, and importance to the overall operations. This classification will guide the creation of segmentation boundaries.

- Traffic Monitoring and Analysis: Employ monitoring tools provided by Microsoft Defender for IoT to analyze network traffic. This enables the identification of normal patterns and anomalies, aiding in defining effective segmentation boundaries.

- Security Policies: Develop and enforce security policies specific to each network segment. Microsoft Defender for IoT provides security recommendations and threat mitigation techniques that can inform the creation of these policies.

- Access Control: Implement strict access controls and permissions for communication between different segments. Ensure that only authorized devices and services can communicate across segmentation boundaries.

- Isolation of Critical Assets: Isolate critical IoT assets within dedicated segments to minimize the impact of security incidents. This ensures that even if one segment is compromised, it doesn't immediately jeopardize the security of essential components.

- Regular Audits and Adjustments: Periodically audit and adjust your network segmentation strategy based on the evolving threat landscape and changes in your IoT environment. Microsoft Defender for IoT can assist in continuous monitoring and analysis for ongoing security improvements.

Organizations can significantly enhance their IoT security posture by establishing network segmentation boundaries in line with Microsoft Defender for IoT, reducing the attack surface, and better protecting critical assets from potential threats. This proactive approach aligns with best practices for securing IoT environments and contributes to a robust defense against evolving cybersecurity challenges.

By default, the hostnames of IoT Hub are associated with a public endpoint featuring a publicly routable IP address accessible via the Internet. This design facilitates sharing the IoT Hub public endpoint among various customers, ensuring that IoT devices connecting through wide-area networks and on-premises networks can seamlessly reach your hub. Nevertheless, there may be scenarios where restricting access to your Azure resources becomes imperative. In such cases, Azure IoT solutions offer support for IP filtering and virtual networks, providing effective measures to enhance security and regulate access as required.

- Protect Access to Your Devices: Minimize device hardware ports to avoid unwanted access and implement mechanisms to detect or prevent physical tampering.

- Build Secure Hardware: Incorporate security features like encrypted storage or a Trusted Platform Module (TPM) for enhanced device and infrastructure security.

Monitoring Recommendations

Monitor unauthorized access to your devices: Utilize device operating system logging features to monitor security breaches or physical tampering.

Monitor your IoT solution from the cloud: Observe the overall health of your IoT Hub solution using Azure Monitor metrics.

Set up diagnostics: Implement diagnostics to log events in your solution, sending diagnostic logs to Azure Monitor for enhanced visibility into performance.

Azure Resource Logs Integration with Microsoft

Azure Resource Logs integration with Microsoft Defender for IoT enhances monitoring capabilities by providing comprehensive insights into the activities and events within your IoT environment. This integration leverages the powerful features of Azure Resource Logs to deliver a unified and centralized view of telemetry data, allowing security teams to detect, investigate, and respond to potential threats effectively.

Critical Aspects of Azure Resource Logs Integration with Microsoft Defender for IoT

Unified Telemetry Data

- Integration: Azure Resource Logs seamlessly collates telemetry data from various Azure resources within your IoT infrastructure, including IoT Hubs, devices, and related services.

- Advantage: This consolidation provides a unified source of information, facilitating a holistic understanding of the security landscape and potential vulnerabilities across the entire IoT deployment.

Real-Time Monitoring

- Integration: The integration ensures that telemetry data is collected and made available in near real time, enabling security teams to monitor events and activities as they occur.

- Advantage: Real-time monitoring is crucial for promptly identifying and responding to security incidents, minimizing the impact of potential threats on the IoT ecosystem.

Customizable Logging

- Integration: Azure Resource Logs offers flexibility in configuring logging settings to capture specific events, actions, or data points relevant to the security posture of your IoT environment.

- Advantage: Customizable logging allows organizations to tailor their monitoring strategy based on their unique security requirements, ensuring that pertinent information is captured for analysis.

Correlation with Defender for IoT Insights

- Integration: Telemetry data from Azure Resource Logs can be correlated with insights and alerts provided by Microsoft Defender for IoT, creating a comprehensive security picture.

- Advantage: Correlating data enhances the context around security incidents, streamlines the investigation process, and enables security teams to make more informed decisions.

Threat Detection and Analysis

- Integration: Security teams can leverage the integrated telemetry data to detect patterns, anomalies, and potential threats within the IoT environment.

- Advantage: Enhanced threat detection capabilities empower organizations to proactively identify and mitigate security risks, reducing the likelihood of successful attacks.

Incident Response and Forensics

- Integration: The combined capabilities of Azure Resource Logs and Defender for IoT assist in incident response and forensic analysis by providing detailed insights into the sequence of events during a security incident.

- Advantage: This aids in understanding the root cause of incidents, facilitating remediation efforts, and improving overall incident response effectiveness.

In conclusion, integrating Azure Resource Logs with Microsoft Defender for IoT offers a robust monitoring solution for IoT deployments. By leveraging this integration, organizations can gain deeper visibility into their IoT environment's security posture, enhance threat detection, and respond effectively to security incidents. This unified approach contributes to a proactive and resilient security strategy, essential for safeguarding IoT assets and maintaining the integrity of connected systems.

By adhering to these recommendations, you fortify your IoT solution against potential security threats and align with Microsoft's commitment to robust security practices.

Summary

The concluding chapter of *Design and Deploy Microsoft Defender for IoT* focused on empowering readers to embark on their journey with IoT security and effectively manage their Defender for IoT systems.

The chapter was divided into critical subsections.

Getting Started with Microsoft Defender for IoT Management

This section laid the foundation for users, providing essential insights into initiating their Defender for IoT management journey.

Manage Your Defender for IoT System

This section delved into the intricacies of system management, offering practical guidance and strategies for optimizing the performance and functionality of Defender for IoT.

Security Baseline Microsoft Defender for IoT

The final section was crucial, emphasizing the significance of establishing a robust security baseline. Readers gained valuable insights into the recommended security practices, threat mitigation techniques, and adherence to Microsoft's shared responsibility model. By following the comprehensive recommendations outlined in this chapter, users can strengthen the security posture of their IoT deployments and ensure a resilient and well-managed Defender for IoT systems. The chapter is a comprehensive guide, encapsulating the essential elements for a successful and secure IoT management experience.

Index

© Puthiyavan Udayakumar and Dr. R. Anandan 2024
P. Udayakumar and Dr. R. Anandan, *Design and Deploy Microsoft Defender for IoT*,
https://doi.org/10.1007/979-8-8688-0239-3

Printed in the United States
by Baker & Taylor Publisher Services